HOW TO BUSINESS

HOW TO BUSINESS

Pieter van der Merwe

Copyright © 2019 Pieter van der Merwe

First edition 2019

All rights reserved. No part of this book may be reproduced or transmitted in any form or by any means, electronic or mechanical, including photocopying, recording or any information storage or retrieval system without permission from the copyright holder.
The Author has made every effort to trace and acknowledge sources/resources/individuals. In the event that any images/information have been incorrectly attributed or credited, the Author will be pleased to rectify these omissions at the earliest opportunity.

Published by Pieter van der Merwe using Reach Publishers' services,
Johannesburg, South Africa
info@howtobusiness.co.za

Edited by Colleen Figg for Reach Publishers
Cover designed by Reach Publishers
P O Box 1384, Wandsbeck, South Africa, 3631

Website: www.reachpublishers.co.za
E-mail: reach@reachpublish.co.za

Contents

Dedication		7
Why I wrote this book		9
Author Bio		11
Introduction		13
Author's Note		15
1.	Trust Yourself	17
2.	Common Sense	24
3.	Understand What You Do	29
4.	Focus on How	35
5.	How Much Homework?	41
6.	Lean and Agile	47
7.	Fundamentals	53
8.	New Hires	61
9.	Interview Questions	68
10.	Marketing	74
11.	Take Opportunities, Not Risks	80
12.	Mindset and Attitude	86
13.	Sway and Bias	92
14.	Good Spend vs. Bad Spend	98
15.	Candour	104
16.	Little Things and Focus	110
17.	Value Creation	115
18.	Business Comedy	121
19.	Entrepreneurs	128
20.	Small Things – Big Impact	135
21.	Chemistry	141
22.	Energy and Drive	147
23.	Pricing	154
24.	Pricing Sweet-spot	160
25.	Franchise and Remuneration Structure	166

26.	Snappy Quality	172
27.	How We Make Judgements	178
28.	Deal Fatigue	185
29.	Exceptional People	191
30.	Negotiations	197
31.	Capital Raising	204
32.	Running a Business	210
33.	Delegation	216
34.	Management	222
35.	Luck	228
36.	Dishonesty	234
37.	People	240
38.	Getting it All to Work	247
39.	Talent and Talent Management	253
40.	What is Success?	258
41.	Sticky Situations	261
42.	Indicators	267
43.	Risk	273
44.	Hopeful and Staying Humble	279
45.	Communication	285
46.	Work Environment	291
47.	Gems	297

Dedication

This book is dedicated to my father, Piet Van der Merwe, who has run his business successfully for more than sixty years. Thank you for teaching me to focus on what I do and for giving me the opportunity to observe and learn from you. I have learned so much from your incredible, natural ability to deal with people

Further, I dedicate this book to my wife Almarie. Thank you for always believing in me and motivating me in everything I do.

I also dedicate the book to my two sons Joha and Liam. I'm so grateful for all the business discussions we have had over the years—your curiosity about business helped to inspire this book.

Why I wrote this book

Being a business lawyer and an experienced businessman, I have found myself and my clients at a crossroads many times between expansion, downsizing, next phase of growth, capital structure, and global expansion. I have had to ask questions like:

- How do I do this?
- How do I achieve that?
- How do I provide a solution for this?
- How do I provide a solution for that?
- Should we start this business?
- How can we plan for the next twenty years?

After years serving as a trusted advisor to individuals and businesses both locally and overseas, I decided to compile this book of what I deem to be the most valuable tools for business people. It is practical, it is implementable, it is easy to understand, and I am sure it will create value for all readers.

Author Bio

Pieter was born in 1973 in Prieska, Northern Cape province, South Africa. The first part of his school life was spent at Prieska Primary School, followed by Kimberley's Eureka Primary School, and then he went to High School *Diamant Veld*, Kimberley.

He went on to study a law degree in the Free State and started working at EG Copper and Sons Inc in Bloemfontein. After deciding to become an attorney, he worked as an associate at a firm but then transitioned to a role as a conveyancer and a notary during this time. Furthermore, he enrolled in a Master's degree in a law programme in Johannesburg.

Upon graduation, Pieter worked at a firm called Mervyn Joel Smith and during this time, he initiated the expansion to three new offices with great success. After seven years with Mervyn Joel Smith, he moved to a commercial boutique law firm for a short time before founding VDMA Attorneys.

Pieter grew up in a house where his father had been a businessman since 1932, running a successful business for over fifty years. His mother was also involved in the same business and managed very fruitful property investments. She also founded an extremely successful real estate agency.

His siblings (an older sister and brother) have also started their own prosperous businesses in their own right. His brother is currently working in a senior position in a leading agricultural processing company.

Pieter also initially invested in the app-development company, Appify, which produced apps. However, after the app market failed to show the revenue growth needed for success, he pulled out.

Introduction

The main reason for writing the book is that in recent years an increasing number of people have been asking for my guidance on business matters, leadership matters, and investments. It became apparent that over the years, I've accumulated a lot of business knowledge, information and insider tips. Besides having read most of the leading business books around for many, many years, I have also run a successful investment business since 2004.

In addition to that, I was the founder, in 2010, of VDMA, a leading corporate commercial law firm in South Africa. This endeavour was nothing short of a David and Goliath situation where all the corporate commercial law work was basically attended to between the five big global law firms, and then you had VDMA. VDMA soon made its mark in the market and has grown its areas of strength ever since.

In addition, I have also been on the executive board of several companies and have been a committee member on various committees involved in deal-making, investments, lending and the like.

Being a business lawyer means that you work with start-ups; you work with established businesses to help them grow to the next level; you help listed companies become bigger, and you help companies downsize when necessary. There is also restructuring to be handled when these companies are not doing well. You help clients merge acquisitions, and you get involved with the development of the composition of companies in terms of committees, corporate governance, and looking after compliance and regulatory matters.

It also means working with international companies and local structures, inbound investments, outbound investments, working with family businesses, and sometimes third- and fourth-generation family businesses that want to grow bigger. Also, it means supporting multi-jurisdictional businesses and companies where there are sometimes problems in terms of fraud and dishonesty. And of course, it means handling the employment side with high-profile people such as directors, chief executive officers, as well as sophisticated and unsophisticated clients.

Since much of this work has been in specific industries or has involved setting up investment funds, jurisdictional funds, and looking after existing investments, there is very little that I haven't come across and dealt with multiple times over the span of twenty years in practice and fourteen years in investment. Our law firm has also been rated among the top law firms in South Arica in a very short space of time with regard to unlisted mergers and acquisitions work.

I don't write this book from the point of view of an entrepreneur; I write it from the point of view of what I have observed and experienced in business.

The points I raise in the book are a combination of my experience with transactions and business-related matters. While the book considers the banking and finance transactions I have been involved with—conservatively US$3.5 Billion in transactions, it also deals with certain business principles surrounding professional relationships. For it is not always the size of a deal that determines the complexity, it is sometimes the people who are involved, as well as a number of other factors.

Author's Note

Never stop dreaming! You could be running a direct spice sales business today but a spice bottle labelling company tomorrow because you identified a more viable opportunity. Never limit yourself!

Being a business lawyer and an experienced businessman, plus a trusted adviser to entrepreneurs both locally and abroad, I have travelled the road between expansion, downsizing, the next phase of growth and capital structure on many occasions.

These include:

- Finding strategic ways forward for businesses on matters such as global expansion;
- Finding new, unique methods on how we approach and do things in business;
- Providing solutions on matters when a way forward seems hard to find;
- Looking at the best platforms for businesses to get started; and
- Structuring long-term planning (for example, over a twenty-year period).

I hope that my knowledge and experiences noted in this book will create a mind shift that will empower you to take your business to the next level, or will encourage you to start a business that will change your life!

Pieter van der Merwe
22 March 2019

CHAPTER 1

Trust Yourself

Trust is when one believes in a person, situation or thing.

Trust is a big word – and a critical one at that – but it is often mismanaged due to overthinking. So often, you will find yourself with far too much information at your disposal. Being almost too experienced in your industry, you will overanalyse situations and the 'trust' part will go out of the window.

We all want the route of safety, comfort, and predictability but we don't always get it. Many people's minds have been programmed to follow commands rather than to think and trust their own judgements. Of course, this differs from continent to continent based on cultural upbringing, but the key take-away is that many people don't trust their subconscious decisions when they should.

Let's throw in a number to make this more concrete: People in business should trust themselves 30% more than they currently do!

Businesses don't come with a manual 'trust your gut feel' mode or way of thinking. Some things in business are just not meant to be analysed; they are meant to be felt.

Here are some ways to force your mind to trust yourself:

See yourself as a leader—Envisage yourself as the boss, even if you are not.

Confidence—Never be short of this. A client will spot a less confident person with ease. We all feel safer with a confident and knowledgeable business person by our side.

Know the worth of your products or services—A lot of money has gone into building your business, so don't back down on the actual value of your work—even if your mind starts telling you to do so for fear of losing a client. Clients come and go. Another one will appear who will appreciate your offerings for what they are worth.

Trust that gut—If it feels good, then go with it and vice versa.

Don't overthink—If a client says "no" to your proposal then so be it and move on. There are loads of other clients out there who will say "yes" *and* for your price.

Learn to live with consequences—Sometimes your gut feel will take you to the right decision and ultimately success.

The truth is, on occasion, you will be let down. And it will be due to changing business circumstances, not your own fault. This is a part of life. It is a learning experience. Treat it as such.

Now let's take a closer look at the word 'fear'.

For example: When you buy a business that is not doing well, the buyer will always have the fear of whether (or how soon) the business can be turned around to profitability.

There are several possible reasons for this:

- Experienced and knowledgeable management might leave the business.

- There may be a drastic currency change in the market.
- Competition in the market may increase.
- More funding may be required, and there may be a struggle to raise the cash.
- Outdated assets may need to be replaced.

There is some good news, though. Statistics show that 85% of fears are never realised. So, the 'fear' aspect shouldn't even be in the business owner's mind in the first place because the risk and business were there before he or she bought it.

So, what is the best way forward?

It's simple—control your doubts, use positive thinking, and take the lead.

Remember, 'fear' won't go away! It is your approach that counts!

Two months later, you will probably sit back and laugh about it!

Let's spend some time now looking at some of the reasons why business people do not trust themselves enough.

Many people push themselves to the absolute limit and end up working a five-, six- or maybe even a seven-day week but still end up believing that they have not done enough in the business space.

The reasons behind this behaviour boil down to a lack of confidence. Perhaps a person who behaves like this is worried that if he or she agrees in his or her mind that enough work had been done, then he or she will have settled for mediocrity. This type of person will tend to bank the successes he or she has achieved and instead focus on those worries. It's a case of obsessing on the possible problems rather than enjoying the successful moments.

Even if the project has made millions of dollars, this type of person will still believe that the cash return isn't enough.

Every business person wants to go out there and make things happen, but there are limits to how much one can do before burnout sets in. As a business owner I hate to say this, but there is more to life than sitting in an office day in and day out and working your fingers to the bone. If this is how you operate, you have lost the enjoyment element in your job and, when this happens, the lack of trust will eventually kick in.

The lack of trust element will be even more present when you are called on to make big decisions. Suddenly you will start to rethink the obvious or not trust your gut feel (something we often address in this book). Instinct will fly out the window and will be replaced by doubt.

You will have lost your ability to take a risk on a huge opportunity, preferring instead to turn it down.

If you are battling to come to terms with your confidence level due to a lack of trust, then how can you expect the clients to trust your judgement?

Remember that an experienced business person should be able to make effective business calls based on trusting his or her knowledge and experience. He or she will understand that others are looking to them to lead the way, particularly when it comes to strategic calls. If it is your business, if you are the boss, don't let the big decision-making moments be hijacked by others. At the end of the day, you are responsible for the final decision.

This means having more than one arrow in your quiver. A good business person will not go into a big decision-making meeting with only a Plan A at his or her disposal. He or she will also have at least a Plan B and Plan C to fall back on.

Don't go to the extreme and have too many backup plans though. Otherwise, you will tend to complicate the matter.

That said, being flexible in how you can adjust your mindset and levels of confidence when certain decisions are being made will enable you to have a bigger impact on the wider scenario.

Trust the data that is at your disposal. Like anything in life, the outcome is not certain, but you are the maker of your business destiny.

Clients tend to respond to confidence. You are only as good as yesterday's performance in the eyes of a client, and there are many other vultures out there just waiting to take that client or a piece of business away from you, so approach everything that you do with the greatest level of confidence, and the client will notice. If you trust yourself, then this will not only help you but will also rub off on those around you.

Now let's check out why a person ends up in this lack-of-trust situation.

First, back yourself and don't just follow other people's views. Even if another person on your team is an authority in his or her area of the market, you still need to be able to make your own mind up.

Then analyse those big opportunities. Yes, they do often come at great risk, but follow your gut feel.

You will only understand this afterwards, but sometimes making a mistake does lead to eventual success. In other words, the lessons that you will learn from a failure could well be the key to taking you to success next time around. So, mistakes are not always serious errors, rather, they are learning opportunities.

Hesitation is a key to disaster. Trust yourself to make the bold move forward on a project or pitch or else that piece of business could be scooped away from right under your nose.

Don't live in regret. Rather make that call and leave the office knowing that it has been done and the future will be an exciting one. The old saying is that 'he who hesitates is lost'.

Just because you don't have a degree doesn't mean that you can't come up with a cutting-edge business plan to land that huge piece of business. Many of the finest staff are self-taught and don't have diplomas or degrees. Keep in mind that what one learns from the textbook at college or university often differs significantly from what happens in the real business world.

Once you have decided to go for that huge opportunity, now is the time for logic to kick in. Make a list of all the business tools that are needed to complete the project successfully. Then make another list in which you determine which of those tools are 'nice to haves' as opposed to 'really necessary'. Sometimes the mind wants what it sees rather than what it actually needs.

Trust yourself to make these correct judgement calls.

Remember that you are not a genius in all areas of the business, so don't trust yourself to the extent of being penny wise and pound foolish in terms of, for example, handling the accounting elements when you know that you are simply no good at it. Get the right support around you in the right areas to make a success of the project.

Work out the worst-case scenario in terms of the amount of time that it will take to complete a project. Then trust that you and your team are more than capable of finishing the tasks well within this timeframe.

Another area where trust is of importance is when it comes to delegating tasks. Are you able to share tasks with those around you, or do you feel that you are doing everything by yourself?

Is doing it yourself the way to go because you have peace of mind that it will be properly executed? This is a difficult call to make as your reputation is on the line, and so is your time, but at the end of the day, you need to be able to trust those around you. After all, that is why they were given jobs in your business.

Sometimes this is difficult as the client may have given you the business because of you, not your company. Here you can see just how important the mentoring of staff in relation to skills transferral is. After all, there are only so many hours in a day and in order to live a healthy lifestyle you need to become a good delegator so that you don't drive yourself into the ground.

All right, let's move to a level of positivity when it comes to trust.

Power comes from knowledge. Use the staff and other resources available to you to the best of your ability. Focus on those strategies that have been flooding through your mind for days, months or years. Trust yourself to make the right decisions.

Your business set-up needs to be done in such a way that both you and your employees will enjoy the day-to-day work.

Trust yourself to make this happen for the sake of your own sanity and those working around you. This will also make your business more controllable.

Trust comes from your inner soul. If your heart is fully invested in what you are doing, then trust becomes easier. If you have employed the right people in your business, it also makes it easier to trust. If you don't trust yourself to make the right decisions in business and life in general then who else will?

Trust yourself to pull off those big deals. Remember that your mind is your power!

CHAPTER 2

Common Sense

Let's first understand what is meant by common sense. Simply put, it is solid judgement concerning daily matters.

Common sense really asks us to think clearly about what needs to be done, and what the best outcome would be, given the decision required for the matter at hand.

Don't obsess about the end goal. Instead, focus on what is in front of you. It sounds simple enough, but in practice this is difficult for some to apply.

Many business people and people involved in business struggle to apply common sense. People must be empowered if they are to have any chance of being able to apply common sense. People are naturally too subjective in their approach to matters.

Being objective is essential to fostering common sense; this asks that you do not think with your experiences, background or genetic composition, but rather based on what needs to be done and what is objectively required.

You can't win with emotion clouding your judgement. Subjectivity won't help you in business. Objectivity will.

Here is an example: Last Saturday I attended a barbeque at my brother's house and his friend, Johnny, told me he was making tons of cash selling television satellite dishes in Kenya.

I loved the idea, but was this true? Common sense tells me that many African people are struggling with poverty and a satellite dish is surely a luxury, not a necessity.

On the other hand, Johnny could well be right and may have found the upper end of the market in Nairobi to sell the dishes to. I tell myself that I will need to learn more about this before offering to invest in Johnny's business.

Now let's get back to reality.

I have thought this through way beyond the notion of common sense because I believe that one should always remember that if something sounds too good to be true then it probably is.

Trust your gut. Don't trust your brain too much, and always give preference to your gut feel when you are pondering a decision. In short, don't overanalyse a situation.

Unfortunately, this isn't always the case, as we are taught from an early age to think things through carefully, but too much thinking suppresses common sense. So you have to unlearn some bad habits and work hard on your common-sense muscles.

Common sense is snappy, and one should make that decision quickly to really get the benefit of 'gut feel'. But, that said, common sense is the lowest quality of decision making, and we aim for great above-common-sense decision making too.

So, let's take it a step further and use the three wise men (or women) principle.

Surround yourself with knowledgeable people. Find three people who are independent of each other.

Speak to them separately and get their opinions on the matter that is weighing on your mind. Make sure that the three people in question are the right individuals for the job, and that they are people who have your personal and business interests at heart.

Once you have listened to them and heard them out, only then will you be in a position to decide. You are basically using the principle of 'trust' here, as these people are providing independent and objective input into your life or business.

Don't rely on your own understanding or knowledge on the matter. Your knowledge can be your own worst enemy because you think that you know too much, and you could be wrong. Think of yourself as a boxer. You can win against a person twice your size or height, but you need to be clever and listen to your instinct when it comes to throwing punches.

Finding the right balance in your thinking and then following your common sense gut feel is the best path to success. This is particularly apparent when it comes to hiring staff for your company, a big business decision that will be covered in greater detail in the chapter on 'New hires'.

When interviewing candidates, your gut feel will tell you if the person is right for the job, or not. It's not always about how well the person did in their final exams. You could end up with an absolute genius, who is not client-friendly and doesn't get along with anyone in your office—hardly a team player.

If you stop to listen, your gut feel will give you an indication of the right course of action. This intuition is often more accurate than any document in front of you can ever be. Remember, that your gut feel works in tandem with common sense.

Also, remember that running a business can be extremely stressful and it is important that business owners put the correct tools in place to help keep them and their staff stay motivated. Staff members need to receive sufficient training sessions and be surrounded by the best superiors and quality colleagues in order to deliver at their optimum.

Achieving this also requires common sense. Ensure that you are realistic about output and productivity expectations and that you tie that in with achievable timeframes and deadlines.

Don't promise a client that you will have the product to him by tomorrow when you know that it is not humanly possible to deliver by that time. Promising clients delivery or committing to other timeframes just to please them can come back to bite you if you fail to meet the promise. And it can also put your staff under unnecessary pressure.

You should also encourage your staff to adopt a common sense approach to their roles. Let's check out some points that should be foremost in the mind of a business leader when it comes to staff members making use of common sense.

First, set goals and hold people accountable. The staff need to understand that the workplace is not a playground but a business where jobs can only be secured if there is client satisfaction and money in the bank account.

Second, be calm when dealing with staff. Some staff will understand things better than others, but the ones using common sense are likely to be of the most value to your business. People are different and see and understand things differently, so business leaders need to walk a tightrope when determining levels of common sense and how to respond to good and bad decisions.

Never forget that the average business day is usually made up of several controllable elements as well as those that are uncontrollable. Those awkward moments that usually require urgent decisions to be made can usually be divided up into three categories. The first being what will take place, followed by what can happen, and lastly, what the uncontrollable element could be.

You can put all the strategies and plans in place, but it's very difficult to determine how others in your team will react in the face of an unforeseen development. This is where common sense steps up to the plate and can ultimately save the day. So, remember the cardinal rule of getting the most out of your common sense: Surround yourself with business colleagues who have a common sense approach to decision making.

Remember to be realistic – to exercise common sense – when it comes to your product offering or service to customers.

Ensure that you have the ability to deliver on what has been promised to your clients. Apply common sense when working out these plans.

In conclusion, the more experienced you are, the more you will think that others around you are lacking on the common sense front when they make errors in the workplace. As a senior person, you may need to remind yourself that you also started at the lowest level and may too have made similar mistakes. In 'getting your fingers burnt', you learned from the errors and became a more experienced and skillful business person.

Therefore, in remembering your own career progression, ensure that those individuals in your organisation are empowered to use and apply common sense.

You get this right by investing in your workforce. The more training provided to staff, the more they will understand your business and the tasks they need to complete. Common sense takes a person up to a certain point, but additional knowledge is still required.

CHAPTER 3

Understand What You Do

Understanding can be defined as the perceived meaning of a situation.

This is one of the simplest but so often forgotten rules of a company: Don't buy a business that you don't understand. You cannot rely on hope and luck when it comes to business. You need to understand it yourself and not rely on people who appear to understand it. Don't get involved if the outcome is not reasonably predictable.

Bear in mind, too, that to understand in the context of business must be understanding of the objective nature, not subjective. There is a difference.

In short, the trust you have in a person is no substitute for your lack of understanding. If you understand the business you are in, then the chances are that you will make the right decision. The end goal always looks very appealing and easy to obtain. Believe, me, it will be even easier if you understand the company and the market you are focusing on.

All right, now that we know what 'understanding' in business is all about, let's try defining the opposite.

The definition of 'not understanding' is lacking knowledge about a certain topic. This is important because if you don't understand what you are doing, you may just put yourself and your company at risk. You will also allocate capital to the wrong projects, which could lead to losses.

Remember that markets differ, so the US market is extremely different from the way business is conducted in West Africa, for example. Just because a product or service sells well in North America, doesn't mean it will meet with the same positive results in Nigeria or Ghana.

Business understanding doesn't mean that you must read as many books as possible on a certain topic. It means that you need to know the product, service, and selling market well before taking the plunge! This is why I say it is crucially important that you never invest in a project or business you don't understand.

I refer here to objective understanding because, in many instances, people think they understand something only to find out too late that there are holes in their understanding.

Not surprisingly this can only lead to frustration and tears.

If you for example don't understand the stock market, then don't try to invest money there. Rather use an experienced broker to manage your affairs on the market. The same goes for business.

Certain aspects of a particular market can be extremely complex, so you need to ensure that your level of understanding is on par with the complexity of the business. For example, imagine trying to produce hospital monitors or other technological equipment without having a solid understanding of what these pieces of equipment do and, more importantly, how much money you will be investing in the project.

There is a reason why certain types of specialised equipment or products are manufactured in hubs around the world, such as vehicle production in Mexico, South Africa or Japan. First, there may be more expertise in those regions due to technical trade schools, and educational institutions. Secondly, the cost of manufacturing may be cheaper there than in other locations.

Considerations like regionalisation and specialisation are just one element when it comes to understanding. Each business has its own unique circumstances. Just because you worked for a huge restaurant chain doesn't mean you will make lots of money if you start a similar business on your own.

It may look easy at first, but each business industry has its own challenges and surprises, which, if you are committed and able to think outside the box, can be overcome.

What must always be guarded against is looking for the 'quick fix' in business. Sometimes a business fails just because people are trying to be too clever about the way that they do things. Simpler is always better!

Many people leave university with a business degree or an MBA qualification and think they can solve any business problem. They soon find out that textbooks and lecture notes differ greatly from the way that business is done in the real world. Business is a living creature, it is ever evolving and changing, which is why it is fascinating.

The evolving nature of business also means that you will inevitably keep learning throughout your career. If you are a people person and can interact well with your colleagues or individuals from other companies in a similar industry to you, then you will absorb a great deal of extra knowledge from them, as indeed they will from you.

The key is to be open to these exchanges.

Don't fear that you might not understand something or look a bit silly when interacting with people on an issue, topic or concept you don't (yet) understand.

Rather, make the effort to learn about that part of the business.

Another cliché to summarise this is that 'no question is a stupid question'—unless the person who signs your pay cheque says so.

Understanding also extends to human interactions within the workplace, in other words having a happy and motivated staff. Losing experienced and knowledgeable staff can be a serious problem that can impact productivity and deliverables. If you don't understand the human aspect of business, then you will come up against this wall time and time again.

So, let's dig a little deeper in order to fully appreciate and understand this important aspect of your business.

First, keep all staff fired up for the tasks at hand by allowing the staff to give input as much as possible and don't limit the 'thinking' element to senior management only.

Younger staff members may be less experienced but could well come up with the next million-dollar idea for your product or service.

Teamwork is key to any organisation so encourage all staff members to work as a team. The old saying that 'many hands make light work' never loses its relevance. Diverse groups of people will hold different views and a good leader will appreciate that real value can be found in the input from a number of people.

Debating is always healthy, so encourage debates. Through debating, the business leader will also learn who truly understands what they are doing and who doesn't.

Suggest staff take notes in meetings because ideas put down on paper usually have a higher chance of turning into action than ideas that are simply discussed and then forgotten. Note taking also gives staff something to refer to in the future.

Try to avoid conflicts during meetings. Everyone needs to understand that they are around the meeting table to add value and, if the business has employed the right people, the meeting should consist of constructive input. Diverse ideas often bring about innovative business decisions, even though one may not think so when ideas are being tossed back and forth.

Highlighting the benefits of constructive criticism can be healthy if it is in the interest of generating a better service or product, but it can turn ugly if this form of criticism is used as a platform for one staff member to downplay the efforts of another.

It is important to encourage intra-organisational dialogue. Individuals from different departments, who work on different aspects of a product or service, may understand things differently. The business leader needs to adopt the mindset that 'no idea is a stupid idea'. All individuals around the table need to be respected.

Listening is one of the skills that many people from all walks of life struggle to get right. Many prefer talking to listening. You will be surprised how much you will learn through listening and, quite often, what you take in will clarify any questions that you may have about your tasks. It is, however, important to be open-minded in order to achieve the most from listening.

Sometimes in meetings it is difficult to keep quiet, particularly when you know more about a certain topic than the speaker does, and you know that he or she is giving incorrect information on a part of the project. So, don't take things personally. Rather use your understanding to your advantage when it comes to discussing action elements.

If you see that a colleague is not meeting expectations on certain issues, don't attack them in a meeting, but do understand that you may have to cover for them for the project to succeed. Some people talk a good game but struggle when it comes to delivering.

Remember the saying 'what goes around comes around'? You would hate to sit in a meeting with immense knowledge at your disposal, but then make one mistake during a presentation and have this being pointed out in front of senior management. So, don't point out mistakes made by colleagues. Rather encourage than resort to finger-pointing. Everyone needs to feel appreciated as this boosts confidence among all parties around the table.

Being well prepared for meetings will further enhance your status among your colleagues and will show them that you understand what you are doing and are serious about your work. Be the leader in establishing spreadsheets and online feedback sessions. This can only enhance your image in terms of professionalism.

If you are unsure of something, then ask. It's preferable to ask and obtain the information than keep quiet and struggle to complete your work when you get back to your laptop.

Knowledge is power, and you will become a more experienced and skilled business person by being a seeker of advice rather than keeping quiet and pretending that you have the answers to everything when you actually don't.

Understanding what you do is a vital ingredient if you intend on rising above the rest in the demanding business industry. Understanding is multifaceted: it relates to knowing the business inside and out, understanding human behaviour, your own strengths and weaknesses, and the global context of business.

It requires constant learning and refinement, being open to new ideas and viewpoints, and the humility to stop and ask if you are in doubt.

CHAPTER 4

Focus on How

'How' can be defined as the way, manner, and means by which you reach an objective.

When it comes to business, too many people get stuck on the 'what' and 'when' elements and do not put enough emphasis on the 'how' part.

'How' is the actual hands-on way to move a concept from A to B. We call it the 'know-how' element of the process. When employing staff, the 'how to do' element is foremost in mind as one needs to analyse the abilities of candidates.

So, here we go. Let's bake a cake. How we bake this cake is the process. Do we have the correct ingredients, heated oven and time to achieve this objective? How we mix the ingredients is crucial too. Then there is the fun part of how we put the icing on the cake.

As you can work out, paying attention to the 'how' element is crucial because it leads to the end result—which is what the client will see.

Let's take a look at the 'how to run a business' element of the daily life of the leader of a business or a CEO. When a leader has been in a position of power for a long period, he or she tends to memorise their tasks instead of putting them down on paper or on a laptop. This is all well and good until the company hits a point of succession. The leader is about to retire and the new person taking over has fresh ideas but does not necessarily know all the daily tasks that the predecessor did.

In fact, the person taking over may be in for a rude awakening and will soon realise that the new job has a great salary and perks but has a list of responsibilities longer than his or her arm!

Note the importance of putting things down on paper or on a computer and not just storing the 'how' information in one's head.

If you are the leader and unfortunately get hit by the proverbial bus while crossing an intersection, that could well be game, set, and match for the business, or it could set the company back for quite some time if the important information is not in a place for the successor to access.

While a leader needs to focus on the strategic side of the business, the small things cannot be neglected.

Imagine if you are a restaurant owner and you have been so busy focusing on the range of menus to offer to the clients as well as stocking the pantry to kitchen with supplies, that you forgot to pay the electricity bill. You are grinning from ear to ear on a Friday night and rubbing your hands with glee at the prospect of making big bucks from all of the tables that are filled in the restaurant.

Then the municipality pushes the 'off' button on your electricity because of you being in arrears with your power bill. Ouch, how embarrassing!

The 'how' element is just as important on the basic needs such as paying the rent, water, and light bills as it is in finding the perfect food offerings that will make your restaurant flourish.

Never underestimate the importance of storing the 'how' information so it is always accessible. The fact that you have memorised the steps to run a successful business does not necessarily mean that the same can be said about your successor.

Remember that the smallest details in manufacturing a product or delivering a service could be the difference between success and failure. So, knowing how to properly delegate work will lead to an easier hand-over process, should the leader move on from the company or someone else be put into the position of decision-making.

Unless you are a small one-person business, as a leader, you shouldn't get too involved in the day-to-day operational affairs of the business, particularly if you have appointed a project manager to handle those tasks.

Yes, the wonderful winning formula of just how you want things done is between the ears of the leader, but it is pretty pointless micromanaging the whole business from the leader's desk when a manager has been put in place to do just that.

A sense of trust needs to be present. If the manager was appointed and has the necessary experience and expertise on the 'how' front, then the person should be allowed to run with the operational tasks while the leader sticks to the strategic side of the business.

Goodness knows, the leader is not short of things to worry about in terms of profit projections, monitoring the opposition, studying market trends, setting or adjusting profit margins and more.

Think of it as a football club. The coach or manager of the club is in charge of what happens on the playing field, but the general manager or CEO is in charge of the administrative side of the club. The roles are completely different, and overlapping will cause chaos and, more than likely, negativity.

The leader needs to focus his or her energy on spotting business opportunities rather than meddling with the 'how' aspects of the business. Sure, just like the office cleaner or receptionist, the leader's next idea may be a multimillion-dollar winner and the input will always be welcome.

So, let's take a step away from leadership and look at some important tips when it comes to product development.

First, one can never brainstorm product ideas to excess. If the right minds are around the meeting room table, then the old cliché of 'no idea is a stupid idea' should be applicable.

Sometimes, the corniest idea could turn out to be the one to guide your product to the biggest sales ever. Sometimes, the silliest idea might be the only one that you have and will make millions for the business in the long run.

Of course, you will only know if the product ideas are silly or not when the item is on-shelf or put into practice from a service perspective. How many people thought that Bill Gates was off his rocker when he started talking computer language? If it weren't for his ideas, which many deemed as silly, then modern technology and business wouldn't be where they are today. He had a clear vision and focused on the 'how' element with regard to his product.

No amount of evaluation of ideas can be too much either, but once you are ready to move forward, it's time to evaluate the market. Knowledge is power. Remember that your product may be a worldwide phenomenon, but is now the right time for its launch? For example, if your product is in the form of artificial chocolate, is it going to sell at a time when the diabetes epidemic has been making news headlines across the country?

Or look at it from another perspective. If chocolate is bad for diabetics, is your new artificial chocolate the answer to helping the country address the health risk? What is your research telling you on this front? Is this an opportunity to do a huge amount of business or is it too much of a gamble that could seriously backfire in the face of your new product and, indeed, your business?

What ingredients in your artificial chocolate mix are of such a 'WOW' standard that they will go a long way to making your product into a world first and consequently, put many chocolate manufacturers out of business?

You will not only make many enemies in the marketplace, but you will lose lots of money too.

It's the same as a person who finds an alternative to fuel or oil by focusing on the 'how' element. It could be a serious risk to the person's safety as finding a substitute to fuel or oil could see existing oil and fuel suppliers in the market lose lots of money.

Either way, I cannot stress enough the importance of focusing on the 'how' element. People will remember the product or service for what it is and, as usual, bad news gets remembered longer than good news, so keep the focus on the offering as your business brand is attached to it, whether the product or service carries your company name or not.

I trust by this stage that the leader has got his or her wise men and women around the table and closest to the world-beating product or service to sign a non-disclosure agreement.

Let's look at some of the biggest brand examples in terms of keeping the 'how' formula secure.

Coca-Cola's® secret formula of ingredients was kept in the SunTrust Bank vault in downtown Atlanta, Georgia, US from 1925. Many tried to emulate the Coke taste with few coming close to getting it right.

Another example of this is Kentucky Fried Chicken. The famous 'Eleven Herbs and Spices' recipe was written by the founder of the chicken brand, Colonel Sanders, and is stored in a safe in Louisville, Kentucky, under intense security.

Yes, it is great to have a team of passionate workers delivering a breakthrough, but the leader of the company needs to have the correct measures in place to ensure that the 'how' element does not disappear out of the door with an employee or consultant when they leave for greener pastures in the business world.

So many times, I have heard the story of staff leaving a company, either under duress or for other reasons, and taking the company client database or other key information with them.

Sadly, a sense of greed does enter the minds of some employees. Why should the leader cash in on a multimillion-dollar deal and the employee or consultant only get a monthly salary? As a business leader or company owner, one does need to be extremely cautious from a staffing or consultancy perspective.

One of the best ways is to allocate laptops to staff members and consultants and not allow any company work to be done on privately owned computer equipment.

Remember that your opposition will be just as keen to sign up some of your staff and consultants to work on their projects as you will be to gain some of their acumen in order to become No. 1 in the marketplace.

So, it is often a 'dog-eat-dog' scenario in terms of coming out on top in the 'how' part of the business.

The clever business leader will make sure that key employees or consultants put pen to paper on major non-disclosure clauses before working on any world-beating products or services for the business, so much so that any business transgressions will result in major legal suits being filed against people who take chances.

The 'how' part is the 'cog in the wheel' of any business and needs to operate at a reasonable pace in relation to the ever-changing world of business.

If the leader can drum the principle of 'only my best is good enough' into the minds of all of the workers on the projects and encourage a sense of loyalty and staff happiness as part of the mix, then good times will be ahead for the business.

Lastly, a final tip to keep staff loyal and happy and committed to not releasing any business secrets is to give them the best salary pay and perks in town, and they will be reluctant to jump ship!

CHAPTER 5

How Much Homework?

The type of business you are in or product line you produce will determine how much preparation and research will be required of you on the business front. Again, you will rely on your gut feel in terms of getting into a position where you feel comfortable with your product or service offering, but the general (albeit unofficial) rule is that six to nine months of homework is the minimum for skilled people in the trade.

That said, never 'overcook' on the research front because the more you overthink strategies, the more you will become hesitant to move ahead with your market offering. Again, trust the information in front of you as well as your all-important gut feel.

Once all the fundamentals have been met, and all the boxes have been ticked, you are ready to take the plunge!

Look at competitive businesses, analyse the market, and speak to friends and people in the know, such as your banker and lawyer.

Check out relevant websites and even gather opinions off market-related social media platforms such as LinkedIn, which also allows you to receive overseas feedback. The customer experience is always the key point. Explore how people buy similar products or services abroad and how they rate their experiences.

Since every nugget of information is important, let's explore some key considerations you will want to cover as part of your homework before you take the important first steps into a new market.

Choose the market carefully—a common theme throughout this book is the importance of going into a market that you understand. If you don't understand the oil business, then it would be foolish to throw millions into it, because your lack of knowledge could create a huge risk on your outlay, making business failure a very real possibility.

However, if you have the right advisory team around you and have put in immense amounts of research into the area that you are about to invest in, the risk decreases.

Make sure that you and your team have covered all the bases by studying enough market forecasts, analysis reports, risk management reports, market, and other documents so that you will not lose sleep at night over the cash that you are about to throw into your new venture.

Consider your company's capabilities; that is, does your company have enough know-how and resources to make a success of the business that you are about to go into?

Many business people get so excited about opportunities in the marketplace that they jump into business areas too hastily. A lot of homework needs to be done prior to hitting the proverbial business 'start' button.

Secondly, does your business have sufficient sales channels to generate revenue on this new venture? Is the required infrastructure in place to make a success of this new business channel? If not, do you need to go to market to source experienced professionals with the relevant knowledge to make this project work? And how much cash do you need to outlay on infrastructure to turn your business dream into a reality?

Spot the gap—sufficient understanding of the market, gained through undertaking detailed and thorough homework, will enable you to spot any other potential gaps in the market.

Perhaps other money-making opportunities will become apparent to you; an avenue which other businesses have yet to tap into. The homework element will allow you to make an informed decision regarding how much cash you are prepared to throw at your new venture. It's an 'outlay vs. risk and potential profit' situation.

With your entry into the market, your homework becomes worth its weight in gold. You need to ensure that your business makes a big impact when it hits the market with your new venture. Perceptions can be significantly in your favour, or the opposite. You need to make sure that through solid homework, your business gets things right the first time.

There is no time to carry out damage control on a market-entry service or product when you are trying to take over a certain sector of the industry. By the time you enter the market, all the possibilities should have been checked and rechecked, giving you a solid foundation on which to build.

When entering a market and your homework indicates a risk in the venture, in spite of the fact that there may be potential long-term profits, then perhaps you would feel more comfortable in sharing the risk by entering into a joint venture with another company. This will allow the risk to be shared, but obviously the profits too when they do eventually arrive. So, use your homework to reduce risk.

It is important to ensure confidentiality, so make sure that all your business staff and consultants have signed confidentiality clauses and non-disclosure agreements before working on any of your innovation projects. The last thing you want is to have put in many hours of labour and then have some unethical person to run off with your brilliant idea and take it to market himself, or sell it to the opposition.

It is unfortunate that some people behave in this fashion, but it is the reality of life, so keep your guard up.

Just to throw in a curveball, it is important to understand that there is also a very real danger of doing too much homework on a project concept and generally overthinking things. Sometimes a business does so much strategising that it needlessly delays taking the plunge.

By the time they are eventually ready to make their move, the business opportunity is no longer available. It is important to read the situation; remember that all-important gut-feel?

Sometimes reading too much literature about how other businesses attempted to enter the market in a certain industry could dampen your team's spirit and motivation. If previous companies had done their homework and timed their move to enter the market, they would probably be market leaders by now, but if they failed to capture the market, then you have a clear example of why you need to do things differently.

Don't try to copy business strategies of previous companies in the particular business space. Business is about being innovative and offering the client a service or product that has not been available to them before.

Remember that once a product is launched, it is too late to start worrying about what homework elements your team may have missed. Sometimes new ideas of how to improve your service or product offering do come to mind after the launch phase, but these will need to wait until the next homework opportunity.

With the entry into the market, you move from the homework phase into more of an action or implementation phase. Don't get the two confused. Homework will come around again.

Like all good schooling systems, there needs to be a process to go through all the homework that has been done, called homework review.

This happens in two parts. First, all completed homework should get 'marked' during strategy meetings in the build-up to the finalisation of the service offering or product and prior to going to market. Then, following the launch, the manner in which the product or service is being perceived in the marketplace needs to be analysed.

This will allow your business to understand whether or not the offering has been favourably received and what adjustments (if any) need to be made to improve on it. As much as your research team will have tried to come up with the perfect offering, markets are always changing, and you may find that additions to your offering may only become once the buyers have had an opportunity to experience your dream idea and formulate (and share) their own views.

As with so much in business, the element of gut feel will always give you a stronger indication of the right way forward than the active mind. But that doesn't mean you can't collect the necessary information to support your gut feeling.

So, let's summarise what we have learned in this chapter:

Do enough homework to make sure that your product or service offering will make a huge impact upon launching.

Don't overdo homework. Overthinking can eventually end up diluting a project, rather than adding value to it.

Make sure you have analysed the market to avoid any potential risks or traps. As you will, in all likelihood, be laying out some large amounts of cash on your venture, do everything you can to protect your business from possible risks by identifying them upfront.

Don't focus too much on how other businesses attempted to enter the market. Instead, keep your eyes on your own innovation, and you can turn the industry in your favour.

Always remember that it is better to be a seeker of advice than to operate in a reactive manner.

Students who do their homework diligently generally have a better chance of success in an exam compared with those who do the bare minimum in terms of work input.

Remember that out in the marketplace it's a real dog-eat-dog world. People will do anything and everything to come out on top at your expense. It's all about chasing the almighty dollar with the focus firmly on the bottom line of the income statement or balance sheet. Many people out there in the marketplace will claim to be your friends, but there is a fine line between friends and business.

Finally, be aware that the more success your venture achieves, the more people will be keen to see you brought back to earth with a bang. Success on your part will often be met with jealousy from others (usually those who didn't want to put in the hours of homework or money in terms or research, and who thought that success in life or business just comes easily).

In spite of these different reactions, never let your focus be distracted away from the bigger picture. You have done your homework and it's now up to the market to react to your product or service offering.

They say that fortune favours the brave, so it is better to go out there and try your best in a well-informed manner – having put in the necessary hours of homework – than not trying at all.

Never let homework deter you from action.

CHAPTER 6

Lean and Agile

So how do you transform your business into a lean and agile structure? It's simple really. Cut away all the 'fat' in terms of additional expenditure.

To understand the term 'lean', let's look at the opposite, which is 'fat'. This is when people are doing the wrong things that they don't have the abilities for, which means that you need to employ extra people or put additional resources in place. This makes your business 'overweight' in terms of staffing.

The 'lean' process of a business is about getting the right people into the correct positions to avoid carrying too many staff and additional spend. Some business people refer to the process as getting your business 'correctly configured'. Think of it this way: One staff member who is great at what he or she does is worth more to your company than four average employees.

Quality staff is just one key point, but there are others to help keep your business 'lean and agile'.

Outsource as many of your requirements as possible. This will reduce the risk of overstaffing your company.

Don't be people driven. If your dream is to have a huge workforce, you need to understand that it carries risks. What if you employ the wrong people and it impacts on product and service delivery to clients?

Abide by the slogan 'less is more'.

Lean-staffed companies tend to have great working environments and managers are able to get more out of their workers if they look after them well.

But never make the mistake of taking good workers for granted, since good staff can often be hard to find. Look after them and you will find that they will be hungry to succeed. Pay ten people well rather than paying fifteen people poorly.

If you are still battling to get to grips with 'lean', then consider the following example. An individual goes into business to sell dog kennels. In this context a 'lean' set-up would mean: Selling through an online portal like Amazon, having no staff, no office, no outsourced accounting, no outsourced marketing, not carrying any stock, and getting the supplier to ship directly.

Now that you have that example in your head, let's go a little deeper in understanding how to become a lean business. Let's look at some of the principles.

You need to decide what you can provide to a customer that is unique and will keep your business top-of-mind. A lot of businesses get tied into making products with additional features and actually forget about the basics in the form of what the client actually wants.

A good idea is to target twenty to thirty clients and carry out your own survey. This will give you a good idea of the client's mind-space when it comes to your offerings and it will save you money and resources so that you don't produce what a client doesn't want or sees as peripheral.

Because bringing to market is expensive, the above point will help you to work as economically as possible. For example, it is always good to check out the shelves for competitors' products.

If you have developed your idea of a product based on your own concept, then you may have already thrown a few million dollars into the water. Now that you have seen what your opposition is up to, you should have an even better idea of not only how to meet the needs of your clients, but also how to go one or more steps better than your opponents without wasting budget. Remember, keep it lean!

Remember the importance of investing in R&D. It is important to have a person or persons handling improvements, not only in your products or services but all aspects of your business. This includes client service, accounting, transportation and more. Each member of your business is an ambassador for your brand. Naturally, as has been detailed elsewhere in this book, the more job descriptions a staff member can carry out, the leaner your business will be too.

But, when in doubt, circle back to how to treat and retain staff: 'lean' only works well if you can retain these key staff members.

Now we've cut the fat, let's look at the term 'agility'. Agility is closely related to the ever-changing business world. Your business offering needs to be agile enough to shift with the market trends; be it pricing, competitiveness or other market movements.

You must understand that the way that your business was run in 1995 is probably not relevant today. One needs to be flexible and agile to move with the times. This means being open-minded around where your business will be five years from now. It requires embracing continuous change and being open to evolution.

It is often said that the only constant in business is change! Change and growth go hand in hand.

Applying agility to our lean dog kennel business might result in the business adding an in-house dog food brand to their sales offering. This will bring with it some new requirements, like adding the support of a nutritionist, for example. What else will change?

The appointment of a dog food nutritionist, the office space required, the fact that the business must carry stock (so additional funding must be sought), shipping costs must also be considered and the business will need to beef up its marketing department.

But it doesn't stop there. Setting a business up to stand head and shoulders above the rest in the industry also comes with these agile requirements.

Staying in touch—As a leader, it is important to stay in touch with modern market trends as well as modern technology.

As the CEO of a business, it could be rather embarrassing if you are the last person to find out just how impactful Instagram or Twitter was to get your brand message out to the market.

You would look foolish if you'd never used these free platforms and instead ploughed money into other publicity campaigns that weren't as impactful as social media.

Have a clear goal—A company's goals need to be cast in stone. Many businesses change their objectives far too often during a year, and this makes room for inconsistency. You need to know where you and your business are headed.

A positive attitude from a positive leader will filter through to all involved with your company. You may end up with staff members of different age groups all working on a product or service offering.

Some people can think more outside the box than others, so always remain open to ideas from all parties. The business leader needs to be agile in his or her approach so as to get the best ideas and productivity out of all involved.

Based on the extended example above, adding a dog food element to our fictitious business impacts negatively on the 'Lean and Agile' running of the business. There may be a positive financial return, but only in the long term.

However, evolve we must.

If we are not agile in our business thinking, I am a firm believer that we run the risk of being outmanoeuvred by the 28-year-old yuppie go-getter who does his business off his laptop with no company overheads, while sipping a cup of coffee on top of Table Mountain in Cape Town.

This mobile go-getter is our fiercest competitor since, without overheads, he can offer much lower prices to the market, and, quite possibly, quicker turnaround times too.

This opponent didn't exist 5 to 10 years ago, but he is now a huge risk for eating away at the client base and profit margins of more established companies. Some clients remain loyal to their suppliers, then again some don't. It is, unfortunately, not always about loyalty.

The words 'profits' and 'savings' stick in the minds of clients, irrespective of how long they have enjoyed a good relationship with their suppliers.

So, let's keep company expenses to the minimum but use our staffing as effectively as possible.

In this era of modern technology, much of the outsourcing mentioned earlier can be done via the Internet; for example, writing documents, doing research, strategic planning and more.

As mentioned earlier in this chapter, would you rather pay ten people well or have fifty staff on your books but pay them an average salary? Which scenario will bring about greater productivity within your business?

We are living in an era where money talks and loyalty is often tossed out of the window, unless the business leader can really make the workspace into a place where people just don't want to leave.

Some businesses use perks within the 'lean' element to retain top talent. Perhaps instead of offering huge salaries, perks such as retirement policies, medical aid, and vehicle allowances can be offered instead. There are also other perks you might consider, such as mobile telephone and entertainment allowances. Many of these perks can be written off to tax.

Ultimately, the package being offered should be so attractive that staff members do not want to leave your business because elsewhere they might earn more but would lose these perks, which in the bigger picture at month's end in their personal lives actually means that they might end up with less cash after all the bills are paid.

Note that as a business leader, you are still running a 'lean' operation. It is just that you are 'boxing clever' from a business sense.

Lean and agile businesses tend to be the leaders in the marketplace. All it takes is a bit of common sense and strategic thinking to get your business to that level.

All business leaders started at the bottom or close to the bottom of the food chain in terms of employment, so they know how it feels to slave away but not earn the big bucks.

Sometimes the staff feel used and abused, but by running a 'lean' business, there are ways and means to make the workplace into a better space.

From an agility perspective, the more agile, the better. It allows for quicker decision-making and implementation in the market.

In conclusion, make sure that your business is agile and flexible enough to adapt quickly to the changing needs of your clients, and you will ensure that your business and brand stay one step ahead of the rest in a highly competitive market.

Clients are not fools.

They know a good service provider or product when they see one.

CHAPTER 7

Fundamentals

Building a business is undertaken for one main reason—to generate cash, and, when it comes to existing businesses, to increase cash. I do not refer to profit because you cannot bank profit, or pay with profit; profit is an indicator of viability. A business runs on cash.

This is the first fundamental of business. But it is not alone. There are other core principles which need to be adhered to and understood if you are to master this journey. If you always remember these and act on them accordingly, then you will be well on the road to creating a good business structure.

Before I discuss the fundamentals, I think it's important to note how crucial mindset is when it comes to business. Always be positive and optimistic. Yes, that's hard, but working on developing the attitude that every single day is a miracle which offers new opportunities to you and your business.

Every step of the way, you will meet new people, so be ready to show them your enthusiasm and never underestimate the importance of relationship building. The old cliché that first impressions last forever has been around so long because it is true!

So here we go with the fundamentals.

Cash flow

As mentioned, the ability to generate cash. This will be discussed in more detail later in the book, but 'income will always be greater than expenses' and the big C-word – cash flow – should be filtering through your brain even when you are asleep. Quite frankly, some business ideas don't have the ability to generate cash. Say, for example, you were to start a business that sells VHS videos. Honestly, it's a dead duck, because it doesn't fulfill any need; nobody needs it anymore. Ultimately, your business model would be inherently flawed from day one.

So, let's examine the basic rules when it comes to monitoring your cash-flow situation.

Never run out of money—If there is no cash, you do not have a business. It's as simple as that. Always manage your accounting system with care.

Cash flow is key—It's not about what invoices have been sent out to clients, as there is always a chance that some clients may not pay on time or at all. What is important is the cash in the business bank account. The old saying is right, 'cash is king'.

Always know the levels of your cash balance—Always know what your cash balance is. How can you make sensible business decisions if you are unaware of how much cash is in the bank?

The risk of managing according to bank balance—There are two types of indicators on this front, and they must not be confused. The first is the bank balance, and the next is the cash balance.

Don't run your business according to the bank balance, but rather according to the latter. You use the bank balance to reconcile financial matters.

Six-month cash balance—This is where long-term planning comes in. What will your cash balance look like in a good few months from now?

Cash flow setbacks—Some business owners turn a blind eye to potential cash flow issues in the belief that the problems will go away or rectify themselves. Perhaps they think that the problems are too small to warrant sufficient attention. This factor links with the previous point mentioned here. What will my cash-flow situation be six months from now?

Taking care of clients—Cash in the bank eliminates stress in your life. Some say it's a blessing to have clients who pay on time, so these relationships need to be nurtured to bring about growth.

Working out cash-flow charts—These projections need to make wise and profitable sense.

When operating a business, it is essential to keep costs in front of mind, but it is equally important to nail down this business fundamental from the start when you are first establishing your business.

General Considerations

Consider some of the following expenses you need to think about from inception:

Consultancy fees—If you are planning to start a small- to medium-size business, the chances are that instead of employing a large staff, you will make use of several consultants (for example, a design company, advertising firm or public relations specialist) to make your business visible to the market.

Then there are the most important consultants of all in the form of contracting an accountant and a lawyer.

Rent—If you are renting office space, it's not only the rental you need to consider but other bills as well, such as water, electricity, and gas.

Insurance—This is a key element that often gets overlooked or regarded as only covering vehicle and office equipment and furniture insurance.

Promotions and events companies spend a fortune on public liability insurance in the event that some form of injury or damage to a person or a person's property occurs at one of their events.

This is also necessary at your office. It is easy to put up signs stating that people enter the property at their own risk, but these do not always hold up in a court of law when something goes wrong.

Staffing—At the beginning, keep things as trim as possible until you have solid cash flow from earnings, not from loans or capital outlay.

Marketing—This is usually the first budget to be cut back when times are tough, yet it is the budget which has the potential to get your business out of the hole and on to greater things.

One good marketing element (be it social media, a mainstream newspaper article about your offering or perhaps a radio interview profiling your CEO and your brand) and the game can swing in your favour, so never underestimate the power of marketing.

Stock—There is always a fine line between how much stock to purchase as it brings with it potential warehouse expenses. On the other side, you don't want to purchase too little and run out when items are racing off the shelves in the stores.

There are variable costs to consider too.

Transportation—After all, you have to get your products shipped out or distributed to retailers; you need to factor in this cost from inception.

Demand

So, step one is to determine if there is a market for your product or service.

The key here is to first establish if a market exists for potential sales of your services and products. Sometimes you end up with a brilliant product, but no market.

Other times you might spot the perfect market, but not have the right product for it. You need to understand your clients' needs. Determine upfront how big your market is, and consider the likelihood – or risk – that it may change, for either the better or the worse.

As an example, imagine you are about to sell milk in Arizona. The first step is to make sure that the people of Arizona buy, like, and drink milk. Also, just because these people bought milk there ten years ago, doesn't mean they will still buy milk today.

You need to analyse the market and also keep an eye on what your competitors are doing in that selling space.

Sometimes people take it for granted that they have a big market, especially when they think they have a great product. In other words, sometimes they are under the mistaken impression that their product solves the needs of many people.

Never take this for granted; determine up front who makes up your market and ensure that your market is big enough to create lasting growth opportunities.

Say you want to start selling fizzy drinks in Namibia. Your first step must be to determine if people will use your product, if they will buy from you. Then you need to ensure that there are enough people who will buy your product on an ongoing basis. Never settle for a small market.

Balance

Aim for balance at the start and throughout. Don't buy more stock than you have sales for, and don't sell more than you are able to deliver. You should keep adjusting to ensure the correct balance between input and output throughout the growth of your business. Your parents probably told you, back when you were a child, that you need to crawl before you can walk, and you must walk before you can run—well, the same logic applies to running a business. Be positive but also be realistic.

Don't try to rush things unless you really spot a billion-dollar opportunity in front of you. Remember the C-word—cash flow. 'He who controls the purse strings controls the game' is another old, but true, saying.

Balance means being lean at the start, keeping things simple, and ensuring overheads are at a minimum.

Balance in this context means being realistic. So, if you are just starting out, appreciate that you probably won't have a lot of sales to begin with; therefore, you need less by way of expenses than you will need when you have grown into a big business. You must only market to the extent that you are able to produce and deliver.

Research and Development

R&D implies constant planning for the future and guarding against stagnating and becoming outdated. In fact, 5% of gross profits per year need to be budgeted for R&D.

It is important to analyse your market and possible new opportunities as you go along. Markets may change, and the needs of customers may change. Your market may alter over time for various reasons.

So, you should continuously position yourself for the future, be ahead of the curve, and ensure that you evolve in tandem with your customers. Don't wake up too late in this regard.

Execution

Let's call it like it is—if you can't execute to a client's satisfaction, then shut the door now and throw away the key. This point cannot be compromised on. Here is a quick top-of-mind checklist. What does the client expect? Why does the client think your product is so great? How will the client feel about your product a few months down the line (is he or she still so excited and enthusiastic about your offering)? Based on this checklist, you will know what to do or change to ensure that your client remains just that—your client.

Packaging—How you choose to package your product for sales is vitally important when it comes to winning over the minds of the clients and appealing to the right audience. The right packaging costs money.

Wages—These could change from week to week depending on how many people you need to sub-contract at your business.
This may also work out on a project-to-project basis, so there may be times when you need more staff to be paid on a weekly basis while other months of the year may be quieter.

Ideally, your operations will be self-funded, meaning that you need minimal cash to start off with.
The business may also open your eyes to other opportunities. If you see a bigger business in making the labels than selling the spices, then you have a choice. Either close down the spice-selling business and start making bottle labels or keep both as streams of business. Always be open-minded.
So much for the small guy, now let's think of the big ones!

You just bought a window-frame business for US$73,870,000. The company's books show that the business has been running at a US$5,500,000 loss and has recently not been operating at all. It is difficult to pull yourself out of this loss position by just doing the ordinary; your only choice is to do exceptional things, and you need time to make these interventions work.

Most people jump to the conclusion that they need to fix all parts of the project rather than focusing on one part at a time. The truth, however, is that you can't fix everything at once. Start with a blank page and find out why the business is struggling. Then draw up an action plan to remedy the situation one element at a time. Or even better, work out a five-year expansion plan with a 30% gross margin.

Perhaps the business needs another product to help it attract buyers and to generate more cash? What about selling door handles either as an added value to your current well-priced window frame or at minimal additional cost?

Now, look at your cash-flow reserves. You need to stabilise them. Part of the underlying cause of the loss being experienced by the business could be that the previous owners were carrying too much stock.

You will need to have a good credit record too, in case you do urgently need to buy some stock. Always make sure that you have about a 15% cash cushion on hand, as this is crucial for the execution phase.

Fundamentals are key to anything that is done in business or life. Stick to the principles and use common sense. That is our next chapter.

CHAPTER 8

New Hires

Hiring is the backbone of running a business. When you hire someone (or take on a new supplier or contractor), you obtain the temporary use of their services for an agreed payment.

Gone are the days of the human resources manager simply employing a new staff member based on experience, knowledge, punctuality, general image and cleanliness, being a team player, and intrinsic motivation.

In today's international world of business, the boxes you should be looking to tick when hiring a new staff member include; a 'good fit' for the team – so that all persons working on the project can produce at their maximum – a caring attitude, focus, and a serious outlook to the task at hand.

Additionally, strong-mindedness is needed for a person to handle criticism and also say what they think; and, lastly, honesty.

Fresh ideas and frequent injections of renewed enthusiasm are needed to stimulate growth in any business and it highly likely that modern-era talent will be more in touch with modern market trends and will be able to add more value than the person who has been with your company for twenty-five years.

It may sound cruel, but business is business.

Hiring can be a stressful aspect of running a business, but it really doesn't have to be seen – or approached – that way.

When busy with the interview process, some human resource managers or CEOs focus more on the structuring of the person's CV rather than the content. So, the first point to remember is that it should really be the other way around.

Once a shortlist of candidates for certain posts has been drawn up, some companies let the persons stay with them for a day to see how they adapt to the new environment and, through their interaction with existing staff members, determine if they are team players or not.

As the day draws to a close, the potential candidates are then put through what is known as an 'exit test' to gauge their feelings about the day spent at their potential employer.

At this juncture, many questions can be asked regarding how the person felt working on the various aspects of the business throughout the day.

It is often a good idea for the exit test to be carried out by a neutral person, in other words, by the personal assistant to the CEO rather than by the CEO or the human resources manager. This will allow the candidate to give a neutral opinion in their responses.

While this is a good way for both the potential employee and the company to get a sense of one another, the bottom line when it comes to hiring is that companies look for people who can fit into their business culture. So, again, the gut feeling you have regarding the person's work and work culture should lead the way when you are making these important decisions.

Quite often a business advertises a post because they want a 'different' type of person from the individual they already have in the role. The CEO and human resources manager know exactly what type of person is required, but the key element in their minds will always be that their clients must be able to trust that person.

A nice person is not always the best for the job as there are so many other factors that need to be considered.

Here are some of them:

Many companies believe in pre-screening candidates before they arrive for the first interview, while others rely on their gut feel during the first session. So, it's important to work out your employer-recruiting strategy.

Look for someone who is extremely dedicated to their line of work by allowing the potential staff member to do a writing task at home. Some people take chances and pay others to do the task for them to impress a would-be employer, but that defeats the object of the exercise. Good jobs are scarce out in the market and some people will go to any lengths to succeed.

Ensure that there is compatibility with the way the person operates and how your company does business.

Check out the social media profiles of potential candidates. This is not being sneaky but rather falls under the category of getting a better feeling for individuals and how they live their lives in general.

As an example, if a person posts on their Facebook page that they party during the week until 4am each morning, then he or she is hardly likely to be in a fit state to be giving their best in the workplace between 9am and 5pm Monday to Friday.

Hiring interns is naturally a cheaper route to follow for any business, and while many of these former students may have less experience than you might want, the question you need to ask is: Can they be groomed for greater things with a bit of time and patience?

Ideally, new hires should spend a day at your business as an observer, and if they are currently employed, they should take leave for this purpose. This is an extremely important step as it enables both potential employee and employer to evaluate a future working relationship. This will help you to make an informed decision about new hires.

Remember that your business values should be built around top-class work, quality service delivery, and professionalism. The first member of staff that you hire for your business will be the yardstick for either good hires or bad hires. He or she will be the measurable element for future hires, so choose carefully.

Bear in mind that the staff hiring process is far different from how it was a few years ago. Today we enjoy far more access to information from a digital perspective, which allows for greater analysis of potential candidates.

Sifting through piles of CV profiles used to be a tedious process, but with the use of digital software packages this can now be done within minutes, giving your human resources expert time to weed out the 'fly-by-night chancers' and focus only on those quality candidates who stand a chance of being shortlisted for the post.

Gone are the days when candidates could only apply for a job through newspapers or magazines.

These days the best candidates are the technologically proficient ones who usually apply for posts using online portals.

In a large business, new hires often tend to become just a number in a large staff complement. While in a small- to medium-size company things are quite different, with each member being a cornerstone of the business and a building block for the future.

In both cases a good candidate is important, but particularly so for smaller, more streamlined outfits. So what traits will a good candidate possess?

First, ask yourself: is the new hire's mindset aligned with what my business wants to achieve? Your human resources person should get a good idea on this front from the interview process, as the CV profile is often nothing more than a carefully crafted document which is often not even written by the candidate but by a third party.

A face-to-face meeting will allow the hirer to decide if the candidate is likely to be able to align with the vision of the business or not.

Second, how willing is the candidate to keep learning? If the candidate believes that he or she has all the answers, then it may be a bad fit. Even the most experienced CEOs or business leaders will tell you that they learn something new about their line of work each and every day. In life, one never stops learning.

Next, is the person willing to be accountable for their tasks and able to handle additional responsibilities? Some people go to work based on a 9am start time and are homeward bound by 5pm, while others are prepared to handle additional responsibility as they look to grow in the business.

It all depends on the mindset of the candidate. Your human resources person should be able to get a good feeling about this from the face-to-face interview session.

Friendliness, punctuality, and confidence are traits that are hard to teach.

You either have it or you don't, so the presence of these elements should make a potential candidate stand head and shoulders above the rest during the interview process.

Your human resources expert should also be able to learn from the interview how focused and ambitious the candidate is. "Where do you see yourself five years from now in the business?" is always a good question to ask during the interview process.

The answer will determine the candidate's mindset. It may even give the human resources person a good gut feel as to whether the candidate plans on using the business as a stepping stone or a port in a storm, or whether they want to build a long-term relationship with the business.

These days, most businesses operate at a decent pace, so the art of multitasking has become crucial. Can a potential candidate work on two or more projects in a short space of time and be successful at it?

Of course, the more a candidate can multitask and achieve successful outcomes, the more he or she should be looked after by the business in the long run.

Some business leaders like to hire a candidate who is just like them; who reminds them of themselves. If the CEO is arrogant, he or she may like to hire an arrogant candidate, or if the CEO is diplomatic, he or she may favour hiring someone who has similar personality traits.

This can be a good or bad thing in the long run for the business, which is another reason why the CEO should not be involved in the interview process.

Some business leaders may go the opposite route in terms of hiring. If the CEO is arrogant, then they might look to hire the opposite type of person – maybe a diplomatic sort – to balance things out.

Research is increasingly telling us that diversity in business is a positive step; it allows for different thinking and innovation. Having a team comprising the same traits and talents will not encourage outside-the-box thinking.

Next, is the candidate looking to earn praise all the time? Some candidates play this game and end up being frowned upon by their colleagues, while others use it as a form of motivation to keep a high level of work. It depends on the personality of the individual.

Some candidates are shy and less forceful or pushy than others. Again, this doesn't mean that the candidate is not good at what he or she does. Some of the more introverted people in this world make the best hires. However, they might not always be the right choice for interfacing with the client.

This is why your human resources department needs to be flexible when it comes to getting the right people into the correct positions and securing the right talent fit for a project team.

Remember that you are hiring a person to improve your business and add value in specific areas. You are not just hiring a person as a replacement for the previous one that left the company. You need to hire a person who can do a better job than, not a similar job to, the previous person.

Hiring staff can be a tedious process, but if done properly, this can be one of the most important tasks that your business will ever carry out. It's a rat race out there, so your human resources person needs to find the gems in the market before other businesses do.

We live in times where many countries are going through recessions and industries are shedding jobs, so many people will go the extra mile to make their CVs look better than they actually are in terms of what they can deliver.

Human resources must be mindful of this desperation on the part of some candidates as they focus on landing the right candidate. Otherwise, they'll be repeating the same process within a few months if the candidate they selected left rapidly after being unable to deliver according to the expectations.

In conclusion, this brings us to the point of expectations. When it comes to the expectations of business management in relation to the candidate, often these are poles apart. The candidate may see the job description as easy, yet the business leader may understand the deliverables to be extremely complex. This is often the case when hiring new talent straight out of university, as what is taught in the classroom and proclaimed in college textbooks is often quite different from the reality in the actual world of business.

CHAPTER 9

Interview Questions

Employing new staff members is not as easy a task as it's made out to be, but over the years I have found a few important principles to keep in mind, especially when it comes to placing candidates in key positions within a company.

Client interface is probably the most important role within a business, so when interviewing candidates it is important to remember that you do not only employ the right person with the right fit for your business but the right person who will meet the expectations of the client base that your company serves.

Whether a candidate is employed in the back office or in the customer-facing day-to-day operations of your business, there is bound to be interaction with the clients at some time or other.

A competent CEO or human relations manager will know that they have to put personal likes and dislikes aside when going through the hiring process. Over the years I have learned not to study the details of the CV profile of the candidate that is coming in for an interview too much, as this will lead to a pre-determined opinion when meeting with the person.

I see the potential employee interview process as having three phases. First, inform the candidate that you are going to ask about their personality, background, and personal interests. It is always good for the potential employer to know as much about the candidate's background as possible.

Typical questions are in the form of: What personal interests does the candidate have? What does the candidate do in his or her spare time? Does the candidate have any other side jobs or other business interests?

The second phase is targeted at the career objectives of the candidate. Then the third part will see the person answering questions as to why they find the advertised position appealing and what their career objectives are.

Then we move on to what I call the 0 to 10 questions. The idea score on these questions would be 7 upwards. When looking at personality, I would gauge an introvert as a 0 and an extrovert as a 10. There is nothing wrong with either, but I would be happy to score a 4 to 5 here. The next question is based on how intelligent you think you are. The mark on this one needs to be 8 upwards. Emotional intelligence should range around 8 and then the ability to be a likable type of person should sit at 8 upwards. Then I would look at how well people would connect with the candidate, which should also be at 8 upwards.

How much insight does the candidate have? That should also be at 8 upwards. Then it's a case of getting 7 or more based on how successful and self-driven the person is. Is the person happy internally?

This should also be 7 or more. Communications skills are important in most jobs and the candidate would need to register 7 or more on this front. Trustworthiness is something that cannot be compromised on and a 9 or more is required here.

The final question here is the ability to not only do a good job but to add value. Going the extra mile is a key element that many candidates understand, yet others don't. It basically depends on the type of person that one is.

Remember that experienced candidates are great to have in your team but don't necessarily bring with them the answers to all the challenges that have to be faced on the projects front.

There is often a big difference between what a candidate has placed on his or her CV profile and what he or she is actually capable of doing.

Here are some more questions that get frequently asked in job interview situations.

If you had to choose one specific skill that you have which makes you the perfect choice for the job, what would it be? The candidate should respond with a skill that is in line with adding value to his or her day-to-day tasks should he or she be appointed. If he or she mentions a skill that does not quite fit in with what he or she would be required to do on a daily basis, it doesn't quite help to land the post.

Another key question to ask is what major achievements has the candidate accomplished? This is a tricky one as in many cases awards are won by teams of people. Now, did the candidate that is hoping to be employed do most of the work towards the winning of the award or did he or she just accept the glory while others did all the thinking and implementation? This is another reason why reference checks are of such importance.

Now let's take a look at the person's ability to solve problems.

This question is not always the easiest for the candidate to solve, especially the younger, less experienced ones, but it has to be asked as a day in the business world is quite often not straightforward and poses many challenges to be overcome.

Does the candidate work better on his or her own or as a team member? The reality is that a company needs a person who can work well on either front, although teamwork is usually seen as the best way to go.

Is the potential candidate the type of person who is able to work directly off written or verbal briefs? Time is money in the business world, and as much as the team leader would like to spend the maximum amount of time briefing in each of the tasks to the team, sometimes it just isn't always possible.

There may be times when the candidate, if appointed, may have to do some problem solving on his or her own, although the leader's office door should always be open should further advice be required.

Then comes the crunch question: Why are you looking to leave your current place of employment? The worst thing that a candidate can do here is bad-mouth the current or previous employers. This would be an automatic red flag to the interviewer that this person is the wrong one for the job.

In which areas would the candidate require additional training in order to excel further at his or her job? While most office-based workers have average or top-level computer skills, some may wish to enhance their abilities on this front by taking other computer courses. It certainly wouldn't be a good idea for a candidate to state in the interview that he or she does not require any further training, as any form of knowledge is power.

The more knowledge a person has, the better. This is not a trap to find out which areas a candidate feels that he or she might be weaker in, but rather to establish in which direction the person feels able to grow.

The big question—what excited the candidate most about the job that being applied for? Perhaps the job package offers benefits in the form of health care, pension/retirement and others, which were not offered at the person's previous place of employment. Or perhaps the job offers the person the chance of local and international travel. The answers here could vary.

Some businesses believe in head-hunting personnel from other companies in order to fill key positions. Irrespective of whether the candidate is head-hunted for the post or whether he or she has sent in their CV profile based on the post being advertised, the abovementioned interview process is still worthwhile in order to get to know the person's background, aims, and objectives as best possible.

When it comes to senior management positions, the interview questions will become more complex as they could well include talks about shareholdings, benefits, bonus potential, severance pay, and other elements that may lead to this individual leaving his or her place of employment to take up the job offer.

The 'how much are you expecting?' question also crops up more often than not. To be honest, there are two lines of thinking at play here. First, the candidate will know his or her worth. The person's salary expectation is not based on how much their previous employer paid monthly but how much they feel they are worth. Second, the pre-screening process will be able to save the interviewing panel a lot of time and energy here if the expected salary is way out the proverbial ballpark. If the company is offering US$4,000 a month and the person is expecting US$10,000 a month, then it is not even worth going ahead with the interview.

Of course, some candidates will request inflated salary figures, knowing full well that they are likely to be negotiated down, but they also stand the chance of losing out on the job if their asking fee is far too unrealistic.

Many skilled interviewers will be able to tell over the telephone whether the candidate is a good fit for the job.

Following the initial interview process, the interviewing panel needs to go back and draw up its shortlist of potential candidates for the job. It is at this point that reference checks take place on the CV profiles belonging to the people who are to be called for during the final round of interviews.

If the pre-screening process is not managed correctly, the interview process may end up with the panel being forced to analyse the candidates according to the two words that start with a 'D'. Are the candidates being interviewed the perfect match for the job according to the word 'Determination' or are they taking a chance in the quest for employment based on the word, 'Desperate'?

Throughout the interview sessions, many human relations people or other decision-makers on the panel may get that gut feel towards a person who is aligned close to their own personality. Now it is time for a subconscious question to the interviewer. Does the company need another person of the same mindset as the interviewer?

Hiring someone is a big decision and needs to be done correctly the first time based on the interview questions asked. Getting this right is a 'must' as it could have a big positive impact on the bottom line of the company over time.

In conclusion, it is best to leave the interviewing sessions to senior staff members in the company.

It would be a good idea to bring project leaders on to the interview panel from time to time as they are the ones most likely to 'inherit' the new person. Make sure that they gel with this individual as they will work with them daily.

Don't rush the interview process. Finding the right person, with the right attitude and skill set is not always a task that can be completed overnight. Think about how long it took to build the business brand or to land your big client. Doing so will help you to understand the importance of getting the right people aboard, irrespective of the pressure that the team may be facing chasing a deadline.

Patience and common sense need to prevail in order to get the right person signed up, who will add value to your team over both the short- and long-term.

CHAPTER 10

Marketing

Marketing is a powerful word, but in short it means to 'package' a business product, service or situation in the best way possible to make it appealing to the buyer.

From the cleaning staff to the personal assistant to the CEO, we are all in marketing. It is all about how we interact with other people.

Let's look at the example of a personal assistant.

If the person has good marketing skills, he or she will be of major value to the company, which means that there will be promotion opportunities for that person. When he or she leaves that company, they will be in a position to exit with a good referral letter from their manager.

The term 'marketing' can basically be split into two different fields, namely internal and external marketing. While these differ in terms of focus, they both link back to the word 'reputation'.

Remember the Golden Rule—you always market to the decision maker, not to the client's brand.

Remember to work smart. You can't rely on luck in a crowded global marketplace. You need to nurture your brand. Later in this book, I will describe why I think Colonel Sanders's Kentucky Fried Chicken recipe was rejected 1009 times by investors before someone finally agreed to back him.

When we get there, just remember the word 'marketing' and the two golden laws that rule successful marketing: The first is that word-of-mouth advertising is always the best! Social media or any other form can't beat it! Second, always give the client more than he or she pays for.

Many suppliers have become so focused on profits that they have forgotten the importance of added value. We call this going the extra mile and, yes, clients notice.

So, let's look at the two main types of marketing and what you can focus on both internally and externally to market your brand effectively and efficiently.

When it comes to internal marketing, mingling works best, if done properly. Get some of your staff to mix with your client's staff, and you will be amazed at just how much you will learn about your client's business.

You may learn about new projects the client has on the table and will be in a position to forward carefully worded messages to their CEO about future business in other fields.

Lastly, sending cards and correspondence to clients from time to time is always a winner, where internal marketing is concerned. Always send a personal, handwritten note—don't email it! Such notes can be posted, or hand delivered to your client's office and can be displayed proudly in their office or lounge.

Where external marketing is concerned, the use of social media is vital. Platforms such as Facebook, Instagram, and Twitter are great platforms on which to follow potential clients. But, as mentioned earlier, your clients and competitors can also follow you, so be careful what you post from a reputation perspective.

When it comes to sending messages to potential clients on social media, one needs to be strategic. Different markets react differently to messaging. Don't overdo messaging to high-level senior management clients, who may see your continuous communication as a headache rather than relationship building. Think about it.

Investors communicate by the hour, but the CEO of a large

company probably less often. So, position your messaging and the quantity thereof accordingly.

Use conferences as both a networking and a marketing tool. Let your staff fly the flag for your company at these external events by handing out business cards and talking up the company.

Does the 'free lunch' aspect still work when it comes to impressing a client? Yes, indeed. Impressions stick in the mind of most clients. Just make sure you take the client to lunch at a proper restaurant and not a fast food chain. You don't want your brand – or you, for that matter – to be seen as cheap. Always keep in mind what a client is really looking for when considering a supplier. It's quite simple!

Clients look for suppliers that can handle reputation solutions and execute campaigns effectively. They want suppliers that can be trusted to carry out their deliverables, as stipulated in agreement contracts entered into.

Have faith and pride in your company and product and your client will too. Ultimately, reputation is key, so treat yours with respect.

In sports terms, they say that 'you are only as good as your last game' and the same applies to business because you will be judged according to your last piece of work.

One needs to keep in mind the difference between public relations and marketing. If your business makes use of a public relations firm to handle the publicity and media elements of your campaigns, you need to remember that they are only going to be as effective as the marketing plan that they are working from.

Marketing people usually take aim at two different parties in the industry.

There is the decision-making person who needs to be convinced that your product or service will add major value to his or her business. Many CEOs or business leaders are usually tight on the budget, so your marketing pitch needs to be mind-blowing in order to get you through the door.

Then, there is the next level of marketing target which is the person in the CEO's business who knows that your product or service will make the world of difference to his or her work or offering.

The person will have to take your marketing pitch to his or her team leader in a bid to get sign-off to make use of your product or service.

Undoubtedly, the person will be put through twenty questions or more by his or her superior, so your marketing pitch needs to provide all the necessary answers that the person will require in order to stand a chance of getting the go-ahead.

The key questions are the simple ones. How is your offering different from other solutions on the market and how cost-effective is it?

Many businesses spend hours on preparing their marketing documentation; from the colours being used to the wording or imagery, and then the training of staff on exactly how to position the product or service when they interface with a potential buyer.

Getting all of your business staff to understand the company's brand and offerings is vital as the marketing aspect is carried by all—from the CEO right through to the cleaning staff. You just need someone to say the right thing to the right person at the right time, and you could have an interested party.

Many businesses go the 'penny wise, pound foolish' route when it comes to saving money. The first budgets that get cut in this situation are the marketing and public relations, yet these are the ones that showcase the products or services to the industry.

A business can never do too much marketing. Sometimes, the results don't happen overnight, and it takes a form of repetition to bring about success. To ensure that your marketing materials do not become stale, be prepared to tweak them from time to time. Use trailblazing words that will catch the attention of the audience that you are targeting.

Then, there is the 'freebies' element.

Everyone likes to get something for free so be prepared to hand out some business, product or service items like branded pens, diaries, memory sticks, and more. These items are a small price to pay in order to market your brand for the right reasons. Don't underestimate the branding on your social media either.

Most astute business people, who happen to land one of your branded promotional items and are remotely interested in what you are offering to the market, will Google their way through your brand information on the Internet to make sure that you are a legitimate business.

Marketing is all about image, so dress neatly and when it comes to your social media platforms, make sure that all content is spell-checked and aligned or formatted. If you make a spelling mistake in your marketing content, how can you expect the client to trust your product or your service?

Your product or service offering needs to be as flexible as you are because you never know where the next call or email could come from.

Your closest friends or family members are usually the best marketers of your offering as they know you best and should be aware that you will not take a second-rate offering to market.

Word-of-mouth marketing is still the best form of advertising, at any level.

The business leader will need to reassess the marketing plan of the company, product or service from time to time so that the promotional marketing materials are always in touch with the offering. What is today considered to be marketing excellence could well be rated as standard in a few months' times as innovative platforms come to the market (for instance, Facebook is now being eclipsed by Instagram).

Remember that irrespective of how much marketing you do and how big your budget may be, brands take time to build.

For instance, if you are a fried-chicken restaurant, you will get your regular customers if your offering and price are right, as well as an increase in sales if the marketing is spot on.

However, you won't pull all of the customers away from the burger joint down the street as not everyone enjoys eating chicken.

Marketing

Sometimes, people can get carried away on the marketing front, and their expectations become inflated. It is important to remain with your feet firmly on the ground.

Chasing the bigger picture with marketing and other platforms 365 days of the year can become tiring and one can lose hope. Stick to the basics, but focus on delivering well-designed marketing campaigns targeted to the ideal client.

CHAPTER 11

Take Opportunities, Not Risks

An opportunity in business arises out of a need, and this need gives rise to a market. A risk represents the downside to this scenario. If there is doubt about the market, then there is doubt around the need for your product or service.

Opportunities in business circles can derive from various avenues, some as diverse as considerations around children, or as a result of death or divorce. Such opportunities usually fall into two categories: 'scarcity in the market' and 'disaster'.

Scarcities could well happen.

A major drought in a winemaking region and worldwide in 2018 would push up the price of wines and increase demand.

Using the same analogy, what if 2017 was a super year for the harvest, but not 2018? Quality wines will certainly be able to charge a premium on the 2018 harvest, especially if they can keep standards high.

An investor might consider the outcome of buying bottles of 2017 wine, after all they will be worth a lot of money in four years' time because of the scarcity in 2018.

So what is a good business opportunity? And how do you know when one is knocking on your door?

As always, your gut feel will play a key role on this front by helping you to assess whether or not an available opportunity has the potential to be successful. Sometimes, one can become overly enthusiastic when being presented with an opportunity and in such instances, the old adage of 'if it sounds too good to be true then it probably is' certainly comes into play.

The hindrance in most people's minds at this point is a fear of missing out on an opportunity only to find that someone else takes it up and makes millions out of it. You have to look beyond that 'grabbing' reflex and approach the opportunity with care and precision.

First, for any opportunity to be a success there must to be a need for the product or service.

Keep in mind that certain opportunities will work in certain areas of the market or regions in the world, but they might not in others. For example, if fried pork dishes sell in bulk in the US, that doesn't mean they will also in the North African countries of Algeria or Morocco, which are largely Muslim.

Of course, having the capital and other resources needed to back the opportunity is crucial. You can't go out and buy a Porsche but then not have the money for the gas, oil or insurance. The car comes with certain overheads that need to be budgeted for. So too is the case with the business opportunity. It doesn't only boil down to having the resources, but also requires the time and energy to make the opportunity achieve its ultimate objective.

Next is the ability to provide the product or service at the right price in the market. If, for example, you are in the business of home renting and you build a two-bedroomed home with a kitchen, bathroom, and lounge in one of the less-wealthy areas of the US, then you will probably not achieve the rental return you want for the cash outlay.

This is because the lower-level-income group of people who live in the area just don't have the resources. So gathering all the information you can is of prime importance if you are looking to buy a company.

Always get as much historical data on that business and its products or services as possible before you even begin to consider deciding. And take the time to scrutinise this information carefully and methodically.

Finally, let's look at timing. If the economy is going through a form of recession and there are job losses, taking an opportunity to produce luxury goods could well be a bad call, since sales may be on the slow side while the economy rides out this cycle.

Still taking opportunities into account, let's broaden our discussion now to consider the example of 'risks'.

Never take risks, always take opportunities.

Risk in and of itself represents negative thinking and is unpredictable in nature, so there must always be a positive trade-off. Although certain risks may be associated with opportunities, never take a risk without an associated opportunity.

The best way to illustrate this is by way of example. Say, for instance, that you've just bought an Italian pizza and pasta business from Mr. Fabrizio who was the owner/manager of the establishment for the past fifty years. The business bears his name: Fabrizio's Pizzeria, but Mr. Fabrizio has now decided to retire.

Let's consider some risks.

You may have a shortage of understanding of how the industry operates as the information is all in the head of the previous owner and there has been no form of skills transfer during the sale.

Mr. Fabrizio's son, who worked in the business for fifteen years, has decided to open up his own pizza and pasta restaurant down the street from this business.

A large pizza brand is reportedly coming into the area with a new restaurant backed by a huge advertising and promotions budget.

Customers may come to the restaurant because of the familiarity of Mr. Fabrizio; but what will happen when he is no longer there?

You may not be able legally to continue under the name. What then?

Using the same example, let's circle back and consider some of the opportunities:

You could get Mr. Fabrizio to continue with the business for two years, working with you to help create a smoother transition.

You could restrict Mr. Fabrizio and his son from competing against you in a similar business in the same town. You have fifteen years of financial data at your fingertips and, on face value, a loyal customer base exists. If you maintain their loyalty, this is something you could build on.

Ask yourself: What did that gut feel tell you before you paid out good money to take over the pizza and pasta business?

What homework did you do before purchasing the company? Surely you wouldn't have taken a major financial risk if you followed the two underlined points mentioned above, which have been analysed in detail in previous chapters in this book?

Taking risks is the trap that everyone tries to avoid, but inevitably we all fall into from time to time. It doesn't help that the notion of 'risk taking' has been somewhat glamourised in the press because it sounds very entrepreneurial indeed. But this is exactly why I strongly recommend against it.

The mere word 'risk' indicates that the final outcome is uncertain, and that's no way to go into business.

Business is about mitigating risk, not running towards it.

Now let look at buying a business.

When you commit to taking on an existing business – like our pizza and pasta joint – while there will always be a certain amount of risk involved, the positive side is that you are not starting a business from scratch and there should be some sort of track record to fall back on so as to improve on ways of doing things.

From a positive perspective, when purchasing an existing business, the company should have an office structure, inventory and sales client list already in place. It is certainly easier to start with these elements in place, than from scratch. Certainly, when it comes to obtaining finance for the business, lenders are usually more likely to assist an existing company than one that is just being launched, and has no history and performance data on which to draw.

As mentioned in detail in one of the other chapters in this book, never go into a buying deal blind. You need to make sure that you have some knowledge of the industry in which you are about to invest.

Never put yourself in the position of being in the hands of your staff, especially in they hold all the industry knowledge.

Some of your employees may take their jobs more seriously than others and, if the business folds, they can just move on while you are stuck with a failed opportunity on your hands.

Another important factor when purchasing a business is to find out precisely why the previous owners are so keen to sell. If the business is so great, then why are the current owners opting out? Sometimes the reasons are legitimate: Perhaps the owners feel they have had their innings and are now going into a retirement phase of their lives? Perhaps they are emigrating?

Often, however, owners are looking to cash in because the opportunity that they thought was a super one turned out to be less than they expected and has cost them money, and brought stress and trauma into their lives. Do you want this headache?

So, when purchasing a business, keep an eye out for any obstacle that may be looking to trip you up. Business debt is usually the first thing to consider.

Also, watch what your competitors in the market are doing and then you will be able to work out just how much of a slog it will be to catch up and pass them to capture greater market share.

Once you have weighed all the risks against the opportunities, only then will you be in a position to take an informed decision on whether or not the 'super opportunity' you've been presented with or stumbled upon is as super as it sounded in the first place.

Is the opportunity worth the cash outlay in the long run? And just how long will it take you to register a profit?

When it comes to the delicate interplay between opportunity and risk, the most important consideration is that emotions need to be set aside. You are looking to run a business, not a charitable organisation. The aim at the end of the day is to make money and to see your business, and its products or services, going from strength to strength in the marketplace.

The business industry is no place in which to make soft, emotional decisions.

Time is money and cash flow is king, and you will need to be accountable as to whether you made the right call in backing an opportunity or not. Even the most experienced and astute business people make the wrong calls from time to time, but naturally these are far less frequent based on their knowledge of the sector in which they are working. When in doubt, never be afraid to walk away. Sometimes that's the best approach you can take.

Finally, always keep your reputation in mind. Nobody wants to be known as the captain who was at the wheel of the ship that sank. Even in political circles, influential people only hang around with politicians who they believe will win elections, and the same applies to business. People will judge you according to your last game; so be sure that when you come to bat, you come out swinging.

CHAPTER 12

Mindset and Attitude

A mindset of an individual can either be positive or negative, but this is usually determined by a second person or group of persons that the first individual is in contact with.

So if there is a clear link between mindset and attitude, it is vital from a business perspective to employ the correct-minded people in a company.

Positive-minded people or people with positive attitudes will generate an energy of the sort that will further motivate others in the office. This will lead to camaraderie and friendliness that will also add value to the business mix.

The opposite sort of mindset or attitude leads to chaos in the office space and in many situations, problems spiral to the brink of being unfixable.

In life and business, you will find people with negative mindsets or attitudes.

The sad part is that sometimes these individuals don't even realise that they fall into this category as they live their lives that way.

It is best to weed such people out of the system sooner rather than later since their negative contribution once in the workplace tends to spread like a virus among other people, even after the negative person is long gone. Office gossip is the biggest killer of team spirit.

Hanging on to highly talented personnel with poor attitudes often leads to the downfall of companies or the loss of key clients. While the business may not wish to lose a highly talented worker, the risk of retaining the individual is just too great.

Sometimes the damage done is based on facts that are far from the truth, but repairing the situation and rebuilding the trust among staff members takes time and effort.

People who create problems in the office space are pretty easy to identify, but one must be cautious too, since the people who report such behaviour to their bosses may have their own agenda in terms of climbing the company ladder.

Having a positive mindset and attitude is vital for survival in the workplace. Remember having a positive outlook doesn't necessarily lead to success as there are many other factors that also need to be considered.

First, you need that positivity to be able to manage the daily business world. You will soon learn, if you haven't already, that in business, the only constant is change. Industries move at an amazing speed, and you will often find yourself in an 'adapt or die' situation.

You will need that positive energy to be able to deal with daily tasks, fellow workers, and other variables that come your way. You will have your own goals to reach, but some of these will become difficult as you will have to rely on the work rate or input of others in order for you to get to where you need to be in terms of work delivery.

The positive mindset and attitude will help you to keep your feet on the ground and see your way through the frustrating times.

Think of yourself as a book. Your mindset and attitude will be the cover of the book and people will remember you for this. The inside contents of the book will only be known to people when they get to know you better.

Let's think of the mindset and attitude from a sales perspective. Right, so you walk into a supermarket and find a product that you really want to purchase, but the item does not have a price on it. So you call over the nearest shop assistant to find out the cost of the item.

Unfortunately, the shop assistant is not a friendly person and is more interested in finishing his or her shift than helping you. The person heads off with the product to scan it at a register to find out the price, but then doesn't return. So you call over another shop assistant. This one seems more helpful, but also seems to have never smiled in his or her life.

Soon you find that no matter how helpful the person wants to be, they know very little about the product that they are selling.

Is this the type of service that you are happy to receive? Will you eventually buy the product at this store or will you politely say, "thank you" and go and buy it elsewhere? Then comes the big question: Will you ever return to this store even if it is the only place in the city where a certain item that you desperately want is on sale?

A positive mindset or attitude can win a deal while a negative one can lose customers for a business.

There is a saying out there in the world that 'confession brings possession'. In other words what you say with your mouth is what you will get in life and your mouth feeds from your thoughts. If you want your life to change or wish to land that big business deal then believe it, speak the right words and think the right thoughts.

Let's look at ways and means to keep a positive mindset and attitude.

Set clear objectives for your work. Don't make the goals impossible to reach. You don't need to stretch yourself to the limit every time. Make sure that the goals are positive ones. Try to keep your mind in that positive space so you can grow not only in business terms but as a person too.

Hit the 'reset' button and re-evaluate the way that you look at challenges and tricky circumstances. Approach all of these with a positive mindset. Think of innovative ways to get things done rather than coming up with a million reasons why some goals or projects cannot reach finality.

Always encourage people around you. Remember that teamwork

is a better business module to reach your goals than working as the 'Lone Ranger'.

You may find people who hoard information and don't want to empower others as they have been left out of a promotion before when they shared and acted as a team player.

These things happen in life but being a team player is the way to go and you will get more business breaks and other opportunities than the ones that may slip away by following this principle.

Everyone needs to learn the industry from a more experienced person. This is called 'mentoring'. Find that positive, experienced person to teach you the business and you won't look back. The person may even show you some shortcuts or easier ways of doing things that they learned along the way, which will save you time and energy.

Believe it or not, there are easier ways to do things in business which are not always shown in the tertiary level textbooks that you once studied from.

While the mentor will show you ways and means to handle things, all that you will learn from the person still needs to sync with your positive mindset and attitude. You can be the best in the industry, but if the mindset and attitude are wrong, you will struggle to gain a form of consistency in your delivery of work and won't stay at the top for very long.

Think of it from a sports perspective. The best in athletics, football, rugby, and other sports have been given the talent to play, but 80% of what they do is in the mind, while only 20% is on the track or field.

The best in the industry, be it sport, business or other, have worked out that if they can master their craft in their mind, then they can deliver high quality on time, every time.

Remember to keep meetings short and sweet. They are there for the purposes of brainstorming or sharing information, but these need to be handled in a highly positive manner to get the most out of team members in the time provided. Yes, there will be times when you will sit in meetings with the most negative people, but your positive approach and innovative ideas may just sway those individuals to change their mindsets and outlooks on business, and indeed life.

Always keep in mind that knowledge is power. One can never do too much market, product or service research. The more knowledge that you have at your disposal the more you will be helped to make the right decisions but it will also play a role in increasing your confidence.

Keep thinking about ways and means to change negative thinkers into positive ones. Don't leave the mind-changing element to the next person to do. You need to be the catalyst rather than sitting on the fence waiting to see how things will work out.

Make sure that you go about your daily tasks with the utmost respect for people, both internally and externally in the business. You may not think this now, but the weakest link in your business just might grow in time to levels that you will not believe and might be the person to give you your next job. So it is important to treat people with dignity and not burn any bridges as you travel along your business career path.

Another old saying is, 'if you do something wrong once, then learn from it, but if you do the same thing wrong twice, then you are a fool'.

Be the one to teach people the right way of doing things. Perhaps the mentor others learned from wasn't as good as the one who taught you.

Many hands make light work, so the saying goes, so be the one to help keep others from sinking in business terms. Remember that if you have the knowledge and experience, you may be able to complete certain tasks at a much brisker pace than others.

What may look like a mountain of work to some, will be a small job to you, so be the team player that can take the workload off the shoulders of others.

As I am sure that you have worked out, motivation partially comes from the leadership of the business but mainly from oneself. A positive mindset or attitude is often developed in one's younger years, but despite the age of a person, it is still something that one can always work on. It is a case of thinking 'what is right with something' as opposed to 'what is wrong with something'.

So you will also have worked out that hiring talented people for the sake of it is not always healthy. This is why those job interviews are of such importance as the CV profile of a person often gives an inflated opinion and distorts the real picture or abilities of the individual.

In closing, having a positive mindset and attitude could play a greater role in getting your next client or job than your talent can.

Companies and clients need positive-minded people that they can rely on to get the job done. If you are one of those and have the talent to go with it, then you will always be at the top-of-mind when it comes to receiving work or even promotions.

You know the old cliché—'good help is hard to find'. Be assured that the 'good help' are those with positive mindsets and attitudes as it is highly unlikely that a multimillion-dollar company will be pleased to hand over or outsource big-bucks work to a negative-minded person. The company's reputational risk will be far too great should the project crumble.

CHAPTER 13

Sway and Bias

To sway a person or a course of action implies the ability to control or influence the outcome. Bias, meanwhile, talks to a preconceived inclination or prejudice, often one that is considered unfair.

Remember that if something sounds too good to be true, then it probably is! This is never truer than when we are considering the balance between sway and bias in business.

Here we have to stop and remember the difference between gut feel and emotion. Gut feel is your instinct, while emotion is based more on your heart or feelings. Emotional decision-making is dangerous, so when in doubt go with your gut.

Don't allow yourself to be easily swayed. For example, if a school teacher you've known for over thirty years approaches you to partner with him or her to open a tennis academy, then you need to put all emotional links aside when deciding on the best course of action.

Yes, he or she may have your best interests at heart, but this is now a business decision, not a personal one!

Don't be swayed by personal relationships with people. Church people, social friends and other individuals you know may want to network with you for the right reasons, but that is still not a guarantee of business success.

Also, consider the decision to take up a bank overdraft or a business loan. It sounds super at the time as it will give the business much needed financial scope, but there is an inherent risk. Likewise, the loan idea sounds great—it's just the repayment procedure that isn't too pleasant. Don't be swayed too easily towards finding additional funding. Remember that the market of today is not necessarily the same as tomorrow. Business has a way of springing surprises on you.

Both of these are also good examples of bias coming into play, or preconceived notions and ideas influencing a key decision.

Bias is when one leans towards a particular element of a service or product offering because of an existing inclination. For example, if you are a successful pet shop owner, you may be more of a dog lover, than a cat-, horse- or cattle-friendly person. So when it comes to buying stock or new equipment for the shop, you may be more interested in spending money on dog-related shop equipment or stock than buying the same for the other animals.

In this case, you have an emotional link which forms a bias towards the dog department of the business, even though the other sections could potentially generate more income.

As a business leader, one can easily become too emotionally attached to a project. This is where the danger of emotions comes into play, particularly when you consider the risk in allowing emotions to outweigh logic.

Presuming is dangerous and opens up the element of risk. We are all human beings and do make mistakes in judgement from time to time, but business leaders, in particular, need to limit these errors as they could turn out to be quite costly.

Staff members too need to be aware of the sway and bias interaction within decision making since any decision taken within your company – be it by the business leader, a staff member or another supplier who is presenting to your company – will have major financial implications for the business in one way or another.

Many top business people rely on their gut feel to such an extent that they are able to arrive at decisions instinctively; this sets them apart from other leaders who want the luxury of time to think things through before determining the best course of action.

Often, however, those who hesitate will look back on their pausing moment in time and wonder how far down the line their business would have been if they had made the correct business move without allowing any form of sway or bias to be factored into the decision-making process.

This approach has a lot to do with an ability to read a situation, and this comes with a degree of experience in understanding the marketplace and the needs of your business, product or service offering.

Do you really understand the opportunity that is being placed in front of you? Will you take it or hesitate and allow the presenting team to go and pitch the idea to your opposition?

Remember how your body works in terms of decision-making. Your eyes see an opportunity and your brain has to decide. Because we are human beings, sometimes the brain looks for shortcuts to make things easier for this overloaded organ. This is where the bias elements creep in. There is another word for it: laziness.

The bias element is a way of processing information quickly, based on preconceived ideas. But this can be dangerous and limiting.

Most business people spend about two-thirds of their lives in the workplace, striving to build a better life for themselves and their families. So they will need 100% decision-making power and cannot allow the bias element to force them one way or the other; simply because the decision feels 'comfortable'.

Successes are born out of making the right decisions. But what about the times when a business or project has failed to reach its objectives? What sparked those decisions? Did the business leader wear blinkers and ignore key advice offered by the team? Did the leader go with his or her own view and shut out any other input? Or, as per this chapter, was the leader swayed away in another direction prior to deciding?

There is another element on the bias side which may also have impacted the leader's inability to make the right call. This is when he or she gets too connected to certain information and believes that nothing outside of it can be correct. It is always better to be a seeker of advice than to reflect afterwards upon the disaster that has to be faced.

As you can see, there is a fine balance between seeking advice and going with the gut feel. Applying this insight into your decision-making will certainly differentiate you from the rest.

Even the best business leaders make the wrong calls sometimes. This is referred to as a blind spot. Imagine making a wrong call only to find out a week later that the project you gave the go-ahead to invest in has been cancelled. Sometimes the blind spot does work in your favour! But very often it doesn't. There is seldom a free 'out' in business.

So, to avoid such situations, the best thing you as a business leader can do is to remain open to constant feedback from experts in this field who are in your employ and your network. Too many leaders fall into the trap of thinking that they know it all and have seen it all during their umpteen years of experience in the job; they feel that nobody can tell them anything that they don't already know.

If you are a business leader who has developed a tendency to only think in a certain way, then you need a change of mindset to get back into an open-minded approach. As mentioned, the brain does tend to get lazy at times, and the last thing that you want is for sway and bias to dog your decision-making.

One way of staying away from the danger of becoming 'too stuck in your ways' is to constantly monitor the mix and make-up of your team. Is the team diversified enough to offer new ideas from all areas of the market? Having this level of diversity, encompassing gender, racial and cultural inputs, will enhance a leader's ability to gather meaningful advice, and will help to play down any element of bias.

This is key, as all individuals are susceptible to developing bad habits when it comes to business thinking. Biases tend to work their way into your business life without you even noticing, which is why the feedback sessions on the leader's management style are so crucial.

Ultimately, of course, decision-making boils down to being

focused, self-disciplined, listening to your gut, and not being swayed or biased away from your initial thoughts.

Don't allow yourself to be swayed into carrying too much stock, even if your regular supplier is offering the goods at a highly discounted rate. The question should be why are the goods being offered at such a cheap price? Does the supplier know something about the market that you don't?

As a business leader, remember to keep setting goals and revisit them constantly. Be extra cautious should an emotional link come into play. For example, just because the project manager is your brother or brother-in-law, that doesn't mean you should give him extra leeway on the business front.

Finally, sway and bias are not as bad as they might sound on first mention. Both can be controlled with relative ease if you are a disciplined, open-minded business person.

It is all well and good to rely on clients, to seek advice and entertain new ideas, but ultimately the final decision rests with the business leader.

Many CEOs and business leaders end up having sleepless nights because of the sway and bias process, but it doesn't have to be that way. If they are their own people – in other words, they do not allow themselves to be easily influenced by others – then decision-making is not that hard a task. Remember the importance of the gut feel.

Stick to the basic business principles that have guided you and your business this far down the line and don't be distracted. There must be a reason why you have succeeded and achieved your current position in the industry. Don't second-guess the processes and the decisions that have steered you to this situation.

Stick to the basics and avoid allowing your brain to become lazy by looking for shortcuts. If you feel that your brain is tiring, take a short break and then revisit the opportunity that is being presented to you. Note that I said take a 'short break'. Remember the adage that 'the early bird catches the worm' and don't drag out decisions.

Sway and bias are easier to manage than most people think. Believe in yourself to make the right decision.

CHAPTER 14

Good Spend vs. Bad Spend

Starting a business will always be attached to some sort of spend or financial outlay (e.g. cash, investment funding or loans). There are two main types of expenditures: good expenditures (necessary expenses) and bad expenditures ('nice to have' luxuries which are not always necessary upfront).

In your budget, always make sure that 'Research and Development' and 'Marketing' are included in your 'Good Budget' as priorities as these are key in the development of your service or product offerings.

Good spend on a measurable basis will further your business.

Think of it this way: which is more important?

Having one more person on your production line to assist with the packaging of your product? Will this increase your output and speed in terms of production and delivery?

Here is another example.

A steel business is looking to grow its stake in the market.

The directors decide to buy three new delivery vehicles to ensure that clients are kept happy with the delivery turnaround time, even though the volume of business doesn't quite demand the new vehicles at present.

Surely the way forward should be to wait until the volume of business increases before looking to purchase new vehicles?

Many business owners opt to put unnecessary infrastructure in place before the volume of work requires this. This is often done as a forecast of potential work, but sometimes the work is not forthcoming, and the business is left with unnecessary debts to carry.

How often have I heard the story of people who have left major consulting agencies to go it alone, set up their own business with glamorous offices in top-end suburbs without having any clients on their books? The feeling is often that business is easy, and the clients will run to them.

They forget that the market is very competitive and that they need to provide a unique offering before the clients *do* head in their direction.

Meantime, without decent cash flow, they have office rent and other bills to foot. The first principle of business must be top-of-mind: Income must always be greater than expenses.

Lots of careful thought needs to go into the budget side of the business be it at start-up level or any other stage. Many businesses adopt the ESPN philosophy: Every Single Penny Matters.

Good decisions generate a sense of positivity and bad ones don't. It's a principle of life. Good decisions allow a business to move forward and bad calls make a company move backward or remain stagnant. Mistakes will inevitably happen, but it's about limiting these errors to the absolute minimum.

So what leads to a bad spend decision?

The likely symptoms would be poor planning and limited effort made on the research front. Quite often, this is followed by poor communication between project staff or departments working on the piece of business.

As mentioned in the chapter on Sway and Bias, emotions come into play at times and could well overrule the gut feel and logic to bring about a bad decision on spend. Then there is the old problem of not understanding the abilities of the persons in the office workspace. Has the business leader overestimated or underestimated the potential of the staff in relation to making resources available for the completion of a project?

Yes, emotional decisions are made, too often, by trigger-happy decision makers who are frustrated into making a call or are out to impress. Decision making of this sort is usually done without the use of rational data, common sense or experience. Like anything in life, these people end up being held accountable for their actions.

Now let's look at some more reasons why spend can often go pear-shaped. Sometimes, it does seem strange as the decisions are usually being taken by an experienced, knowledgeable business leader.

Of course, all situations with regard to spend tend to be different so no matter how much knowledge one has; it boils down to the experience of whether one has been through a similar situation before or not.

Seeking advice is a key part of ensuring that financial blunders won't happen. So it is always good for a business leader to be on the lookout for someone who can provide the right advice. In this modern era of technology and networking, there is no excuse for a lack of awareness or being caught cold in deciding on a big spend.

So what are the flag points that can help guard against a bad spend?

The first step is to check what the opposition is doing in the marketplace. Then one needs to gauge the state of the economy. This can fluctuate from day to day if not hour to hour, so it's not that easy to make a call based on it alone.

Keep in mind that holiday seasons can either work for or against you, depending on what type of industry you are involved in.

Most service-orientated businesses (e.g. the building and construction industry) usually close over the festive season period, but if you are a supplier to a leading retail store, your goods will probably still be in demand.

Keep a close eye on your sales statistics and how they relate to the previous year's sales. The market is always evolving, and new products replace older ones so be careful not to spend major cash on products that will become out-of-demand a year later.

The clothing industry is another area where spend has to be carefully monitored. Fashion trends are forever changing. Blue clothing may be in this year, but green could be the big selling colour of the new fiscal.

When it comes to food types, this is equally tricky. You don't want to buy a few million dollars' worth of dairy products only for something to go wrong with your warehouse freezers and the food turn into throw-away products.

As you may have noticed, business carries a fair amount of risk. The ones who are the least affected are the consultants who sell intellectual property like lawyers, accountants, stock brokers, and writers.

I mentioned the main rule of business, 'income shall always be greater than expenses', and in certain situations where this is not the case, businesses are forced to shut down certain areas of their operations to cut costs.

This often leads to job losses.

There are times when in situations like this the business leader will need to understand that the profits, if any, from the current fiscal, will be much less than anticipated. It is not an easy thing to explain to a board of investors who have believed in your idea and put their cash on the line in the hope of great profits, but the business world can be a ruthless one, just as much as it can be a bed of roses.

The banking industry often finds itself in the worst position when it comes to good and bad spend. Not that they spend money as such, but they loan out money, and then sometimes the persons who have received the cash are not in a position to repay the amount with interest. The smaller banks usually carry the most risk in this regard.

So what have we learned from the above? There needs to be a ratio between fixed and variable costs in relation to cash available and (most importantly) the potential sales that can be made, better known as income.

Money matters can indeed drive a CEO crazy. I don't think that there is one top-level CEO who goes to sleep at night without wondering what will happen to his company if he loses one, two or more of his clients as this all relates to the good or bad spend element.

The key here is a simple one. Build your service or product around the word 'unique'.

What type of service or product can your business offer to the market that your opponents can't? If you find the answer to this question, you will be well on your way to finding out how to get a client to open his or her bank account towards doing business with you and this should increase your profits and also give you a good idea on how much to outlay on goods or materials needed to deliver services.

As a business leader, you will need to live by the slogan: 'knowledge is power'. The more knowledge you have, the more you will have an edge over others in the marketplace.

So you made a nice profit after doing a good spend this year? Let's not get too hasty or overeager, because there is no guarantee that you will make the same sort of profit next year. It's all about keeping your feet on the ground and reading the market.

Many start-up businesses go about things the wrong way on the 'good spend and bad spend' front. People who have worked for larger businesses all want to take their experience and go it alone.

They all want to have that large plush office with a personal assistant, even before they have brought in their first client.

Soon, they discover the harsh realities of the balance sheet. Salary they used to receive when working for a large corporate is no longer there and the pain is starting to set in. They now have to make their own salary as well as additional monthly cash to pay their office overheads.

Yes, business is not quite as easy as they thought it would be. Budgets are drawn up for this reason, so stick to them.

Remember that at the start of a business it is all about 'baby steps' and keeping things lean. So many people launch start-ups to try the waters and find them too deep and challenging within the first year, which forces them to beat a hasty retreat back to being a part of a large corporation again.

In conclusion, 'good spend' and 'bad spend' are really what one makes of them. Stick to the principles of business and you will inevitably come out on top. Like anything, there is also going to be a bit of luck involved too. You need to be in the right place at the right time to link with the right person to get the right presentation and then it's up to just how much cash you are prepared to throw at this opportunity.

It is often said that 'money talks'. If that is the case, then you will hear the cash telling you when a spend is bad or not, not necessarily in words, but again through that instinctive gut feel that you must never go against.

The word 'never' is a tough one too because you will often find yourself doing things or spending money on items that you said you never would. Keep that sense of open-mindedness and you will be well on your way to making the right calls on the budget front.

Even the best CEOs make mistakes but its better to be positive and try than not to try at all. The keys to good business are solid business principles accompanied by a solid business plan.

Good spend and bad spend are not an art but an everyday occurrence that you will begin to get used to and manage in an ever-evolving business world.

Just do your best to manage those budget figures and you will learn that fortune favours the brave. Rather be proactive than reactive as that golden opportunity might not be there for you any more when you return to it. Back yourself up when making the right calls.

CHAPTER 15

Candour

To be candid is to be open and honest; to be frank. Without candour, without openness and directness, a business cannot advance.

Candour should never be seen as a form of criticism or a sign of a lack of respect. Staff members, for example, need to be able to speak freely about their company and its products without fearing victimisation by their superiors if what they have said about the business is not appreciated.

Sometimes the staff members of a company are so concerned about saying things that they see as adding value, but a superior may see as criticism, that they carefully phrase their sentences before heading into a meeting. Freedom of speech is therefore restricted in the mind of a staff member who only has the best interest of the company at heart.

People should display the same degree of candour that they do at home and should be able to get their views across without fear of upsetting senior management.

Open communication is the cornerstone of any good relationships, so it is unfortunate that this principle is often not applied in the workplace out of fear of potential repercussions.

Here is an example of squashing candour in the workplace:

The CEO of a successful business is ruthless.

The CEO speaks first in a meeting and the rest follow, fully understanding that they must say what the boss wants to hear since he/she doesn't take criticism too well.

The CEO speaks for 60% of the meeting.

In the eyes of the CEO, no new ideas are good ones, unless they come from him/her.

Let's look at how the CEO should have handled the situation:

The CEO is open-minded and listens to the staff when they give input.

The CEO is open to criticism, knowing that any critical views could help to grow the business.

The CEO is an understanding person.

The CEO collects information since he/she understands that knowledge is power!

Staff can speak openly in meetings without fear of having their well-intended ideas or views rejected.

In these two examples, it is clear that a culture of candour needs to be created in the business with the CEO leading on this front. In this way, the business will grow.

The CEO needs to understand the saying that 'no idea is a stupid idea'. Committed staff will be open to contributing in meetings if they feel that their opinions and ideas are well respected.

This will also contribute towards a happy workforce and will make staff feel that their opinions have a role to play in the business. Candour leads to better decision-making and directly contributes to growth.

Business leaders need to understand that time cannot be an issue when it comes to candour. For example, when trying to find a solution to a workplace issue, the worst thing that a business leader can say at the start of a meeting is: "Let's use this time constructively as I only have forty-five minutes until my next meeting". Business decisions at any level need to be made in an emotion-free, time-free state of mind.

Employees are quick to work out if a business leader is genuinely serious about solving a problem, or just going through the motions because the company constitution or laws says he or she must. If that is the case, then perhaps the business leader is not the right person to mediate in situations.

Perhaps there is another less-stressed person in among senior management who will be able to find the middle ground to solve issues of this nature.

What about ego-driven business leaders? Some project leaders work hard to get their junior staff to come out of their shells and speak up at meetings, only for their ideas or opinions to be shot down by the ego-driven boss. This is often a case of more than ego. It could be a situation of the boss not knowing the junior staff well enough or forgetting that the he or she also started as a junior many years back.

Every business needs to have an open and honest working culture in order for all involved to perform to their maximum.

The key word here is 'transparency'. If the business leader is serious about building a fair amount of trust and confidence among the team, then he or she needs to be open-minded.

Let's look at ways and means by which a business leader can gain the trust of the workforce to bring about the achievement of meeting project deadlines and success.

The more transparency exists within the leadership and the team, the more the chance of meeting the business's stated objectives.

Remember that open-door policy and that 'no idea is a stupid idea' philosophy mentioned earlier? In fact, as mentioned elsewhere in this book, the next client to be signed could well come from an idea put forward by a member of the office cleaning staff and not senior management.

Also, remember who made the choice to employ the current staff. So, they need to be encouraged to deliver. The best way to achieve this is to make people comfortable in their place of work, so that they work more effectively and produce higher levels of success.

Never disagree with any form of input or feedback from staff members with regard to projects or the business in general. Instead, thank them for their input and leave them with the idea that the input is being taken into serious consideration.

This is a far more preferable approach than shouting them and their ideas down. If the input of an employee is pushed aside in his or her presence, especially if this is done at a meeting, then he or she is unlikely to give additional input in the future.

Most businesses are built on the back of long-lasting relationships with clients, and the same principle should apply to the interactions of the business leader and his or her employees. After all, each member of staff is as much a part of the company as the boss.

Similarly, it is up to the business leader to also keep his or her promises. If an employee has been motivated by a potential increase, bonus or promotion upon successful completion of a project, then the boss must make sure that the reward is granted once the project has reached its success point.

Quite often the endpoint is reached, but for a variety of reasons often not communicated to the employee, the reward is delayed or, even worse, not forthcoming. How does the employee react? Often by sending his or her CV out into the market or stirring up discontent among other staff members by fuelling the gossip machine.

One of the challenges for any business leader is that he or she gets so caught up with the balance sheet and chasing the bottom line, that staff matters become secondary. This is a common error with some business leaders, even getting to the ultra-frustration point of thinking that if the employee leaves another can quite easily be found. After all, the leader believes jobs are hard to come by in the marketplace.

Irrespective of how stressed the business leader is, he or she must always keep a clear, calm mind and be tactful at all times.

From an employee's perspective, he or she also needs to differentiate between constructive criticism that is aimed to help them to grow in the business and downright nasty remarks from the boss.

It is always a good thing to pencil down a list of your own strengths and weaknesses and to revisit these on a regular basis to see just how you have grown in the workplace; this will also enable you to assess whether input is indeed constructive or part of another agenda.

So how does one apply candour in a situation where you really don't get along with a colleague? This is never a pleasant position to be in, particularly as you will be watching your back the whole time and will constantly be unsure as to whether or not the other person will sabotage your work or promotion opportunities.

As touched on in the chapter on Exceptional People, each person needs his or her own space in which to perform.

If all job descriptions are properly drawn up and post-project analysis is applied, it should be clear who delivered in which areas and to what extent. It is then just a case of keeping your space free from the person with whom you don't see eye to eye. Sometimes a little distance is all that is required. Many people in these situations actually go on to become the best of friends or business allies; it just takes putting some boundaries in place.

If you encounter this problem, it is always a good idea for the business leader to meet with the two parties over coffee to find some sort of common ground rather than just sending through the job description via email. It is better to be proactive rather than reactive in these sorts of situations. All parties need to remain professional and think objectively.

In conclusion, candour is an important element that needs to be present in every successful business. It is closely linked to the integrity of the company, which, of course, stems from the people who are employed there.

Remember that good business reputations are built over years and bad ones are broken within seconds, so the basics of the business structure need to be correct from the start.

This is why it is so important at the time of hiring of candidates, to pick the right people who will fit into the culture of the business as there is little time for damage control to be actioned later on. Candour can be described as being 'worth its weight in gold' as on the business scene, time is money.

CHAPTER 16

Little Things and Focus

There will always be little things that will take your focus away from what you really should be concentrating on during your business day. The secret is to force yourself to focus on the essentials. Train your mind to concentrate on two or three big items each day and treat anything else as secondary, as otherwise you will always struggle to reach your daily goals.

Let's not misunderstand this. Small things are of great importance, but in business, prioritising is a fundamental skill.

Take, for example, this scenario: Parking bays outside your office are of major importance but nobody regards them as especially significant. We all think about the products and the services that are being offered.

It is only when a customer comes to your office and has nowhere to park their car that the issue suddenly goes from small to big in your mind.

When it comes to determining what is a 'big' and what a 'little' priority, start by dividing your office thoughts between physical and experience items.

Physical: These include elements such as the quality of the coffee that is served at meetings or how comfortable the seat is that someone will sit in at your office for three to four hours of each day.

Experience: This aspect includes how people are greeted over the phone at your business or making sure that the potential customer is transferred to the correct department.

Another point could be making sure that your email server is always in good working order, since there is nothing worse than a client sending correspondence to you and it bouncing back 'return to sender'.

All of the above elements will matter greatly when the client decides on whether or not to hire your company. The client will not only remember the quality of your product or service offering but also the client-care element, and if the supplier is just interested in the client's cheque or is prepared to go the extra mile in terms of added value.

Little things can make a huge difference in giving you and your business a major advantage in the industry. When it comes to clients, you'd be surprised just how much little things can create long-term and top-of-mind awareness to a client. There are many things that you may take for granted, which other business people, namely clients, don't.

While your day needs to be prioritised, the smaller things (which can often be more time-consuming) cannot be forgotten. Examples of these include: Sending a 'thank you' card to a person who referred a client to your business. Or sending a personalised message and card to a client for a birthday.

Remember, your relationship lies with the person not necessarily with the company.

Getting to know the stakeholders of a client's business is important because it expands your horizon for networking. In a situation where you lose a client, you will have their stakeholders at your disposal and may potentially grow your client base with them.

Keep in mind that small businesses grow to become big business because their leadership understands the philosophy of 'small stones build big bridges'. That is why it is important not to overlook the small things. In fact, I would go as far as to say that you should keep a focus on these as if your business's life is at stake. After all, business is not just about delivering a product and taking the client's cash. It is about how to retain that client for the next job or sale.

In our modern world of innovation, technology, and efficiency, this approach also extends to small considerations like payment structures. You would look a bit foolish if the customer gets to the register in your supermarket and the cashier is still using a 1980s lever-type register instead of a modern era touch-screen device. Or if the slip printed out from the register prints at the rate of one slip per minute while modern registers print in a split second.

These are just some examples of little things that clients don't even think about, but which we expect to happen. Would you do business with a company that wasn't in step with progress?

It's the little things that encourage a client to return.

These touches give the client the peace of mind that he or she is working with a highly professional supplier who is committed to delivering the best service or product.

Of course, small things will also link to cost savings along the way. How many times have you heard a CEO or business leader complaining about the cost of ink cartridges, telephone bills or other office expenses? Well, as far as the ink cartridges are concerned, many businesses are becoming eco-friendly and printing as little as possible with all important information being kept on the cloud in cyberspace. This is an example of how sweating the small stuff can save you in the long run.

Surveys also indicate that today's employees are not always after bigger salaries or perks. They also enjoy the small things, particularly the newer generations who are motivated by working for a caring employer. Just a small gesture of keeping quality coffee in the office makes a huge difference. Add fresh milk instead of powdered milk. Already the employees will get a feeling that they are working for an organised, caring business.

Similarly, how many times have I heard from visitors to my own office that the coffee we serve tastes better than the refreshments served at many other offices? It's the little things that make a huge difference in the mind of the visitor.

Another point is to ensure that all staff members in your business, whether senior or junior, have business cards. They are, as we outline in these pages, ambassadors for your brand and your next client could well come from a word-of-mouth motivation by your company cleaner, and not necessarily the CEO.

Keeping staff front-of-mind, even by means of small touches, is both easy and effective. Here are some ideas:

Many businesses keep their staff motivated by placing posters featuring 'power words' from world leaders down their passages. You will be surprised how these words will be read and remembered.

Don't forget to make the right amount of stationery freely available; plus branded pens and notepads make perfect giveaways to clients or potential clients.

Don't underestimate the power of branding.

It is pointless putting out notepads and pens if your business logo is not on them. Your logo is a representation of your business's vision. Remember that people may remember your logo before they remember your business name.

From a customer perspective, it is important to get to know each person you work with better. If you are an agency providing a service, you need to know what your client likes or doesn't like. So don't carry out a great proactive initiative by buying your client a set of golf balls for his or her birthday if the person hates golf.

If your client does like golf, then by all means send the pack of golf balls, but be careful not to send the cheapest ones on the market. Small touches can work in your favour, but you never want a good initiative to backfire.

There is no room for error on this front.

When interacting with a client or customer, always speak and act in a positive manner so that the person knows that you are in charge and on top of your game. Walk boldly, think at speed and talk confidently.

Furthermore, be open to constructive client criticism of your service or product as you are looking for ways to improve on your offering. Never become defensive.

Finally, when you are with a customer always give your undivided attention. After all, he or she is paying for your time or is about to buy your product or service; so for that brief shining moment make him or her the centre of your world. That means no mobile phone calls, no checking emails, and no interruptions. This small gesture will not go unnoticed.

Lastly, little things may cost some cash, but the return is evident when you consider the relationships you can build with both staff and clients—something that is undoubtedly worth much more than any financial outlay.

Sometimes the little things come at no cost at all. Just having an air conditioner in your boardroom, which you paid off five years ago, may make the world of difference in a meeting on a hot summer's day. Perhaps parting with a fine bottle of wine that you received as a Christmas present could be a deal clincher in the mind of a client who is something of an aficionado. Or how about opening that box of Swiss chocolate that you received from a client and sharing it around the office?

As I mentioned earlier, small stones build big bridges. Keep in mind that if you remove the biggest slab of cement from a wall of your building, the wall may openly tilt to one side, but if you remove the smallest stone, it may collapse completely. Small things are of major importance and the old art of attention to detail cannot be overstated. Put yourself in the shoes of the customer and ask what he or she might want or expect from your business. Then make it so.

CHAPTER 17

Value Creation

Creating value for a customer is the main aim of any business. The value element plays a key role in helping to push the sales of products or services. This creates the platform for an increase in stock price while making certain of future capital availability to fund operations.

Value creation can be achieved through various means, including an increase in sales, a saving in cost, a better quality product, a better quality service, an increase in client happiness and an increase in staff happiness.

Of course, a combination of the above will also lead to value creation.

The focus of a company is often directed towards generating more sales, but this doesn't necessarily equate to value creation as there may be value negativity in other areas of the business. So it's important to understand all elements in the business.

It's also important to pinpoint where the growth of a company comes from.

For instance, when a company grows, it doesn't necessarily mean that you'll have a bigger business, because there may be a higher operational outlay on the other side of the balance sheet. Again, you need to understand the interplay between all factors to get the full picture in terms of value.

To understand the balance at play in business, it's vital to get to grips with Income Statement and Balance Sheet matters.

This breaks down into two areas, namely cash versus expenses on the Income Statement and assets versus liabilities on the Balance Sheet. The Balance Sheet (assets vs. liabilities) is, in fact, an outdated way of looking at the liquidity position of a business. For example, if you buy a business for US$1 million but the business has US$800,000 in liabilities, then that means that the company is not in a great financial state.

This tells us that assets may look great on paper, but that this does not reflect true value creation. The important barometer for any business to focus on is cash versus expenses.

Let's sum this up.

There is no point in increasing turnover and carrying an increase in major expenses at the same time. Those balance each other out and don't increase the value of a business.

Also, remember that value creation is not built in hours. It's a process of collecting data and other forms of information for strategic purposes in order to come up with a solution that will be miles ahead of anything that your competitors are offering.

The key here is to return to check your data on a regular basis so as to make sure that your value creation idea is still on target with your plan. Some businesses draw up their strategies and have them approved at meetings. They get so excited during the production phase that they forget to go back to verify that the big idea is still in line with the strategy.

Don't think of value creation as if you are giving something away for free. Rather look at the bigger picture as to how this small investment of cash or time can elevate your business, with the backing of one or more large-scale clients who love the value element. It is all about going the extra mile. You might not think so, but clients do notice these things. The trick is to make sure that the client doesn't begin to think of added value as the norm.

This often happens when there is a change of staff at the client's office and the new person doesn't understand that your additional offering is just that, and not a part of the deliverables in the contract.

So your business had its big idea and the client loves it. Today is taken care of. What about tomorrow? What if you or the person who devised this value-creation concept is no longer with the business? Do you have a succession plan? As much as you may hate to think about it this way, you won't be on this planet forever. What will happen when you turn sixty-five and retire? Does the show come to a complete standstill? Or is there a longevity plan?

Your business principles relating to the value creation element of your company will always be your foundation or cornerstone of the organisation. But this asks you to ensure that you've covered all your bases, including strategic, leadership, sales, marketing, financial and the legal aspects of your business plan.

As a business leader, it is essential to keep an eye on your business's recurring revenue streams. Ask yourself: In which areas of my business are clients likely to keep making use of the existing products or services?

Should I consider cutting back on those areas of my business that are not producing a profit? Is it still worth continuing with these lines? If so, do these areas require more capital to be grown into profitable units, or should they be cancelled immediately?

So the race is on to keep costs down while still looking for the big idea that will generate value creation. Don't fall into the trap that many companies do in this regard. Many keep looking ahead to land the next big client and forget about the current clients on their books.

Remember that it is often on the backs of your smaller clients that your business has grown to where it is today. Quite often it is better to have five to ten small- to medium-size clients on your business's books than one huge client.

If you lose one of these ten smaller clients, then your business should still be able to survive without too many job cuts, but if you lose that one huge client then it's often a case of (to borrow from the tennis term) 'game, set and match'.

Now let's look at the 'added value' part.

Added value, whether in terms of your energy and hourly input into a business or in the form of cash, speaks to attributes that add major value to your company or the business for which you work.

Take a look at the business market where you are aiming your company's products and services and see what additional value can be added to these offerings to make the client's decision to go with your company a no-brainer. Make the offering so attractive that the client would be silly not to hire your business or buy your products.

Of course, cost will always come into it. You may develop the best product or service, but if the price is exorbitant it will be a tough sell, unless you are sitting with something that will put the client's brand head and shoulders above the rest for the foreseeable future.

Always look for a way to generate added value to a product or service in the most economical way possible. Keep in touch with modern market trends.

Are there new forms of equipment available to manufacture your added-value idea at a cheaper cost than the resources available to you at present?

Make sure that you don't fall into a stereotype situation with your suppliers. Sometimes if you use the same supplier for too long, you tend to trust them too much and don't always pay attention to price increases.

Try to be a part of the leading brand that will change your specific business industry forever. Be the powerful force behind this business revolution. This is often more difficult for smaller businesses when a large corporation has launched a world-first big idea into the same market to add value. So, as a small business, you will need to ride the wave and wait for the market to return to a sense of normalcy.

You will find, however, that the smaller the business, the quicker the turnaround of an added-value element to the product or service offering due to the flexibility of the business size when compared to a larger corporation.

Of course, the waiting game is also a dangerous one as other opportunities may pass you by. But there is always the reality that you may be handicapped by the amount of capital you have at your disposal. Because of their larger resources, some bigger corporations can add more value by splashing out cash on projects that they believe will add major value to them over time.

Let's adopt a client-first approach to value.

When it comes to value, always take the time to question yourself and your strategic focus. Put your mind firmly out into the market from a client's perspective. What does the client really want from you as a supplier? What added-value element would swing the client's or buyer's mind in your favour to allow you to make the sale?

In most cases, a client wants your innovative product or service to reduce his or her costs. It's that simple. There is nothing stopping a small business from landing such a 'golden goose' idea. In fact, this often happens which makes the little guy the envy of all the big corporations who have spent time and money chasing a particular client's big budget.

If your offering comes with warranties or guarantees, then even better. It's also important to ask: How easy is it for clients to access your offering? Is your product available for purchase online? The easier it is to access, the higher the chances that the client will use your business. The key to making it in business is to stay one step ahead of your opponents.

When you build your product or service strategy around the principle of customer winning or retention, you will find yourself automatically generating value.

Some think of the value-creation element as a nice to have add-on. It's not that at all. It's the element that attracts clients to your brand. Even if thrown in at minimum cost, it's a small price to pay to attract clients who will hopefully develop long-term relationships with your brand.

Value creation links closely with added value and is the reason why clients become brand-aligned. Some clients believe in the 'if it ain't broke, then why fix it' philosophy and become so connected to a supplier that little can shift their mindset. This is why your added-value proposition had better be classy enough to knock the socks off the decision-makers.

Customisation is crucial in this respect. If you are able to tailor your big idea into the perfect fit for your buyer's requirements, then you will inevitably score the big deal.

If your pricing is too cheap, will it impact on a client's decision-making? Probably so, as it means that you have gone from one extreme to the next in terms of pricing.

I have to admit that I would think twice if I spotted a product on a shelf that was two-thirds cheaper than at another store. *There must be a reason why the retailer is trying to get rid of the stock*, I'd tell myself. Is the manufacturer of the stock going out of business or quite possibly already in liquidation? If your clients start thinking like this, then your value creation attempts just fell flat.

Value creation needs to be one of the key areas of strategic thinking in your business, whether you are part of a small, medium or large company. Anything to do with value creation will impact on your brand in a positive or negative sense. Remember too that you are playing a mental game here. Value adding is a perception to many clients. Any business person will tell you that in the market, there is 'nothing for nothing'.

So it boils down to how you package your big idea in terms of product and services, and how you run your day-to-day business in terms of strategic longevity.

Value creation, in both your home or work environment, is a major principle that will make a huge difference to your life and your business.

CHAPTER 18

Business Comedy

Don't involve yourself in things in the business industry that you don't understand! There should always be a fair amount of predictability in the outcome.

No financial discipline leads to comedy!

Example: If you buy too much stock, this often leads to the need to repack in order to on-sell. To cut costs, unskilled people are used here. But this decision comes with risks, for example—no control, no discipline, no data, and no skill.

These risks can lead to business comedy. And it's not at all funny. So, here are some pointers to avoid getting caught up in a business comedy.

Don't fall into the trap of paying too much for a new business. The unofficial rule of buying a business (but a rule that you can trust) is that a good deal will be the asset value minus 20%. Also, make sure that you don't pay more than two years' revenue.

Everyone wants to sell their business for the maximum amount, so sometimes prices do get inflated. Make sure that you have sufficient understanding of the industry you are entering or else it may be very difficult to gauge the price.

Get a valuation from an independent party so you know exactly what the true standing of your potential buying is.

Make sure that the business you are buying has the correct mix of skills. Get the right people into the right seats! Your business needs competency and energy. People must be appointed on what their current abilities are, not according to what they studied twenty years ago. Don't get swayed by appointing someone who worked for a big corporation. This doesn't mean that once they get into an office at a smaller company that they will be able to meet all of the expectations.

Make sure there is a healthy cash buffer. Consider seasonality and micro indicators. These are just two of the factors that could handicap your business if not understood and managed correctly.

For example, if you go into the printing industry, printing is currently on the down cycle due to the threat posed by the digital era. You need to have a good understanding of all cash-flow requirements.

All businesses go through cycles, so you need to make your purchases at the right times.

Don't get involved with businesses with bad leadership.

Don't get involved with someone who did a great deal five years ago and is still riding on the fame of that transaction.

Any business deal that you enter into should include growth opportunities.

Make sure taxation and all other stakeholder obligations have been met.

Understand the standing of the business and its reputation in the marketplace. Good word-of-mouth referrals travel fast. Unfortunately, criticism of a company travels even faster.

All Intellectual Property (IP) needs to be in place when you buy a business so that you won't have people who resign and who are critical to the company (e.g. people who will leave with valuable IP that could cause major setbacks to the business).

By sticking closely to the fundamentals of a business, using common sense, taking advice from quality people around you and following your gut feel, you should be on the right track to make well-informed decisions on the business front.

The only way to explain why businesses might find themselves in desperate financial trouble is because of a lack of discipline on the financial side. In most cases, financial discipline is the No. 1 element to avoiding business comedy.

Remember the principle of 'income (cash generated) shall always be greater than expenses' that I have already mentioned on several occasions in this book. Going in pursuit of a big idea and splashing cash on it like there is no tomorrow is almost certain to put your business in a bad space.

Every business owner needs to bring his or her own form of work culture to the company and important elements such as gut feel, common sense, self-discipline, and punctuality are just a few of the important ones that need to be ever-present.

All big businesses were small at some point in their history, so do the basics well to get to the next step in terms of business growth without becoming the talking point of the market for all the wrong reasons. Of course, like many things in business, this is often easier said than done. So let's have a look at some ways to make this happen.

Does your business hire the right staff for the right positions based on their CV profile or have reference checks been done on the individual to see if he or she is really as good as they claim? Many people beef up their profiles for that big job interview. I have interviewed so many promising candidates in my life.

Many are fresh out of university where they obtained splendid marks in their exams, yet when it comes to the workplace they battle to string a few sentences together when drafting a document.

This can be quite comical if such a person is exposed to a client because the business leader doesn't have enough time in a day to check every document that a staff member sends out.

Spelling is also a major challenge these days with the shortened words used on social media platforms such as Twitter and Facebook proving to be one of the main reasons for the poor language quality.

If a staff member battles to type an email in decent language to a client, how will he or she draft a quality document of high importance?

And what about the financial manager who came into the office in a bad mood on a Monday morning and didn't double-check his budget calculations before sending the document through to a company board meeting? It is a pity that he didn't double-check the numbers on the page and that the expenditure total of US$3,000,000 was mistyped as US$30,000,000.

Then there is the refreshments lady in your business with the habit of serving tea or coffee to visitors but forgetting to put in the sugar.

These may appear to be little things, but they make a world of difference in the bigger picture, particularly when one is dealing with major clients.

A former colleague that worked in the PR industry at a firm suffered from dyslexia, which is defined as a difficulty in reading words, letters and symbols. While dyslexia is a learning disorder, it is not insurmountable, but it does require greater attention to detail by the individual in question before documents or gifts are sent out to clients. In this case, a checking system could be put in place where another member of staff could read through the work to avoid any problems and dodge potential faux pas.

Another good idea is to keep your laptop locked and your computer password to yourself at all times.

The last thing that you want is some staff member who has an axe to grind with you, getting hold of some emails that shouldn't be seen in public, and sending them out to the world.

In 2001, a leading cellular network wanted to send a radio DJ to Antarctica on a ship, with his daily broadcasts to be done using state-of-the-art equipment. The media launch in Johannesburg was scheduled to take place at the local zoo in the panda bear enclosure.

The PR agency representing the broadcaster was not seeing eye-to-eye with the marketing agency of the sponsor and wanted the DJ to be photographed with the panda bear.

This would have been a bad move as the panda bear is a wild animal and would have torn the DJ to pieces.

This is an example of why understanding the environment is so critical before you make ridiculous suggestions in a meeting.

It is also essential to grasp the culture of the market. For instance, in the Black culture (and market) in South Africa, burials are a very serious matter.

So when another cellular network went big with their football sponsorship campaign and put roadside banners all over Johannesburg ahead of a big tournament stating, "Life will never be the same again, we have come to bury (the opposition)", it didn't go down too well in certain circles.

Another example of this is when the same cellular network put, "Yebo Bolo" on their billboards to promote a sports sponsorship. In township lingo, "Yebo Bolo" has little to do with sport but is more a reference to an intimate part of a man's body!

Creativity is great but what may seem innocent to you might not be to the next person. Where are those checks and balances? What happened to the research element?

Even on the sales side there are elements of business comedy. There is a man in the Democratic Republic of Congo who made newspaper headlines for selling spiritual apples. The apples, once consumed, were supposed to bless your life and take you to new levels.

There is a catch though. The spiritual apples only last for one day. So if you buy one and don't consume it that same day, you will need to return the next day to buy another one to gain the benefits that allegedly go with it.

That sounds like a very good sales gimmick rather than a means of changing one's life.

Yes, everyone is looking for that hook or angle to make bucks in the business world.

In closing, business comedy does have the ability to entrench your brand in the minds of clients and members of the public, but just be careful that this doesn't happen for the wrong reasons.

We live in an era where most people are trying their utmost to be politically correct and inclusive and the last thing that you want to do is to offend someone by inadvertently insulting their race, culture or creed.

Keep in mind that a business you supply to has put in many years, months, and days into carving out their place in the market and they cannot afford to have a trusted agency making even the smallest of mistakes which could leave them in an embarrassing position.

Let's go back to knowing the market.

If you are a car dealer, don't make a fool of yourself and buy a large supply of vehicles because they are being sold at an extremely cheap price. Why is the price so cheap? Are these vehicles about to be discontinued or recalled due to deficiency issues?

When a product is priced way below its usual market value it is always a good time to question why this has happened.

People don't sell products at discounted prices without having a good reason. If it is about bringing a new product into the market, moving stock and getting noticed, then that is different.

However if the product has been on the market for a while and is now being sold off at discount prices, it is a good time to be suspicious before signing off your budget only to be lambasted by your business leader for wasting cash.

Business comedy is not always that funny, especially if you are the butt of the joke. Businesses are always waiting for their opposition to make a mistake on which they can capitalise. Don't be the one to make the error.

Maintain your ethics and work standards and stay true to the ideal of adding value wherever you go in life. People will get to know you for your abilities and understand your weaknesses.

Take on a job with the mindset that you always want to leave your current employer knowing that you contributed to making their business a better brand than before you joined. As we've touched on previously in this book, people will always remember you not necessarily by what you achieved over many years, but by your 'last performance' on the business front.

Like any comedy show on television or in the theatre, the idea is to build up to a climax; accelerating from one small event to the other.

These comedies may be fun to watch but in business the secret is plain and simple: never let anyone else involved in your business perform in one.

CHAPTER 19

Entrepreneurs

An entrepreneur is a risk-taker, meaning someone who spots a business opportunity and looks to capitalise on it, quite often using the funds put down by an investor.

In my opinion, there is a significant difference between a BUSINESS PERSON and an ENTREPRENEUR.

A businessman or businesswoman goes into a venture with a carefully-thought-out business plan to action around the company or project into which he or she is investing money. Such individuals apply sound business principles with the intention of bringing about value creation. They go about the implementation of this business thinking in an objective manner.

The entrepreneur is someone who takes huge risks in an effort to make money and could well be found dabbling in the oil market today and working in a bakery tomorrow. I see the entrepreneur as someone whose outlook on business is ill-considered, short-lived, and has no long-term value creation.

The entrepreneur is a 'business gambler'. He or she produces world-class pie-in-the-sky-type documents to impress a funder. Then they start a race but often fail to get to the finish line.

But, and it's a big BUT, I must stress that there is nothing wrong with the principle of entrepreneurship. It is the actual entrepreneur, the *individual* who often takes uncalculated risks, that is the challenge in this scenario. Many of the entrepreneurs that I know are jobless and scouting for new opportunities. Entrepreneurs are usually big talkers, have big personalities (in many instances to hide insecurities) and I have found that there is often no substance to them, only noise.

This is why it is difficult for me to comprehend why entrepreneurs write books, talk at conferences and webinars, and have the world at their feet.

I don't think that successful business people (people who understand businesses and value creation) should use entrepreneurs as their go-to advisors for solutions and commentary. It would be wiser to consult successful businessmen and women who understand value creation and the development side of business.

Below are some thoughts on why people get excited when they hear the word 'entrepreneur'.

Entrepreneurship gives the person a great amount of freedom to work for him or herself rather than for a boss. Their own work hours can be set as they go about facing new challenges.

Unlike a staff member of a company who gets a fixed salary each month, the sky is the limit in terms of what the entrepreneur can earn monthly.

You are your own boss which will create a huge amount of job satisfaction.

Here are some considerations to keep in mind when embarking on an entrepreneurial venture. At the start, there is probably little or no money coming in so, if you can, don't quit that full-time job just yet.

If, for whatever reason, you do bite the bullet and go full time into the entrepreneurial field, you will have more time to spend with family and friends than most full-time workers. Yes, the hours of work will be long, but you can decide when they will be. Perhaps you prefer to work the midnight to 8am shift, put in a few hours of sleep and then have the day to yourself? It's your call.

If some money does come in upfront on your project, courtesy of an investor, then you can decide on how much to take as a salary and how much will go to the project. One needs to be cautious on this front as the money will not last forever and you will ultimately have to answer to the investor.

You will be extremely upbeat about the goings-on as it is, in all likelihood, a new territory for you. Try your best to keep your feet firmly on the ground. Logic needs to prevail. Stick to the business principles. Your big idea may be just that for now, but it might be a small idea in a year's time as the market evolves.

There is life outside of entrepreneurship.

Of course, entrepreneurship will probably give you more learning opportunities than most other forms of job. Some learning curves will be tough and possibly even costly, but the lessons will build your knowledge of your industry to will ultimately be worth their weight in gold.

Now let's look at the disadvantages of being an entrepreneur.

It is extremely time-consuming. It is not easy to be an entrepreneur and one has to flexible in terms of a working schedule.

It often entails competing with other businesses. So, in order to make a profit, the business offering has to be unique in a bid to grow a solid client base.

It brings with it the need to make a lot of sacrifices as being an entrepreneur does not guarantee success in the business world.

The biggest drawback is the long hours that have to be put in, which is quite different from the 9am to 5pm jobs held by regular staff employees.

You are your own boss, but with this freedom comes the pressure to generate income. If there is no money in the bank account, then there is no salary on which to live.

Here are some additional considerations to ponder on the challenges side.

Most one-man (or -woman) show entrepreneurs run their small business with one backroom person to handle the administration, telephone, and other odd jobs. It is probably best to do it this way if you can afford that junior staffer, as the paperwork will inevitably start piling up. So here already you have your first monthly expense.

So what makes you think that someone else out there in the market does not have the same big ideas as you? There is nothing to prove that your idea is, in fact, a world first. Again, this is a big risk that you are taking. Welcome to the world of entrepreneurship!

Being a one-man (or -woman) show can be a lonely road to travel. Can you keep the passion and self-belief all the way to the finish line? Many people can't, although there are exceptions.

If you have decided to back yourself in the full-time entrepreneurial route and have forgone the comfort of a monthly salary check, then your knees could end up knocking together sometime when the cash runs out.

This is why I advise you to stay with the full-time salary at your place of employment for as long as possible.

Entrepreneurship sounds awesome, but few understand the hours that have to be put in to make your project into a success. Being an entrepreneur comes with a great amount of stress. It's 'make or break' in the eyes of many.

As we can see from the above, the rewards of being an entrepreneur often look fabulous, but like anything in life the advantages need to be weighed against the disadvantages.

Some people hold top jobs as investors, lawyers or other high levels of professional consultants and then dabble on the entrepreneurial side in their spare time in the hope of landing that big idea which, with the backing of a big investor, will allow them to quit the 9am to 4pm rat race forever.

The odds of achieving this have often been described as the same as winning the lottery. While it can happen, it is a long shot at success and usually cannot be achieved overnight.

Of course, by juggling a full-time job and an entrepreneurial venture, the workload does increase as the individual is now managing two roles.

Many people think that entrepreneurs are a cut above the rest in terms of intelligence and have an uncanny ability to spot opportunities. This is not necessarily true. While passion is great to have, it is essential that there are some serious checks and balances on the entrepreneurial front. Unfortunately, in most cases, these are lacking.

The entrepreneur usually doesn't have a team around him. He is often a one-man (or -woman) show working from researched information. There is nobody to report to. You have probably heard the phrase that 'two minds are better than one'. Well, in this case, there is usually only one mind, that of the entrepreneur.

The inherent risk of working in this sort of isolation is that the entrepreneur will be willing to throw large sums of money at a project not knowing if it will be a success or not, or indeed how the market will react to the new idea, service or product.

Many people who try to become entrepreneurs have described this line of business as a "very expensive hobby". It is something that is usually started outside of one's fixed salary job and takes a lot of time and effort. Often after all the work has been done, the big idea doesn't seem quite so big after all.

The mind of the entrepreneur starts to wonder whether he or she was meant to be an entrepreneur, or if he or she was actually designed to work a salary job until pension time.

Whatever you do, don't quit your day job to back your entrepreneurial dream. I am not suggesting that you won't succeed as an entrepreneur; many do, but the odds are heavily stacked against you. Think of it this way: If entrepreneurial work were that easy, then everyone would be doing it.

Some see entrepreneurship as a 'nothing-ventured, nothing-gained' situation, a real case of making your fortune. But, as can be seen from the above, entrepreneurship is a hustle and not something to be entered into lightly. It's perfect for those with vision, even more so for those who have reached retirement level or received a golden handshake from their former jobs, but it isn't for everyone.

However, if one sticks to the business basics as laid out in this book, entrepreneurship can be a profitable opportunity. Critically, don't be hooked by every person who comes to you cap in hand with what they deem to be a super idea. Don't spread your funds so wide as you will tend to reap far less than what you have sown. Not every entrepreneurial idea will work out in your favour.

Be prepared for some disappointments and several financial setbacks. Entrepreneurship can be as frustrating as it can be joyous, but many people do abide by the principle of rather risking failure by trying, than not trying at all.

There is the other side of the coin that in this day and age of recessions, which bring about job losses and the risk of losing your salary security. Many bosses cut the long-serving loyal senior staff member with thirty to forty years' experience to put in a junior at half the salary.

Sure, the experience and much of the expertise gets lost in the process, but in today's world it's all about the bottom line on the balance sheet.

I'm afraid that loyalty has gone out of the window at many businesses, which explains why more and more people are open to going the entrepreneurial route.

Remember what we have stated several times in this book: If it sounds too good to be true then it probably is. As an entrepreneur, you need to use that invaluable gut feel as well as a good degree of common sense. Only a small percentage of entrepreneurs make it into the big leagues in terms of profits, but again it is not impossible to be among that fraction.

The power is, as always, in your mind, so keep emotions out of the workplace and focus on the bigger picture.

There is nothing to stop you from being the next Colonel Sanders (Kentucky Fried Chicken), Walt Disney or Elon Musk (Tesla), or indeed any of the other big names who have made their mark in spite of being told by many that their idea would never work.

Don't be discouraged. The big idea is your dream and it belongs to nobody else but you. Perhaps the dream is there for a reason and you will never know unless you try.

Believe in your concept and yourself. Business evolves around knowledge and confidence and, despite the odds, you may just have what the market wants. That said, understand that entrepreneurship is not easy and is often a huge risk.

CHAPTER 20

Small Things – Big Impact

Attention to detail is vital when running any business and it is often the small things that create the biggest impact.

When purchasing a new business, excitement sets in and small, yet key, elements tend to get overlooked.

The first question that a buyer should be asking in their mind is why is the person selling their business and how did they get to the selling price?

Let's look at the good old debtors' book as the cash flow cycle is key on this front.

Clients who have not paid within 60 days probably won't end up paying. That is the reality of the situation so don't be caught out when buying a business and inspecting the debtors' book. Clients in a 60-day payment cycle look good on paper, but it will be tough to get the money from them in the real world.

Taxation is the last thing on a person's mind when they purchase a business, but it is probably the most critical. For example, if you are purchasing a US$100 million business, a proper tax structure could save you US$30 million.

Why is a person selling the business and why is he or she offering a specific price? Have you, the buyer, considered how you will be able to add value to the business that you are about to purchase and if it will bring in more money and be a success?

Another small thing that makes a big difference is to have happy people working for your company and to focus on fixing areas where there are unhappy staff.

Here are some other examples of small things that can make a huge difference when it comes to your business.

Make sure that your team is motivated. Offer incentives to ensure maximum focus on the goal.

This doesn't have to be a monetary incentive. Perhaps it could be time off work or gift vouchers for staff members who go the extra mile. You will be surprised to see how staff members react to 'carrots' that are dangled in front of them.

Keep politics out of the workplace. Try to nip discussions on the subject in the bud as soon as possible as politics can break team morale faster than it can be built.

Make sure that your team is cared for. Last Friday of the month refreshments is a good way to show your staff that you are serious about building a team and it is not about superstars or one-man shows.

Make sure there is enough pipeline. Always ensure that there is enough stock and enough staff.

Make sure that your office looks the part as this will help when clients visit your premises. Impressions last long and your staff will also feel more motivated in a well-organised environment.

Make sure that your staff is always well dressed. First impressions last.

Small things will play a big role in creating more trust between staff members and senior management and will go a long way towards building a better experience for clients that you do business with.

Perception is huge in business. This is your picture to the outside world. Is your business perceived to pay small salaries and work the staff into the ground nine to five, Monday to Friday? Or is your company known as the perfect place to work where the perks that go with the salary are so good and the management does its utmost to maintain a happy office?

As the chapter heading suggests, small things lead to a big impact. As a business leader, how good are you at delegating skills? I know you want all documents drafted by the staff member to be exactly as they are in your mind, but remember that most staffers are not psychic.

Just as there are a hundred or more ways to write this book, one needs to delegate and believe when it comes to working with staff. Delegating is a small skill which can move mountains if handled correctly.

Another skill that is essential is your team's ability to manage clients.

You have sold them a big idea that will put them at the top of the market, and now the expectations from your side are huge too.

Will that box of chocolates with a quality birthday card make the client ease up on the pressure that he or she is putting on your team? Perhaps not, but at least the client will know that your business is a caring one which wants to grow the relationship.

The smallest thing that one can offer to a client that costs absolutely nothing is a smile. A smile is a sign of confidence. Let the client know that you are the right person for the piece of business and have things under control. Be that Plan A, B, and C type of thinker and worker rather than just having a Plan A and then stressing out as to how to get the job done.

If you are the one interfacing with a client, keep in mind how the person's business day works. Some clients arrive at the office at 7am and leave at 4pm to beat the traffic. So work according to that schedule. Don't phone the client at 5pm when you know that the person is behind the steering wheel on his or her way home. In the same way, you shouldn't phone a client during his or her holiday leave period. Think like the client thinks.

It's not only birthday and festive season cards that you should be sending to your client to cement a working relationship. What about milestone cards? If a client is spending US$10 million on your company in terms of service fees, the least you can do is to drop a card at the completion of the milestones successfully completed to say: "Thank you. As a team, we will get there!"

Another way of keeping clients feeling that they are a part of the team rather than a figurehead is to ask them for their opinion on certain business-related things. This will make a huge impact and will boost their egos at the right time.

Of course, the ability to go the extra mile and more will be key in leaving a long-lasting image in the mind of the client. This is a fine line as you don't want to end up with this being taken for granted as it's not a part of the contract deal. An example of this is fetching documents from the client's home. Once or twice is fine, but you are a project manager, not a courier. This needs to be carefully managed.

A supplier who responds to emails and other correspondence within an hour will always be more highly thought of than the one who only returns messages once or twice a day.

Let's be honest, time is money and your company is paid by the client for your services, whether it is as a consultant or in manufacturing a product. If you can't respond quickly to a person who indirectly is paying your wages or salary, he or she will find someone else that they can rely on.

Despite our current age of technology, and emails being quicker than a phone call, the latter form of communication is still much more personal. Yes, use the telephone for communication with the client but keep things in perspective. Wrap your questions into one phone call, first thing in the morning and at a regular time.

Again, this will show the client that you are organised and on top of your game.

Never underestimate the power behind good training programmes for staff. As a manager, always be prepared to provide as many training programmes as possible for your staff.

Don't see it as an additional cost to the budget, but rather as 'the water or sunshine that will allow your seeds to flourish'. It's a small price to pay for a system that will empower your staff.

The more knowledge your staff accumulates, the more value they will add to your business, in assuring client happiness at the same time.

Besides being a seeker of advice, you also need to be a solution-finder and take time into consideration. Clients want results as speedily as possible. So if you have to attend a big business meeting at a shopping mall, don't spend time driving around and around the outside of the building because you didn't want to pay the US$2 undercover parking fee.

That fee is a small price to pay for a meeting which will produce a business deal that is about to bring in US$20 million for your business.

When it comes to meetings and crucial stages of a project, make sure your mobile phone and Wi-Fi router are always loaded with sufficient airtime and data. The last thing you need is for your mobile phone to go offline and your Wi-Fi signal to go down as you are about to pull off the deal of your life.

These are small, seemingly obvious things that can create a huge impact on your business, but you will be surprised how many times even experienced business people get it wrong.

You don't necessarily need to fly your current, or potential, client around the globe to land that renewed or big deal.

Also, be in touch with modern technology. If you are sending some form of computer-related gift, like a branded hard drive, make sure it is in line with modern trends. Twenty-five years ago, sending a client a box full of floppy-drive computer disks may have been a good call. Today, floppy disks are museum items.

A project manager should make sure that his or her staff is equipped with all the modern-era tools to do the job. If a worker is not computer literate, then a manager needs to send the person out for training.

Having computer skills is as important as having a driver's license. How embarrassing would it be if a client calls you at short notice to a meeting, but you can't get there because you don't have a license and your booked taxi arrives late!

Remember to throw your connections out there. It's not quite name-dropping, but let the client know that your business is affiliated with various national and international organisations.

It is not about blowing your own trumpet, but hey, if you don't promote yourself and your business, nobody else will.

If you are dining with a client, you will learn a lot too. If you notice that your client doesn't drink wine, it is best not to send him or her a bottle of the best from the Cape wine industry as a Christmas present. Small things make a big impact, but they could turn into nightmares through poor preparation.

In closing on this chapter, everyone has an opportunity to make money in this world. It is up to you as to what you make of it, but if you haven't realised already, then you soon will, that business is a game of perceptions. Sell yourself big and you will be seen as big, even if you are a one-man (or -woman) show.

Do the small things right to convince the client that your offering is the answer. Sometimes, the smaller businesses get the work ahead of the larger corporations because they understand these basics and their prices are cheaper due to fewer overheads.

Yes, small things do make a huge impact. You know the old saying that first impressions last?

Well, when it comes to business, use it to your advantage just like others have done to turn a US$100,000 deal into a US$10 million piece of work. Be confident and stick to the business principles laid out in this book.

CHAPTER 21

Chemistry

When it comes to staff members, we need to accept the fact that how people gel in your organisation is very much about personality and attitude. Some people have chemistry to work well with others, and some don't.

If you were looking to hire someone for a specific post and you had ten candidates to choose from, what would make you choose one person and not the other nine?

You would need to go with your gut feel and senses. Choosing the candidate with the best chemistry to fit in with the rest of your staff would be more valuable to you than just focusing on the person's ability. Remember, a person may be brilliant, but he or she can also be destructive.

Chemistry is not about how qualified a person is. Many of the world's cleverest people with a host of degrees might not necessarily make the grade due to the fact that they cannot fit into a business structure and, therefore, they cannot work to the best of their ability with other colleagues.

Think of it this way: Good people are important, but they are not always likeable.

Ultimately better chemistry leads to better culture in the workplace.

The chemistry element is not only applicable internally but will also be clearly visible to your clients. They will easily see if a person fits into the bigger picture as a supplier selected to handle their business, or not.

Here's an example.

If one staff member who lacks chemistry doesn't get on with the others in the department, then the whole department could end up becoming less motivated and this will ultimately have a negative impact on the business's output and income.

So what are the signs of a person with chemistry?

A team player who gets along with most, if not all, of their fellow staff members.

A good trend to watch out for is for someone who goes the extra mile to try to fit into the environment. This usually indicates a willingness to try to make things work out.

Ultimately, it is up to business leaders to build team chemistry, but finding the right chemistry takes some deep thought. You cannot just throw talented people into a workplace and expect the results to follow. Sometimes talented people find themselves the creators – or part creators – of office power struggles and other politics which break down the chemistry that previously existed in the office.

As a business leader, you will note that good chemistry carries with it advantages. If you get the mix right, you will notice a positive vibe among your workers. People will want to be at work and be part of the team. There will be less absenteeism and workers will frequently go the extra mile as they will all be following their own ambitions to grow within the company.

The downside is that people often stop thinking for themselves when they are next to a highly talented individual. They let the gifted one do all the thinking, and this stifles the creativity of other team members.

Of course, the talented one is so caught up in what he or she is in the process of trying to achieve that he or she will not notice the one-person-show the project is turning into.

Now let's look at senior-level management. Are members of your company management more debaters than decision makers? This happens frequently and upsets the balance of the chemistry at the top level. Some management members go into a meeting hoping that others will make the tough decisions and, when this doesn't happen, things turn negative, causing frustration.

Remember that not all business people think like you do. You may be a highly proactive person, but that doesn't mean that the next person is. Everyone has his or her own outlook on business (some good and some bad). Stick to the golden rule of life: Treat people the same way that you would like to be treated. When issues arise, don't make personal remarks. Stay professional and focused, sticking to the bigger picture. This will retain a positive form of chemistry to keep your respect at the maximum among your colleagues.

Some project leaders get so caught up with tasks that they fail to spot the chemistry issues on their team.

Gaps start to open up and people start to shut down. Suddenly those new ideas that are in people's heads aren't being tabled anymore and performance goes downhill.

Other people who lead teams in business become territorial. It is almost as if they feel that if another person comes up with a great idea, they will be looked down upon by the boss, who may be wondering why a leader who is more experienced than the rest of the team never came up with the idea. The project leader then becomes territorial and hesitant towards the other individuals in the team.

These are some of the negatives that impact company dynamics and chemistry, but let's take the time to think more positively. Surely a good leader would rather be seen as the pioneer of a movement or new service or project than the one who tried to break the concept?

These pioneers are true leaders who, through their actions, create a sense of energy among the workforce. They are always focused on the ultimate goal and bring new ideas to the table. They are also problem solvers who are well-placed to come up with solutions to challenges faced by the rest of the team.

This makes for great chemistry as the other staff will view the pioneer as a pillar of strength and someone they can turn to as a springboard and with whom they can bounce off thoughts and ideas.

They say that 'time waits for no man'. While ideas are being thrown around the table, the clock is ticking.

Time, the abuse of it, or the way that it simply ticks away seemingly at speed during a business day, can play a huge role in destroying chemistry. Time planning is key. This is why many businesses charge their clients per hour and not per project. Think about those long meetings that you sit in. You know the ones that I am talking about. You often end up leaving the meeting having learned little or nothing.

That meeting time could have been better used by putting in the hard work at your laptop or computer.

I am not saying that meetings should be on the banned list. Brainstorming is vital for any business and, if done in a positive sense, will go a long way to boosting chemistry in the workplace. Like anything in business, your ideas on how a meeting or brainstorming session should be run will be different from that of the next person.

Let's take a look at managing business styles in order to promote chemistry.

Have you heard the old saying that 'opposites attract'? Well, it is true in the business sense, so pull those different individuals closer to you. The ones in the office who you think are miles apart from your way of doing things. You will be surprised as to the difference that this makes and how it will boost the chemistry on your team if you get it right. It is not an easy thing to do, as you may feel that some on the team are far removed from the way that you are thinking. Stop and think back to what is mentioned elsewhere in this book.

The next big idea or breakthrough on a project might not come from the CEO or other members of senior management. It may come from the office cleaner, who is also an ambassador for your business brand. So, stay open-minded. Your weakest staff member might just provide the insight that will take your gem of an idea to the next level.

Similarly, how do you handle those obnoxious people who you are basically forced to mingle with at office parties, or on Friday afternoon after-work drinks sessions?

Bite the bullet and mingle. That breakthrough of an idea may just spill out from one of the people whom you don't like to hang around with.

Yes, opposites do attract and even tend to balance the team. Nobody ever said that business is easy. Be open to opposites.

The wise way of handling these 'opposite' people, is to start them on small- to medium-size projects before working with them on the big clients. Do your part in trying to get to know these people better and understand their way of thinking. Who knows, the one you thought worked in opposition to you, might become the strong link in your team.

When it comes to tabling ideas, many people worry about their reputations and often hold back in terms of putting an idea forward, just in case it will be shot down in a meeting. That idea could just be the deal clincher!

It is up to the business leader to bring about an open discussion at meetings. Nobody should be holding back when it comes to the tabling ideas. Likewise, nobody should be punished for their input. Everybody should be working toward a common goal.

Here's another perception. People assume that the one who speaks first in a meeting is the best placed on the current topic. He is thought to be the one holding the most information and understanding of the topic. Wrong!

Think back to that office cleaner who might just know more about the service or product than you think but is pushed into a corner because he or she is nothing more than an office cleaner in the eyes of most. Remember that all people are not the same and everyone thinks differently.

When it comes to building chemistry in a business, there are no quick fixes or one-size-fits-all solutions to the daily challenges faced.

People need to be treated as business ambassadors and not as just a number on the staff spreadsheet for month-end salary payment.

As a business leader, rather work with the mindset that no idea is a stupid one, or you miss out on something really special.

Remember that in your career you will be working with different personalities. Some people will be highly strung while others will be more laid back. Some will be open to sharing ideas while others will be shy and more operations-minded than the client interfacing natural-style talkers.

The good news is that if the business leader handles the chemistry elements correctly, he or she can even change a person's business outlook or personality for the better. People learn from champions, so how do you, as a business leader, classify yourself?

There will also be differences in how people think simply because of their generation. A thirty-year-old will have a totally different outlook on business compared to a fifty-five-year-old. Neither is wrong, and both can actually learn from each other if they are willing to do so. If there is tension between the age groups, then it is up to the business leader to find a way to bring unity to the team.

Perhaps the best way forward here is for the team leader to call a 'Data Research' meeting. The older member may feel that his or her experience on a project is essential, as this will make sure that mistakes are avoided. As explained elsewhere in this book, the older member may be less open to taking risks, while the younger staffer will have a totally different outlook on the market, with risk being part of the mix.

As they say: If you don't take the risk, you don't win. Winning is all about finding the right mix of chemistry between staff of different age groups and cultures.

CHAPTER 22

Energy and Drive

Energy and drive are two important qualities when it comes to growing any business.

Energy relates to people with high levels of vigour and stamina. Some are prepared to work longer hours than others. Think of it this way—if you had to take a decision about employing yourself, would you? You would, of course, have to take the indicators of age and energy into account.

From my experience, younger staff members generally have more energy than middle-aged or older ones. And some colleagues may be brighter than others, but they lack energy.

Energy can be summed up by way of likeability, i.e. is the person likeable and fitting into your business culture? Proactivity, i.e. does the person go the extra mile when carrying out tasks or just put in a nine-to-five working day because their letter of employment says so? Additionally, positivity matters, i.e. do staff members have a positive attitude or do they just moan and look for problems rather than coming up with solutions?

Attitude is the one element that outweighs talent. Many top business or even sports people make it to the top, but the key to success is staying at peak. And this will only happen if the person has the correct attitude, and this goes with mental strength.

The 'drive' element is just as important and is something the business culture needs to embrace. People become driven if the business path is clearly laid out. Offering incentives to staff is just one way to ensure that 'drive' is top-of-mind for them.

People tend to go from company to company if their employers cannot get the 'drive' element right.

To achieve maximum success one needs to remember the formula that rests in three elements: promote, communicate, and celebrate.

Drive needs to be promoted through all elements of the company's culture in order for the business to grow.

Constant communication between senior management and staff members is crucial so that employees can understand growth opportunities within the company.

This will mean that they can focus on achieving their goals and will not have to look elsewhere.

Enjoy the success of achieving the goals which have been brought about through hard work and correct business structure. Celebrate!

In this day and age very few staff members stay with the same company for twenty years or more, and while that may be a good thing in order to avoid stagnation, constant turnover of staff indicates problems in the company structure.

This often means that the senior management has not achieved the correct formula in terms of maintaining the happiness of their employees. As a result, they will lack the ability to retain talented staff members.

There is nothing worse than having a talented staff member and losing him or her to another company. Later, one hears that the staff member who left has just pulled off some big digit deal for the new employer, which could have been yours.

But harnessing their energy and drive for the benefit of both the company and the employee are vital ingredients for success.

Energy and drive may certainly come from within the actual employee, but it is also the responsibility of the employer to make sure that the structures of the company are correct in order for the two elements to be nurtured to the fullest.

Of course, the support offered by a company will always have a deeper impact on an individual who is already driven and energetic. So finding these people is important. Which begs the question: What are the components of this charged-up person who takes the business world by storm?

Such an individual always has a great proactive approach. He or she is eager to work extra hard to achieve personal goals and, in the process, inspire those around them to do the same. Such people also tend to be more appreciative of the work and ideas of others in the office space.

In addition, energy-driven people tend to be better communicators, as they know what they want as well as how to achieve their goals. They are real team people who always seem to have that extra bit of time to help their colleagues on an individual basis.

The energy-driven business person is more likely to be a leader or a leader of the future.

They are able to judge situations and reach decisions faster and more accurately than most.

The energy-driven ones have a way of making the business space more interesting, not only for themselves but also for others in the office or on the team.

They also seem to be better listeners as they take in information and ideas and use the information to formulate improvements on their own thoughts or concepts. If nobody else in a meeting is paying attention to a presentation, be assured that the energy-driven person is. These people never seem to sleep. They are wide awake and miss very few opportunities to improve their ways of doing business.

Since they seem to have more time than most, the energetic ones spend many hours researching material for their next task. Homework is a part of their daily routine. They believe that knowledge is power.

The office space of an energetic person is always tidier than most. They know what they want in the business space, and out of life in general, and their days are meticulously planned. They set themselves short-, medium- and long-term goals to work towards.

These people are gems to have onboard any business team.

They are blessed with a highly competitive element. Finishing second is not an option to them. They are born to win.

That said, do the energy-driven people open themselves to receiving help? Of course they do. The perfect human being has yet to be born. The energetic ones are more than willing to receive help from others in order to gain the knowledge to advance to the next level. They are just as open to helping others. They do not withhold information or try to downplay others in the office. Why should they? The energy and drive elements put them on a different level from the rest anyway. It can be seen from a mile away.

These people are so success-driven that sometimes they don't even realise the value that they bring to a business or a project. Their growth graph is unlimited—it just goes ever upwards.

Being open to accountability is also a huge strength of energy-driven persons. They are not afraid of taking on responsibility, nor are they afraid of answering to their superiors.

One of the biggest downfalls of many businesses is moving an energy-driven person to a management position. While they may be leadership orientated, it may take time for them to adapt from being an operations person to a strategic one.

Take a newspaper reporter as an example. He or she may be the best in landing and writing political stories for tomorrow's newspaper, but when promoted to being news editor, which involves sitting behind a desk running the administration side rather than finding stories, this could prove an obstacle to the growth of the individual and the business.

Most energy-driven people, who operate at non-management level, don't feel pressure as much as the high-level people within the business. Most CEOs live in a world of pressure because everybody in the business is counting on them to deliver and make things happen.

Leadership often brings with it a nice salary and huge perks, but also a form of uneasiness. There is not a night that most CEOs go to sleep without wondering how tomorrow and the future will turn out if they were to lose a major client.

Of course, if you are an energy-driven entrepreneur, then life is not quite as easy compared to working in a salaried job. Entrepreneurs have to make their own money and are, therefore, always going to be involved in a more stressful situation.

But money isn't the only motivator for those with drive and energy, so what *does* make them tick?

First, unlike most, money is not the driving force for these individuals. They are motivated by achievements. They fully realise that the money will flow in as a result of their accomplishments. They do not need to verbally promote themselves. Their delivery and positive attitude gets noticed and markets their abilities quite clearly. They are definitely not attention-seekers.

They are workers who believe in themselves and go out to get the job done to the best of their ability. The results speak for themselves and are remembered by bosses, colleagues, and most importantly clients.

Many energy-driven people enjoy giving back to the industry or the community. They want to leave a legacy. They know how much others may have helped their careers and they wish to do the same for those following in their footsteps.

Unfortunately for them, achievement is often a 'chicken-and-egg' situation as they are so hyped up about reaching their goals that they never really believe that they have made it. They are always striving to go one step better than they currently are in the business world.

A CEO's dream is to have high-level energetic people working for him yet such individuals are not always that easy to find. So, when you do, it is in the business's best interest to hang on to them and keep them as happy as possible.

Bear in mind that not all energetic people have the same

characteristics. Human nature shows that some are more dominant than others. Some can energise the workplace more than other people can. It really depends on the individual's characteristics. Some people have a better sense of humour than others, while some are also more talkative.

One of the leading factors that make energy-driven people stand out above the rest is that they tend to be less judgemental.

As a result of all the positives associated with this type of personality, it goes without saying that energy-driven people are good to have in a meeting when it comes to the hiring of new staff.

They will give you their gut feel of whether the candidate is the right fit for a job or not and the input is usually invaluable.

Energetic people are innovative and always on the prowl for new challenges and to find solutions to problems. They are outside-the-box thinkers who are one step or more ahead of the rest. Again, they need not be persons with high-level university degrees or college diplomas. Some of the most energy-driven people are self-taught, having gone straight from high school into the workspace.

This highlights once again that having a degree or diploma doesn't necessarily mean that one can do a job. The boss will be more interested in whether the individual has the ability to deliver than the pretty degree or diploma certificate that the candidate plans to mount on the office wall.

Having a fair number of energetic people on a team makes the business environment a pleasure to work in, and this is contagious for other staff members. This creates a spark and a desire to be in the workplace, rather than watching the 9am to 5pm weekday drag on with the salary cheque at the end of the month as any sort of carrot.

If the rest of the staff is wise, they will not see the energy people as threats but rather as individuals to learn from and from whom they can absorb energy.

Energetic and driven persons will lead the way in terms of delivery according to deadlines due to their understanding of how business works. Time is money and cash is king. Nobody understands this better than the energy-driven person, which makes this type of individual an absolute 'must have' in the eyes of any CEO or business leader.

The energetic person will achieve his or her goal quicker and more professionally than most. It is all in the mind and nobody understands this better than energy-driven people, for whom the focus is always on the present and the future, and never on the past.

CHAPTER 23

Pricing

The terms 'pricing' and 'value' are closely linked together for one has to price the product or service offering that you are taking to market in relation to the amount of value that the client will receive.

The whole game plan of business is about creating that link between the offering and the consumer. So how do you get to the right price? There is no hard and fast mechanism to work this out. It could take months of research and various forms of planning before you come up with the answer. This involves keeping an eye on the opposition regarding what they are bringing to the market and at what price.

Remember that a world heavyweight boxing champion is only the best until such time as a challenger knocks him out or beats him on points. Few stay as a champion forever. The same principle of sport will apply to pricing in business terms.

Even if you manage to find the right price and the market is swarming in to buy from you, never get too comfortable because there will be someone out there just waiting to better your offering at a cheaper price.

Of course, the higher the quality of the product or service that you offer, the more you can charge. This is a tricky road to go down because you have to consider how your clients will feel when your pricing keeps increasing. Yes, we live in changing times, but some clients forget that what they paid for a carton of milk five years back is a much cheaper price than they are paying today.

They get stuck in a comfort zone thinking that you are their friends and won't raise the pricing too much. You will need to find a smart way to tell them that you, just like them, are running a business for your wealth and not your health!

Another factor that clients will tend to forget is that the supplier costs that you need to pay in order to generate the product or service, also rise over time. So you are not pricing for the sake of emptying the client's bank account, you have some serious costs to cover on your side too before the offering can go to market.

Pricing of a product or service is an art. You need to have a clear strategy as to how you will work out the pricing element and this includes the setting of short- and long-term goals.

It is possible to have both goals in your plan but naturally, you will be looking for a lengthy period of one to five or even more years thus encompassing short- and long-term objectives.

The Cost-Price format is the easiest one to use as it's simply aimed at maximising profits. It's not rocket science to action this one. Work out the sum total of your costs and then add a percentage of profit to it.

Second, you get the Value-Based format. You know your sales market or client base better than anyone else and will be fully aware that some clients will be prepared to pay the right price while others will moan, and you could possibly lose them. So, you will need to be flexible as the price quoted to clients may differ. The biggest risk here is that one day two or more of your clients meet up and end up chatting about you, your product, and the price and then the news breaks that all are being charged different prices for the same quality product.

If you are in a line of business that offers services, like an accountant or lawyer for example, then you may look to charge your clients on a 'per hour' basis.

On top of the hourly fees, you would invoice the client for any additional expenses such as per mile rates in attending meetings, telephone calls, and other costs that run up on the project.

Some clients prefer to pay less on the fee but opt to build in a performance-based clause. This is a sort of bonus type reward to be paid to your business upon the successful completion of the project. Perhaps payments will be made as targets are reached along the way, so these targets will need to be agreed upon with the client prior to the commencement of work.

Pricing services is much easier than pricing products. A service has a value. As do your consultants working on the project. All clients want experienced consultants working on their business so naturally, this would be costlier than having a junior staff member working on the project. Using experienced resources costs money and a client should understand this.

In business, it is very easy to short-change yourself. So it is best to test your pricing module before you go into big time mass production or work on a large project. If you are working with a client who has been on your books for quite some time, then drop them a friendly note to advise on the increase in the price.

You will soon hear if your new price is acceptable or not. If the business relationship between yourself and your client has been a successful one filled with trust, this price increase bridge may be easier to cross than you think.

Like anything in business, surround yourself with knowledgeable people who will give you the right advice at the right time. Let them provide the common sense while you back your gut feel.

I often get asked the question about what to do if your opposition or competitor in the market cuts their price to come in cheaper than you in the eyes of the client. As I mentioned, pricing is an art and there needs to be some give and take. If you feel that your client has been really loyal to you over time and you don't want to ruin the relationship, then you may cut your price to come inside the figure offered by the opposition. What you don't want to have happen is for this process to become the norm as it is actually taking 'food off your plate'.

Unfortunately with long-term client relationships, sometimes the added-value efforts made by the supplier can often be taken for granted and the buyer forgets just how good a service provider or product manufacturer they have on their books.

This is why it's important to stand one's ground on the pricing front. One can only discount so much. Any business is run according to the principles of 'income shall always be greater than expenses' so client loyalty is super to have, but pricing can only be brought down to a certain level before the warning lights start to flicker.

Clever business operators will realise the importance of monitoring the market, and especially the opposition, on a monthly basis. Experienced business people will tell you that the only constant in business is change.

Remember the oldest trick in the book is to only raise pricing on certain products or services and not on all of your offerings at once. Clients are less likely to make a fuss if the price has only gone up on certain offerings, but if all of your company's products or services receive a price hike at the same time, questions may be asked.

Also, don't fall into the trap of keeping your prices at one level for a lengthy period. This will leave you no alternative but to carry out a huge increase well beyond market norm at some time or other, which your clients might not understand.

Don't make the mistake of becoming totally focused on the pricing and cash-flow charts and nothing else. There are so many other areas of the business that also need your attention.

Budgets are drawn up for a reason. Don't spend your days making endless changes to the cash flow documentation as this will, inevitably, force you to make several changes to the pricing structure too.

Make sure that your business accounting system is strong. While the business leader doesn't have to be involved in this daily, you should employ a tough no-nonsense clerk to chase down the outstanding cash. Your pricing module won't feel so bad if the money from the perennial later payers is brought in on time. Any high school kid who has done accounting will tell you of the importance of Gross Profit figures and Net Profit margins.

Those net profit percentages may not be as big as you think or would like them to be, so keep an eye on the gross numbers at all times. They will grow faster than you think due to labour increases, product material hikes and more.

Have you ever been in a situation when a client looks at your pricing and then asks: "Why is the price so low? What is wrong with your product or service?"

If you get this sort of response, then you know that your figures are extremely low and can be brought up a bit before you meet your next potential client.

Another comment to come your way may be: "What a great product or service you have". This is another sign that the client is over the moon and your offering could well be worth much more in monetary terms.

Remember also that pricing often rests on relationships. For instance, writing an 80,000 word book could easily equate to US$0.30 per word.

However, a top-level writer who writes for the CEO of an international bank could well be writing at double that price and the boss wouldn't think twice about it.

Sometimes, especially if one has to fork out lots of cash on the purchasing of supplies to manufacture products, it is not easy to run a company without a bank overdraft facility. There is something strange about this facility. When you go into the red in banking terms, it is always quite a struggle to come out of it to a positive monetary state. Again, this boils down to your pricing. If your 'cost vs. price' is correct from the start, you shouldn't end up in this position. Rather, use suppliers who will allow you to pay over thirty days.

There will be times when you will be relaxing at home and want to kick yourself hard. You costed out a job for a client and crossed your fingers all day hoping that the quotation would be signed off. The client did just that without blinking an eyelid. Now you are disappointed because if you had increased the final total amount substantially, it might also have been signed off just as effortlessly.

At times like this, it is best not to tempt fate. Who knows?

The client may be so happy with the cost that they may tell their associates and friends. Of course, this may not have happened had your initial pricing been too high.

Yes, pricing can, like other areas of the business, make your head spin. Experience will teach you just how to handle your pricing.

Remember that if a client is really trying to squeeze you down on the numbers and you feel aggrieved by it, it is better to walk away. Rather do no business than bad business.

The saying is that 'there are plenty of fish in the sea'. Some clients are happy to take chances. They talk big but haven't got the funds. Choose your pricing as carefully as you choose your clients.

CHAPTER 24

Pricing Sweet-spot

The term 'Pricing Sweet-spot' refers to the most crucial balancing act that you are going to find in the business world. As a business leader or company CEO, you need to find the perfect price that a client will be prepared to pay for your product or service, meaning the price is not too high or too low. It's spot on.

All clients want value for their money spent, but just how much are they prepared to pay? Remember that you are running a business in a cut-throat world. Sure, a supermarket is quite happy to print the prices of their goods for sale in the local newspaper so that the consumers can see their month-end specials and more.

However, you won't find consultants such as lawyers, accountants or insurance brokers doing this as their opponents will simply cut back on commission and undercut their opponent's prices to get the work.

Educating a client is absolutely key as they need to understand the value of your product or service and why it's more expensive (or even cheaper) than your opponents' prices. Don't fall into the trap of assumption.

You thought that your client understood your product or service and its pricing? Well, quite often, you may have thought wrong and lost the client. The buyer needs to know what exactly they are paying for and why your offering is a better deal than others in the industry.

Clients have much more in their daily work and personal lives to worry about than just understanding your product or service offering, so in order to succeed you are left with no other option but to spoon-feed them. You will soon learn that not all clients read emails thoroughly.

A weekly or bi-weekly face-to-face status meeting with the client is the best way to go and it is here where you can entrench the value of your offering in relation to the price that you quoted.

Yes, it's the good old 'quality and pricing philosophy'.

If the quality of your offering as well as the pricing is right, the sales will follow. It's all about getting the buyer to have confidence in your offering.

The principle here is a simple one. Always make sure that the value of your offering is superior to your pricing and not the other way around.

Here's is that word 'assumption' again. I am working on the assumption that you as a business person have full confidence in your offering. If you don't then how do you expect the client to buy into the sale? Always look at the Pricing Sweet-spot from a customer's perspective and not from your own point of view. If you were in their position, would you sign off on the purchase at the price that you quoted?

You need to be honest with yourself. Are your operations costs too high? Is this factor pushing up the sales price? Could this see you lose the deal with the client? If this is the case, which it is quite often in business, then you have bigger problems in your business to worry about than you first thought.

Let's look at some of the factors that will come into play in terms of finding the Pricing Sweet-spot. A lot of market analysis needs to happen before you roll out your offering for sales. Keep in mind that there are a lot of factors which are going to be way beyond your control.

First, is the market ready for your offering? If the industry is going through an economic recession, the time might not be right for you to launch your super state-of-the-art plasma screens. In a situation like this, people are battling to put food on their tables and pay the electricity bill, let alone fork out cash on luxuries.

Does this mean that your price must come down in order to drive sales? Well, it can't come down too much as you have suppliers' costs to pay too and you are in business for one reason—to make money.

Here is another example. There are major labour strikes happening in and around the city. Workers are refusing to manufacture and deliver your supplies to make the plasma screens unless their bosses give them an increase.

It's a chicken-and-egg situation. If the bosses give their workers a wage increase, then the pricing on materials sold to you are sure to go up too. This means that the price that you will charge to the client is also set to rise.

Things are becoming trickier by the minute. As your costs are set to rise, you need to make sure like never before that your client will still buy the plasma screens at the increased price. You need to do such a good selling job that the client will simply feel that the price increase is a drop in the ocean in terms of the huge amounts of cash that he or she will make from selling your screens after purchasing them from you.

As you can see, one needs to be totally aware of what is happening out in the marketplace as one way or another whether it involved your business directly or not, it could impact on your figures at the end of the day.

To understand the market to the best of one's ability, some businesses even employ 'shoppers'. These 'shoppers' don't buy products or services but are consultants who simply walk around studying the market and the trends of buyers.

The old sales cliché of 'see it, touch it, feel it' is very much applicable. If the object on sale is a type of food or drink, the 'taste it' part comes into play. A client is more likely to purchase something that they can visualise or touch rather than a concept that looks good on the boardroom screen during a meeting.

So, how do you find the Pricing Sweet-spot if the value of your

Pricing Sweet-spot

offering is unlikely to bring the price that you want it to?

The answer is often referred to as 'accumulative sales'. If you are selling women's blouses but due to the high material costs, the selling price ends up a bit higher than usual and the clients might not budge, then go the accumulative route. Most women love necklaces and earrings.

Don't go top of the range here, but find something at middle-market level that you can afford to throw into the mix so your product on sale will not only be seen as a blouse but a blouse with added-value accessories. Guess what? You can quite possibly even sell at a slightly higher price than just the blouse on its own.

As long as you are running at a profit, all is well. Remember too that some days your profit margins courtesy of your Pricing Sweet-spot will be higher than others.

Now let's look at the oldest sales trick in the book. Ever wondered why products in a shop end with the numbers 99 at the end of the price? It's a psychological way of getting sales done. A product for sale at US$10.99 looks a lot cheaper and a much better buy than if it were sold at a price of US$11. Or at least that is what the human brain is working on even though the difference is merely 1 cent.

You also need to consider the sales market that you are selling into in terms of the geographic approach. For example, certain products or services may sell at a different price in different cities or suburbs.

If you own a makeup shop in a large shopping mall, where you offer makeovers, you are almost certainly paying high rates in overheads by way of rent, electricity, and more. Therefore, your price per makeover will be higher than the makeup person who is running the business from their home or travels to clients.

It is never a good thing to have two, three or more price lists for the various areas as people talk and soon the one who is paying the most, just because they live or work in an affluent area, thinks that you ripped them off in terms of pricing. However, if you don't have these different pricing structures, you will miss out on a few sales along the way.

Don't ever go too cheap just for the sake of getting the offering sold. Too many business people fall into the trap of thinking that if they go in cheap, they will lose money but will get their offering out into the market. If people love it, then sales will be done in bulk orders with much money generated.

This is a risky way of doing business. Sure, one can go this route if you are a part of a big brand but if you are a small- to medium-size business, it is an immense risk. Of course, people love cheaper prices, but if you price your product too cheap, even the cheapest of clients will begin to wonder about the quality of your offering.

Knowledge is power as I always say. If there is a sudden spike in purchases, you need to know why.

On the other hand, if the products or services suddenly stop being in demand and sales drop off, you need to know the reason for this too. Having this sort of information at your disposal will allow you to work out whether your prices should be raised or lowered, to what extent and also for how long.

Remember that your wonderful offering at the right price is just that, until your opponent latches onto your strategy and comes up with something even better to offer next month. Do you remember the old saying in leadership: 'uneasy is the head that wears the crown'?

You need to cash in while you can as you are only the market champion until the next business person with a big idea comes along to burst your bubble. Then you have to go back to the drawing board to find a solution that will get your offering, or a new version thereof, back to the top.

Television subscription networks and mobile network providers are best known for making use of the penetration pricing concept.

They put a product on the market for a limited time span and with the client interested, they then up the prices. Some customers stay loyal if the service is what it is claimed to be while others will look to find a cheaper alternative.

The principle here is very similar to the restaurant pricing model. For example, hamburger and chips are on sale on a Tuesday at the cheapest price in town, most likely at two for the price of one. The restaurant owner is no fool.

The owner knows that you will order something to drink while you eat, and the drink prices will be through the roof. The restaurant has to make money somehow.

When buying a mobile telephone on contract, you will often find that the phone handset is thrown in for free as a part of the deal. Having read this far in this book, you will know that in business there is nothing free. The money is being made back through the airtime contract that you just signed. The same applies to the television network.

You are getting the satellite dish for next to nothing, but paying for it a few times over through the monthly subscription that you fork out to the television network company.

By now you would have realised that your Pricing Sweet spot revolves around a lot of psychology and perception.

In closing, never be afraid to receive client feedback, whether it is positive or negative. The negative feedback may hurt, but there is no time for emotions in the world of business. Use the negative feedback to fix any areas of uncertainty relating to your offering and you will see your business rise to the next level.

CHAPTER 25

Franchise and Remuneration Structure

Each person in your business must feel like a franchise owner. They need to take ownership of their work, an attitude which will foster a feeling of independence and autonomy.

Take international food chain McDonald's as an example. They have a reputation of honouring the staff members who make the biggest contribution to their business every month. To the McDonald's senior management, it's all about rewarding and acknowledging those who go the extra mile to uphold their brand principles.

Each person working for the company should feel like he or she is a part-owner of McDonald's.

Of course, if you want to create a feeling of shared responsibility and part ownership, then it has to be two-way traffic. The staff will look back at senior management and, quite rightly, ask what the business has done for them.

Similarly, the franchise owner will have drawn up a tick-box checklist when evaluating the performances of his restaurant staff.

Is the restaurant always clean?
Are the staff members always neatly dressed?
How friendly is each staff member towards customers?
The franchise owner will constantly look at ways and means to

build on the incentive schemes that he or the head office has put in place. After all, this is one way to keep staff happy and motivated.

Of course, remuneration incentives don't only have to be in the form of cash. What about allowances for transport, clothing vouchers or staff take-away meals on their birthdays?

The principle of getting top work done and keeping loyal staff members happy is a simple one:

Pay your staff members more than your competitors pay theirs, but then expect top delivery!

Instead of cutting corners, the CEO should look at it as: Pay More and Expect More!

Every position in the company must have an incentive scheme aimed at individual performances.

Now let me give you an example of an incentive scheme that I don't like and then one that I do approve of.

If a company doesn't do well, no bonuses are paid out to any staff member. This is the incentive scheme that I don't like.

Annual incentive bonus reviews should be based on a twofold approach. First, 50% of the bonus should be attached to whether the company did well or not. Then, the other 50% of the bonus should be attached to the individual performance of a staff member, irrespective of whether the company did well or not.

This means that the staff members who did perform will get twice the bonus compared with those who didn't. That's a fair outcome. I like this incentive scheme.

The bottom line is that staff members need to feel valued if they are to perform at their peak. It can never be fair that staff members who contribute are not incentivised due to poor strategy; bonus structures must be individually assessed.

Of course, we need to look at the basics. If franchises don't make enough money, then the whole system falls flat. So the product needs to be of such value that it will always attract interest and be in demand.

Let's look at some tips that will help on the franchising front.

First, if you have a product and create a franchising system, you will be paid either a fixed fee or a percentage fee by the buyer.

Remember that the fee agreed on needs to be applied across the board, so you can't charge one outlet representing your brand one amount and then change it for another. This will create problems if the truth ever surfaces which, in most cases, it eventually does.

Naturally, the operator will only buy a franchise from you if it is viable to him or her, so the offering needs to be attractive enough for the operator to make money and still pay the percentage fee to you.

So keep the entry cost affordable. Don't price yourself out of the game. Keep the percentages, known as royalties, at a realistic level in line with the offering that you have tabled. If the offering requires much-needed support from your side as the franchise, then this needs to be considered when working out the percentage.

If you are a supermarket and someone is buying one of your franchises, you will inevitably include incentive targets on the sales front so that it is as much in the operator's interest to move stock as it is in yours.

Keep the operator hungry to succeed. Don't be 'penny wise and pound foolish' and think only in the short term. Always keep the bigger picture in mind.

The operator needs to provide the franchisee with a comprehensive business plan before they get the go-ahead. Remember that the operator is carrying your brand, so it is never a good reflection if they go out of business.

Clients will inevitably remember your business name going under and not the name of the operator. So be careful who you go into business with.

Also, remember how you go into business. For example, for an operator who is short of cash, you may elect to work on a business model whereby they take on the franchise on condition that they pay you back monthly. You need to manage this carefully and to make sure that the monthly paybacks do happen.

It is always clever to keep an eye on the balance sheet of such an operator, just to make sure that they don't run up too much debt. After all, this could see the business relationship ending on a disastrous note.

There may be times when the operator is cash-strapped and will ask for some leeway in terms of the repayment plan, and the two parties agree upon the terms. Be prepared to offer some form of leniency in terms of the bigger picture, but remember that this is a two-way street.

While there has to be a form of give-and-take, this is business, so the payment plan cannot be changed forever. Think of the change in payment terms as an emergency, short-term procedure to help the operator. This is not a new normal.

Keep in mind that some people are very good operationally, perhaps even better than you are, but they don't know how to make the profits that you have in your head. You may need to do some mentoring, so that you are both on the same page.

Your way of doing business may be completely different to theirs, so try to find synergy.

Don't turn it into an 'I am right, and you are wrong' situation. Learn from each other.

Equally, you want this franchise episode of your business life to be a success, but what form of training are you offering to equip your operator with the necessary know-how to run your brand?

Now let's take a look at what operators need to be successful in the franchise industry. What will business owners require from the operator before going into business with them?

The attitude of the potential operator will have a lot to do with the success or failure rate. A person cannot really be taught to be proactive. It is something that you are born with, just like personality or lack of it.

You will quickly work out if the person buying a franchise is as excited on Day 1 as he or she is in the days and weeks that follow; that's why the gut feel is so important. Once you have signed all the relevant documentation, it is then simply too late to back out. You are either stuck with a winner or a losing horse, so to speak.

Some people talk a really good game, but put them on the field of play and it could be really bad news. So here are some quick tips for any operator wanting to buy a franchise.

Do you fully understand the product you will be selling? Will you be able to work on your own as opposed to being part of a team in a huge corporate? Can you build a team around you and motivate others? How well can you sell a product or an idea? Can you put those hot sales presentations together yourself, or do you need external help? Are you a good organiser who is capable of running this new business?

Franchisees (business owners) need to believe that the operator is not a quitter. As an operator or franchise owner, set yourself a goal of two to three years and make sure you have enough cash flow to get you through the first year at least. You will soon find out if you are cut out for this line of business or not.

Remember, none of the parties involved know all the answers to business. You will learn something new every day, so be open-minded when it comes to acquiring knowledge.

As a new franchise owner ask yourself if you need extra support. There are plenty of tips in this book about hiring the right staff. Make sure you surround yourself with winners in order to remain a champion yourself.

The next point applies to all parties involved in the franchise process. As much as you may want to do everything yourself – after all the perfect formula is in your mind – there are just not enough hours in the day to achieve this.

You will need to start trusting people to do their tasks around you.

Yes, you have been let down before by people and will probably be disappointed again in the future, but you need to learn to trust individuals otherwise you will be working 24-hour shifts, seven days a week. And that is just not feasible.

If you don't regard yourself as a hard worker, then the franchise industry is not for you. A franchise is your business and livelihood, even if you are paying royalty percentages or a fixed fee percentage to someone else.

The first year will always be the toughest since you will have to knuckle down and get things up and running, and people in the right positions. It's about signing contracts with suppliers. Again, you need to find the right suppliers who deliver on time, every time in order to avoid personal disappointment or embarrassment.

The foundation element of any business is always the most important element. If your business model is a healthy one and you have laid solid foundations, then you should have a sense of comfort going into year two.

Try to encourage your employees to be ambassadors rather than just salaried workers. Let them know that there is huge scope for them to grow in the business.

Everyone in life needs a goal, so put those incentive schemes in place to encourage your staff to work towards greater things. All staff want a bit extra in their pocket at the end of the month, just like you did when you worked on a fixed salary for that large corporate.

Finally, never forget that your staff will look to you for leadership and new ideas, so they need to know that your door is always open should they have any thoughts on improving the business or new ways to market a product. Be open to input.

Like most things in life, this seed that you planted which is called a 'franchise', will take time to 'grow' and to reach its full potential. You will need to exercise patience in this regard. I am sure you know the axioms that tell us 'good things come to those who wait' or 'Rome wasn't built in a day'.

The franchise game is an exciting affair, but it is the old story of what you sow, so shall you reap.

CHAPTER 26

Snappy Quality

We live in a world of instant gratification. Gone are the days of snail mail and very few people stand in queues at banks to do their weekly or monthly financial administration anymore.

The time span of *waiting* has decreased rapidly. Our world is built on speed. So when it comes to a product or service, it is not only about what is being paid for but whether the product or service delivers instant gratification.

Here is an example.

Would you pay US$100 for a product which includes free delivery within seven days? Or would you be prepared to pay an extra US$10 (so US$110) if the product can be delivered on the same day it is purchased?

Most people would be prepared to pay the extra US$10, so the service or product provider would use US$3 of the extra US$10 for delivery and the remaining US$7 to cover set-up costs.

Here is another example.

You are looking to secure a US$1 million loan for your business from a bank. For some reason (only known to bankers), it seems to take almost a month to get all the paperwork in place and the loan granted, and this when the client is paying 10% per annum interest.

Would the client not entertain the thought of paying 12% per annum interest if the bank could sort out the loan within 72 hours?

Service and product providers need to understand that speed is essential and not just an add-on or peripheral part of the service.

A good business will be judged not only on its offering but also on its speed. I am not suggesting that quality should be sacrificed in order to ensure speedy service. Both are equally as important, but the speed element, as explained in the examples above, are often forgotten in the midst of the business transaction process.

Once your business is able to deliver a top-quality service or product at speed, you will find that your company will be viewed in the 'Premier League' of businesses and more clients will come your way. Just don't let the bar slip since bad service often creates damaging publicity to your business reputation.

Today's world of business is all about the client wanting everything 'now'! Time is a vital element and in our modern society, patience is something that many decision-makers are short of.

Similarly, when it comes to offering a product in the marketplace, it is important to give the customer instant gratification. Think of the calculator. When adding lots and lots of numbers, it needs to give the total answer now, not in a minute's time like many of the old adding machines used in the 1960s and 1970s.

And what about instant coffee? It got its name for a reason.

It's the same when a customer is paying for goods at a till point. Gone are the days of writing out a cheque. Nowadays, the debit or credit card gets swiped and within seconds, away you go.

Instant gratification is not a 'nice to have' element. It is a part of life. Remember that the chances are that your client base is much younger than it would have been twenty or thirty years ago. Business is done differently and more efficiently due to modern trends as well as modern technology. Basically, it boils down to managing the expectations of the customer.

Businesses should always be thinking about how they can further impress the client by offering snappy quality. In most cases, this applies on the social media front with business looking to find new ways and means to show clients that they are always on their A-game and one step ahead of their opponents.

Clients respect high-quality delivery, but also take note of the intent element in terms of how hard a supplier is trying to move with the times. Believe me, clients notice if a company appears to be stagnant and just waiting for a five-year contract to end so that they can push for renewal. Is the supplier resting on their laurels?

Or are they trying to keep their brand fresh and unique? Is the supplier making every possible effort to give the client the best product or service within the shortest possible time frame?

Building a snappy quality culture requires going back to the basics. Does your company do any form of research in terms of finding out what a client expected in terms of snappy quality? For example, many clients find that the billing systems of agencies are simply too tiring.

Why so much paperwork and back and forth calls just to complete a transaction? Business is about a need or a desire to *have*, so why kill the momentum with piles and piles of emails regarding invoices? It is not like the client doesn't have anything else to do than answer tedious email chains.

If you are a supermarket store, the first thing that a customer would probably judge your brand on is just how clean the floor of the shop is. This is a sign of snappy quality. If you can't even keep the floor clean in a store that sells food, then surely it will be difficult for the customer to have a form of confidence in you on any other level?

The big corporates understand the importance of getting a client's mind to progress from 'need' to 'buying'. The seller understands the importance of speed or pace.

In the snappy quality department, there is no need for error. Remember how a cellular telephone used to be just for making phone calls?

The first ones that came out in the mid-1990s weighed close to a brick. Now through finding out what the client needs and by making use of a plethora of research and development, the cellular telephone is no longer just a phone, it is closer to a life-support system. You simply can't do without your mobile phone that handles calls, text messages, emails, images, Instagram, Twitter, Facebook, LinkedIn, games and more.

This is about the best example of instant gratification that one can get. It's quite simple really. A concept has been planted in one's mind. As a client, you simply cannot do without your mobile phone. Even if you are not using it, it is probably on the table in front of you. Many even start to fidget with it when they are bored at home or in meetings. Many are addicted to social media because it is instant.

Circling back to the basics, ask yourself: How good is your refund system when clients return broken or malfunctioning goods to your store? Do you give them a hard time? If so then they'll probably want their money back and refuse to buy any further goods at your shop. Or do you instantly refund their money and offer another brand or product on the shelf in your store?

If you are a supermarket, the client should be mature enough to understand that you keep a whole range of appliances in your store and he or she might just have got the 'bad apple in the barrel'. But it is how you handle the situation from a client-service perspective that is important here.

As a supplier, it is equally important to keep thinking about the time factor. In which way can you save your client time, as this links directly with energy and stress? The customer experience is seen as a form of science and, like every form of life, there are suppliers who understand this and those who don't. The latter are always the ones who wonder why the others manage to get the business ahead of them.

Snappy quality is no longer a peripheral or added-on element. It is an essential part of the modern-day business when it comes to winning over clients.

This is all well and good when things are going well. But what happens when a blizzard hits Canada in an area where you are doing most of your sales? The delivery trucks can no longer get from Toronto to the outskirts of the city to deliver your products. The best advice that I can give here is for you to sub-contract a quality PR agency that can put a crisis control strategy in place. Think about it.

The client has probably paid a deposit for the goods, which now haven't arrived at the store. Of course, the goods are snowed in, but, for all you know, the client could be thinking that you took the money and ran, or that you went out of business.

Remember the client might not even know you from a bar of soap as your business is based many miles away and, quite possibly, on another continent. The above is a weather issue and a problem which was not yours but has now become a hot potato.

Always be prepared to acknowledge your failings. If a delivery of goods is not on time as per your arrangement with the client, rather say those two very difficult words: "I'm sorry"—even if it wasn't your fault. This will prevent a showdown with the client over something which is quite often quite trivial.

Let's get back to the office side now. You know just how frustrating it can be when your call is put on hold while you are trying to sort out an issue while chatting to a call centre agent over the phone regarding your cellular telephone bill? Then put yourself in the shoes of the call centre agent.

First, how long did it take before the automated voice went away before an agent answered the call?

Then how long did it take for the agent to sort out the issue? How many times was your call transferred from one call centre to the next before you found a person who had some idea of the issue that you were talking about?

Most senior management executives do understand the frustrations that the clients go through, even though they won't be too keen to admit it. That is why many businesses put a service survey onto the automated system so that the client can rate the service that is received.

A similar system also happens when one is carrying out queries with a supplier on the internet these days. These are perfect examples of where snappy quality turns a brand into a winner or a loser.

The instant element of snappy quality cannot be overlooked and is probably one of the foremost elements in a modern-day business transaction which could lead to growing or decreasing business relationships.

The best thing that a business leader or CEO can do is to put himself through the customer experience on a regular basis. He or she will soon work out if they are happy with the product and client service received.

In this way, a leader can work out what is needed to improve the snappy quality element of the system in order to avoid frustrating clients or potential clients. Are you one of the leaders who is proactive enough to do this? Or do you delegate it to someone else and then end up pondering whether your product or service is as great or as poor as the feedback indicates?

The reality is that snappy quality creates a form of top-of-mind awareness which will put your brand first in the queue for new business if you handled the basics correctly.

Let the customer always understand that you are a firm believer in instant gratification.

Remember that key to business success: Always stay one step ahead of your opponents. Always have an A-, B- and C-game plan, because most opponents only have an A-game plan and then start to panic when it doesn't work out for them.

Always go that extra mile for the customer. Sometimes it gets taken for granted, but be assured it never goes unnoticed and is seldom forgotten.

CHAPTER 27

How We Make Judgements

Judgements are made according to three approaches namely (1.) conscious decision-making. (2.) Your gut feel by way of relying on your unconscious mind, and (3.) sometimes a combination of the above-mentioned two points.

Your analytical mind (your conscious mind) works better when you are analysing facts. When you have information which you can access or analyse, then the judgement or decision that you make is based on certain factors.

These encompass the business objective of the decision that you are making as well as the capability of delivery regarding the service or product. Another factor is the amount of capital at your disposal with regard to what you are aiming to achieve.

So the above will indicate to you that the judgement is not only about application but is also heavily based on information.

Your gut feel, or unconscious mind, is far more emotional and less open to analysis.

This approach can be triggered by the people around you, the time of day and how busy you are, weather conditions, the service provider's image and many, many more factors which could lead to a gut-feel decision. In this realm, you often need to follow your senses: sight, smell, hearing, taste, and touch.

Let's look at an example.

When you buy a yacht, you would ask several questions of the salesman. Such as: How far can the yacht sail? What is the interior of the yacht made of? How modern is the sail rig? Most yachts come with an emergency engine, hence there is a fuel tank. So what is the size of the fuel tank? The answers to the above questions would position you to make a conscious-mind decision.

However, your gut feel is often related to judging people, so the salesman's image and levels of professionalism would lead you to an emotional decision around whether or not he knows what he is talking about and if he appears honest. These will influence whether or not you buy.

Often, the difficult part is to know when to rely on either the conscious mind or the gut feel to reach your conclusion.

When it comes to a client who is trying to decide about your service or product, the buyer would have surely done his own homework before taking the final decision, so again it boils down to the right service or product, at the right time and the right place.

Life is a series of decisions and the reality is that no matter how much data or information you have at your disposal, you will be forced to make judgement decisions at key moments in your business life.

Some business people have used their judgement ahead of common sense or logic and made millions of dollars, whereas if they used the data instead of the logic they may have failed. So we have quite a serious balancing act here. There is a role for both judgement and information in the mix. The best advice is: Don't ignore either.

The key in business is not to be emotional. Yes, you will get excited when a great opportunity is put before you. You will probably try not to show your excitement in case the presenter ups his price. Judgement is a time-aligned art. You don't want to hesitate and lose that opportunity that would have made you millions, but at the same time, you don't want to jump in without having thought things through.

Decision making is also an art.

When you consider the pressure to perform when it comes to

judgement, it is easy to marvel at how presidents of countries or major corporate leaders handle making all-important calls on a daily or even hourly basis. The answer is simple. They have a team of highly-skilled advisors sitting around them who are in touch with the latest trends to help the No 1 make the right decision.

Of course, it's not that easy if you are a One-Person-Show-type business.

It is said that top leaders make many better judgements than poor ones. This highlights the importance of developing good decision-making habits. Many business people, for example, choose to break down their decision making. Each decision that needs to be made gets given a name.

Then it's up to the strategy element. They work out their current client base and what impact their judgement will have on that. Then it's time to look at the potential new clients and analyse that carefully. The last thing that they want is to sign up 30% of new business, but lose 60% because the established clients were not comfortable with the judgement decision that was made.

Before a judgement decision is made, and when you are busy putting the strategies in place, it is important to do a full breakdown dependent on the product or service that is being sold. Are more of the buyers male or female? Does your offering sell better in the summer, autumn, winter or spring? In which parts of the world does your offering sell the most? What is the current economic status in that geographical area?

These sorts of decisions are more urgent than the ones regarding the purchase of stock.

Be assured that when it comes to decisions of this nature, they cannot be made via Skype or email. These are make-or-break choices involving the business and need to happen around a table. One error in judgement and the business brand or offering could suffer long-term damage.

It is very unfortunate for those in the decision-making chair that although they might have got a judgement call right in the past, it doesn't mean they can make the same call on the same project. The business world evolves by the minute, never mind by the hour, day, month or year, and each decision needs to be made according to the current market climate.

So how does one find the perfect formula?

So from the above, you can see that the ability to decide is more important than the actual decision. However, the thought process plus the research, data, and logic – plus that good old gut feel – are all the ingredients that make up the art of judgement. Every person has an opinion, but one has to put beliefs and emotions aside when making the big calls on the business front.

Some businesses in the US see judgement as a skill and actually ask candidates about this when they meet to decide on hiring new staff.

Good decision-making needs to be rewarded.

Now it's time for some good news. The general rule of thumb is that if you do make some non-financial errors in judgement that you are able to correct these in time.

However, the right decision at the right time is always ideal. Fortunately, there is a way to make your staff steer wide of wayward decision-making. Highlight an incentive plan for your employees.

If it means that they can make a few extra bucks at the end of the month or year by making the right decisions on projects that will be pleasing to the clients, then you will be surprised at the positive results that will follow at the speed of light!

Some people operate better when they are given increased responsibility. Keep in mind that your 'gems', who are worth their weight in gold to your company, might be great at their jobs but might not necessarily be leaders.

Therefore, these special people might not be your decision-makers but rather your perfectionists in terms of work. So other people may need to be groomed for future decision-making responsibilities.

Quite often the best decision making needs to be done through outside-the-box methods. You may find that the best judgements are made on staff getaways rather than in the meeting room at the office. Of course, sometimes this is not easy, particularly if the decision needs to be made urgently.

There really is no hard and fast 'magic wand' to bring about correct judgement in terms of decision making. Different formulas work for different people. The best advice that I can give is to listen to others and take heed of their advice. As we've touched on in these pages, remember that the best idea might not come from your US$1 000 000 per annum executive but from the tea lady, who takes home US$20 000 a year.

Some people just have the ability to say the right thing at the right time and you will know by your gut feel if this is the right decision or not.

One needs to be open-minded to all forms of opinions.

A lot of decisions go wrong because leaders or CEOs don't consult enough before taking major business calls. Some leaders tend to get into a stereotyped mindset and think that they have seen it all before in the world of business.

They feel that there is nothing that you can tell them that they don't already know. They forget the principle of the evolving business world and that today's business scene is already a step behind when it comes to tomorrow.

Therefore, they are out of touch with decision making. Some even collect information from their research team but don't actually bother to study the data or make their judgement based on what they have been told.

To ignore information that is at one's fingertips does seem a bit senseless

Other leaders find themselves at the centre of office politics. They don't want to use the information or advice provided by a particular person because that person is deemed to be after the CEO's job, according to the office gossip mill.

The reality is that an accumulative amount of information will always put the decision maker into a better position to make a judgement, than not having the information or advice at his or her fingertips. Even if the leader or decision-maker believes he or she is an expert in a particular field, he or she also needs to remember that no idea is a stupid idea.

Again, the tea lady may just come up with the key to the perfect judgement before the highly-paid business executive does.

It often works that way on the sales front with the junior sales person clinching the deal before the senior sales person, purely because the concept, idea product or service was worded in a particular – albeit different – way compared to the manner in which the senior sales representative tabled it.

Remember to keep things simple.

Making a judgement needs to be handled with care, particularly when one is working with large budgets. It is often a good thing to think just how the opposition would handle the situation.

What decision would they go with? Quite often, following the analysis of the information on the table, just by putting themselves in the 'shoes' of the opposition, the leader may be able to make the right decision.

Also, remember to think clearly. Just because the idea didn't work in another country five years ago doesn't necessarily mean that it won't work in your market today. One cannot make judgement decisions wearing blinkers. Your brain makes decisions based on what your eyes have seen, or your ears have heard.

Always keep thinking of ways and means in which a product or service can be improved. This could also lead to the correct decision being made. Perhaps the time is not right now for the launch of your big idea. Perhaps there is 5% of the mix still missing. Would it be better to hold back for six months and re-evaluate the market to send the perfect product or service to the shelves?

It goes without saying that a big judgement decision should be made when the decision maker is in the right frame of mind. Making a big decision after having had little sleep or too many glasses of wine at a party the previous night is also not a good move. The decision maker needs to stay focused and to be at his or her best to access the information, logic and gut feel that will lead to making the right call.

The risks are often high, but the rewards will be greater if the judgements made are spot on!

CHAPTER 28

Deal Fatigue

Deal fatigue is a 'state of tiredness or stagnation' that happens during lengthy negotiating periods. The trick here is to not give in to the demands of the other party for the sake of concluding the deal, but rather to hold out with maximum mental and physical energy to get the outcome that you wanted in the first place.

Large transactions bring a huge amount of excitement with them to both CEOs and staff members alike, but as times passes – be it due to the lengthy process of concluding the paperwork on the deal or the negotiation process – the shine and feeling of glamour and achievement start to disappear.

The process of finalising a large deal is often tiresome and, during this period, people tend to lower the purchase price to get things done faster. They also lose the stomach to see the transaction through to the end and end up focusing on other priorities.

Let's consider the example of a mining firm:

The firm wants to buy a mine for US$100 million.

Time passes by due to the processes that need to take place to satisfy the competition authorities. Seven months later the firm is informed that the tribunal process will take at least another year before its completion.

So let's look at the options available to the firm:

They can pull out of the deal because of the long and tedious process. The second option is that they can work full out on the tough clauses placed in the contract by the tribunal in order to get the deal finalised as quickly as possible.

This brings us to the importance of getting the right people into the right positions in order to keep the wheel turning as fast as possible in order to conclude the deal.

A vital piece of advice is: Always structure a plan with timelines (deadlines) and allocate responsibilities to the relevant persons.

Momentum is key in ensuring that there are no delays in getting the transaction concluded so constant communication between all team members and stakeholders is of critical importance.

Get this right by involving all relevant persons in status meetings to ensure that all bases are covered in terms of deliverables. This will ensure that nothing falls between the cracks in terms of deliverables being forgotten.

Here are some tips to avoid deal fatigue:

Create a data centre on a server which can only be accessed by those involved with this specific transaction.

Don't take shortcuts. When things get tiresome in business, people look for the shortest way to get things done, but this often tends to impact negatively on the quality of the task. Remember that the small print in a contract is usually even more important than the normal size print.

Stay level-headed in the face of shady deals. Sometimes outside buyers will make an offer for your company, not with the intention of buying it but just to get their hands on information that you will include in your documentation. Your gut feel, and common sense combination should tell you if the potential buyer is genuine or not.

Ensure that a time frame for the completion of the deal is in place.

Always be ready for a last-minute rush as many deals often get concluded towards the end of the negotiating period.

This last part of the negotiating period is crucial as you cannot afford to drop your price just to push the deal through. Stick with what you feel the deal is worth and, if the buyer really wants in, they will come to the party or at least pretty close to the asking price.

Now let's look at the understanding element of business deals.

Many business owners who are poised to sell their respective companies take time to jot down the ten most important facts concerning the transaction and paste them in a prominent place in their office. These important points relate to the heartbeat of the business and, in turn, the livelihood of the business owner, so it is important to keep these in mind in order to avoid the dreaded deal fatigue

During negotiations, you often hear someone declare: "I think we are close to a deal."

This could mean two things. First, the other party is trying to psych you out and let you think they are close to agreeing to your terms when, in fact, they actually are not.

Second, after many hours of negotiations, you could be falling into the trap that you are close to clinching a deal, but you may actually still be a good few hours, days or months away from reaching a conclusion on the matter.

It is at this point that fatigue often sets in and to speed things up you may just be tempted to throw an adjusted price into the equation. Don't let that be your reaction. It's always better if the other party is the one to throw in the number. This will mean that you are the strong one and still have many hours of negotiating energy left in your think tank.

The general rule of thumb to remember is that when a seller puts a number on the table, the settling price is usually higher than when a buyer puts the number forward.

Deal clinching is a game that needs to be played to perfection.

During the negotiation process, it is always a good tactic to let the other party know that you have to consult with a higher authority in your business in order to give the final go-ahead on the deal. This will make the other party realise that this could be a slightly longer process than they first thought. What you are doing is keeping the other party's mind ticking over.

Nobody comes to the table to lose the deal, or waste time, so the other party may do anything and everything to speed up the process, including the adjustment of figures in your favour.

If the deal is a large one, then you have every right to take additional time to think through the terms and conditions of the contract. Keep the other party thinking that you are consulting with your superiors or your advisor and you will be surprised at how you will benefit as the negotiation process changes to your advantage.

Don't be afraid to be seen as slightly aggressive in the negotiating phase. You are trying to gain the emotional advantage here. You are showing the other party exactly who's the boss at this meeting.

Remember you are trying to create a situation whereby the other party will be forced to close the deal on your terms as soon as possible. Nobody likes meeting after meeting about the same matter. Believe me, the other party is equally keen to get the business done and will succumb to your terms if you play the emotional game correctly. Don't lose patience in the process. You are in it to win it!

Now we've looked at the process and some of the tactics you can deploy, let's take time to consider some of the causes of deal fatigue.

Quite often, if negotiating timelines are not set out at the start or are not abided by, your meeting will tend to go around in circles without reaching any form of conclusion. This can cause deal fatigue.

Sometimes meetings will be postponed because either of the parties will not be able to get their 'experts' to attend key discussions. Perhaps vital data which was needed for the meetings were not made available on time, therefore forcing a delay. Perhaps the meeting does go ahead, but it is found that the information due to be discussed is incomplete, thus forcing a postponement of the negotiations. More deal fatigue.

The business sector, in step with global developments, is evolving all the time while your negotiations are ongoing. For example, you are hoping to land a major tender deal to provide kitchen equipment to hotels in Libya, but the country has just been invaded and is in a state of war. This changes the timelines of the deal.

You will now have to conclude the tender but will only be in a position to act or deliver when peace and tranquillity have been restored to the country.

Critically, you must be prepared to walk away from a deal if the parties cannot agree on the terms. The sun will always shine again tomorrow, and other opportunities will come your way. Don't sell your product, service or soul for next to nothing just to make the deal happen. Stand your ground and know what you and your offering are worth. Yes, many hours of talks may fall by the wayside but don't sell yourself short for the sake of forcing a deal to happen.

Always be properly prepared for negotiations. Assign the right people to the right tasks. Remember those task sheets and lists of important points? Take time to do that and bear them in mind. Don't only keep the information in your head. Keep it on paper too so that nothing can be overlooked or forgotten.

Make sure that your internal team communications are constant. People are busy with their existing clients too so new clients are secondary no matter how big the numbers are. Bear in mind that, as things currently stand, the new client is a 50/50 possibility until the deal is done.

Sometimes you may feel that the negotiations are taking so long that you just want the process to be over. Quite possibly the other party is feeling the same way, so don't be the one to give in. Stay strong and stand for the terms and pricing that you started out with. It is a case of who needs whom more.

During negotiations, there is always a bit of give and take in terms of making concessions, but don't make these 'discounts' in order just to speed up the process. Concessions are made when acting in good faith to make the deal happen for both parties, not because you are sick and tired of sitting in meetings.

Some parties are so devious that they structure their concessions bids according to time. When they feel that they have the other party pressed for time, they push for the concessions, knowing that the opposition is under pressure. This is not a great way to do business on their part, but all is fair in love and war. One often has to do what is necessary to make things happen.

Mastering the ability to make the right concessions at the right time takes years of experience and practice. It is an art and can swing deals in a matter of minutes.

Deal fatigue is a state of mind. When you feel that you are starting to rush things in a meeting, that is when you know that deal fatigue is kicking in. Try to remain professional, disciplined and positive. You need to defeat the enemy around the table and your mind can't give up on you at this stage in the process.

As tiredness kicks in, maybe you need to look at adding members to your negotiating team. You don't want to miss an important step because you are tired, so rather look at the resources you have available in the office. If you can't spot the answer there, perhaps you need to fork out some cash to bring in an advisor or consultant.

Such a move will also make you look like an even busier and more top-level person in the eyes of the opposition. Who knows, they may even offer concessions and want to complete the deal on your terms right there and then. They also have timelines to meet and superiors to report to.

Deal fatigue has no place in the modern business world, but just like an old headache, it crops up time and again and needs to be treated. Never ignore deal fatigue. Rather give it the attention that it deserves.

CHAPTER 29

Exceptional People

All businesses have those magical individuals; those 'exceptional people' who are extremely gifted but may need to be managed more than others to extract the most you can out of them.

Your place of work is where you undoubtedly spend most of your day, and you definitely don't want to be surrounded by exceptional people whom you don't enjoy. This circles back to the element of greed, where some people sign up for a new job at 10% more salary but then hate every minute of being in their new work environment.

Let's think of it from a positive sense. If you are surrounded by exceptional people who add major value to a business, it will probably bring out the best in you and your work. And quality work usually leads to promotion opportunities.

From a CEO's perspective, it is crucial to have the right people in the correct positions, rather than just having great people in the company who are not being carefully deployed. Sometimes great people can't handle the smaller tasks which will create broken links in your business supply chain.

Disciplinary rules need to be at the forefront in any company. Remember how you discipline your children at home? The same must apply to your workers. But you cannot have general rules for some and special rules for exceptional people. This falls in line with taking accountability for the carrying out of duties, whether or not some people are more talented than others.

When one has an extremely gifted person in the business it is important to treat this individual the same way all other staff members are treated. There should be no form of favouritism, irrespective of the individual's high skill set or work ethic.

It is important to have the trust of all people working for your business, especially the gifted ones.

I have had vast experience working with many specially-gifted business people, from lawyers to accountants, to business leaders and many more. At the end of the day, it is not as much about the subject matter that counts but rather how you make them feel.

Keep in mind that some exceptional people are not necessarily the best when it comes to interacting with the client. They are often strategic make-it-happen-type people, not necessarily meeting specialists.

Exceptional people are usually not great when it comes to meetings. They get bored and just want to get back to their laptops to do what they do best. Note that they hate to be pressured into completing work.

Yes, deadlines are in place for a reason, but they dislike people looking over their shoulders and pushing them to the finish point. The more time that they have to research and work diligently, the better they perform.

Let's look at ways and means to make these exceptional people feel even more important so as to get maximum work output from them.

You will find that the exceptional people will be more outside-the-box thinkers than others. They will be more open to taking risks knowing that the triumph will be huge compared to the goal that management originally set for them.

Remember in life that opposites attract. You will find that exceptional people won't necessarily be that special if you put them in a room with other people of similar talent. You will be surprised as to how people with diverse mindsets actually manage to deliver on tasks.

Here is another very important point when working with exceptional people:

By all means put them in the important areas of a project, but don't overload them with tasks even if they look like they can carry the world's problems on their shoulders.

A business leader needs to be cautious when assigning tasks to staff members. Keep the small- to medium-size ordinary tasks for the non-exceptional people. If not, the business leader will soon realise just how bored a special person will get with day-to-day run-of-the-mill stuff.

Exceptional people can work with almost mirror-like images. They can see the reverse of the project element that they are working on. They can almost sense the client's reaction even before it happens.

In terms of salary, the business leader needs to follow a fine line. Don't overpay the exceptional people. Either way, these people are not necessarily driven by money but rather by getting the job done to the best of their ability. They quite often are more satisfied when being praised for their efforts and results.

It is a status or image profile kick that they get from completing any task to the best of their ability.

Exceptional people will not necessarily become managers of a department. Some of the world's best rugby or football players were hugely talented, but it didn't make them great captain material. This is a mistake that many CEOs often make.

They move their special person to a senior management position and then he or she is not quite as impactful as they were in the engine room of the business.

It may sound rather strange, but some people – such as the exceptional people we are referring to here – prefer to be managed than to be a manager themselves. It has to do with the psychological mindset of the individual.

These people are easy to identify as they are way ahead of the rest when it comes to handling or analysing complex issues.

A leader needs to understand that they must handle a special person with the utmost care. These people are not as thick-skinned as most.

This can lead to office politics with other persons feeling that the special ones are getting all the attention.

The special ones don't enjoy the 'following orders' element of the workplace. Due to their efforts in striving to become better all the time they can run into office politics.

Professional jealousy does exist in most corporates and the business leader will need to keep a close eye on the goings-on in areas where exceptional people have to work with others. Sabotaging of a special person's work does happen. Some people will do whatever it takes to look good in the eyes of the boss ahead of others.

Exceptional people are not always blessed with solid communications skills. So this is another area where the business leader needs to be sensitive when working with these 'gems'.

Always put the special person in a quiet area in the office. They don't like to be disturbed while working.

A special person's biggest fear is failure, and this keeps them ticking over in terms of striving for excellence.

Of course, for a gifted person to be at their best, they need to have chosen the right career path and need the right management in support of them. Let's not fool ourselves, even if a person is special they still need to use a lot of brain juice to deliver the goods.

Anyone who is at the top of their career will know that when they are judged, they are analysed on their last performance.

Even among exceptional people, there are various categories. Personalities and work attributes differ. Some have more willpower and drive than others.

As a result of the high standards that are set by such people, success may be mediocre in their minds. They are looking for even higher levels. Therefore, if they are not able to strive to reach these ultra-high standards that they set, they may see their daily job as being just above average and could look elsewhere for greater challenges.

So when it comes to projects, these special ones need to be able to make decisions in order to move to the next level. The space that the special one has to work in should have as few roadblocks as possible. The more obstacles, check-points or sign-in sessions, the more the person will slow down and lose momentum.

Remember that when a special one fails in his or her work, then they don't drop to average but to the bottom of the graph. They basically fall into the brilliant (where they are for most of the time) or zero categories; at least in their minds anyway.

These people also hate repetition. Doing the same things over and over in the workplace just demoralises them. The special ones will be among the quickest learners on the team in the workplace; they pick up new trends at great speed. Their minds are like sponges as they rapidly absorb new information.

Be assured, that much of what is new in a day's work is researched after hours at home by these people. They believe in knowledge and will do anything and everything to keep learning.

Some exceptional people even prefer to go the self-employed route. These feel that the nine-to-five slog is not for them, as they have the vision to make money elsewhere. Many make it big through networking marketing of products. As mentioned earlier, this shows that there are different types of exceptional people. There is no one-size-fits-all scenario to describe these 'gems'.

Being perfectionists, these people may feel stress and pressure more than most, even if they don't want to show it. They put more energy into their work than many others do, so it is only natural that they will tire some time or other. However, their never-give-up attitude will keep them going until the project is finished to their satisfaction.

So, does a special person work on one project at a time or can they multitask? Multitasking is what they enjoy the most, in fact, as they may get bored working on just one task. Remember, their minds keep moving forward in search of the next idea. Most of them have a wide range of interests in life. They do not believe in being limited in any form.

The not-so-special ones who are bright enough will know the importance of learning from these gifted people. If the second sphere of talent in your organisation is able to show genuine interest, then the special ones may be willing to help or teach them a few things.

Of course, they can't teach them too much as the second-sphere peoples' mind will not be as absorbent in terms of retaining information as is the case with the exceptional people.

Exceptional people are awesome to have in a business, but they also take quite a bit of pampering in order to allow them to work to their full potential in the interests of the company.

There is no doubt that, if managed correctly, these people can make a huge difference to the bottom line of the business. Their proactive sense is something that a business leader will wish all his employees possessed.

The best way for a business leader to motivate the workforce is via financial or voucher incentives. As stated earlier, some special ones may strive for this while others will just want the glory and prestige of having done their task to the best of their ability, which is almost certain to have been at a much higher level than most people in the firm.

It is, therefore, vital to understanding how best to handle each individual based on their motivations.

Either way, the secret is to handle these gems with care. If not, their next employer will doubtless enjoy the benefits of their diligence, skills, and intelligence.

CHAPTER 30

Negotiations

There is something telling in the origins of language. Take, for example, the word 'negotiation'. It has its roots in the Latin *neg* (no) and *otsia* (leisure). This is a reference to busy businessmen who had no respite from their work. The word continued to be associated with business until around the 17th century, when it started to take on a more diplomatic implication.

Far from 'no leisure', negotiation began to stand for an interaction, a dialogue, a discussion between parties with the hope of achieving a mutually beneficial outcome in the face of conflict. And that is our widely-held understanding of the word today.

To negotiate is more of a process than a concept. It is not something which happens at a single point in time. Instead, it is a bundle of engagement exchanges.

Negotiation centres on how we feel, how we make another party feel, and the trust established over a period of time; be it over the course of one or several meetings or many months.

A lot of homework is required before one gets to the negotiating table. Never underestimate the importance of proper preparation.

It is unfortunate that in many instances people do not understand the principles behind proper negotiations and often are not even clear on the outcome they are seeking.

Understand the people involved from your side and from each

parties' side. Know the backgrounds of the other negotiators who will be at the table. This will give you some idea regarding their strengths and weaknesses in terms of their areas of knowledge.

Understand the reality from each party's side. Parties come to a negotiating table with set objectives and sometimes one will be able to negotiate certain clauses in their favour easier than others. One needs to be strategic and to 'box clever'.

Determine where the power lies. Part of being strategic involves knowing the lay of the land: Who needs this transaction more? If, for example, a big multinational is keen for first-mover advantage into a smaller market and competitors are also buzzing around, then who actually holds the power? The multi-national or the small company?

Always negotiate at a place of your choice. Do your best to get the 'home venue'. Negotiating is easier when you control the environment as opposed to going into foreign territory. This will give you and your team additional confidence going into the meeting.

At each negotiating session, understand your bottom line and higher mark. You need to be absolutely sure what your ultimate target is as well as the bare minimum that you are prepared to settle on during talks.

In negotiation sessions always ensure that you appear confident; to reinforce this, you can even be a bit late for a meeting. This tactic is akin to going on a date. Being late leads the other party to conclude that either you are not desperate, or you are a very busy person; hence indicating a sense of status.

Always be friendly and have empathy with the other party. There is no need to be arrogant or unfriendly during negotiations. After all, this might not be the only time that you will sit with the other party or parties to negotiate.

For all you know, this could be the first of many negotiating processes that could make lots of money for your business. Remember one of the greatest philosophies of life is that small stones build big bridges.

Always have good coffee and other forms of refreshments available. The setting of the negotiating room plays an important role in the process. This will make the other party feel comfortable and, hopefully, they will relax a little too much. Any form of advantage, however small, will be good for your cause.

It is important to have references to other deals available to bench the market. This goes back to the homework that you did ahead of the negotiation process. This work will help to ensure that you will not overpay when buying or that the other party will not underpay when selling.

Make small talk. An example is in referring to the other party's social media platform. This will immediately let them know that you have done your homework.

Always let the other party start negotiating first and listen carefully. Give them enough time. As they are guests at your venue, it is courteous that they speak first. As they do, show interest, nod, and maintain eye contact.

The other party will always want to start in a strong, positive fashion. It is always best to let the other party begin so that you know right from the start what is in their minds.

Furthermore, if they come out strong in the beginning, there is always the chance that they might start to tire later in the meeting. That, too, can be an advantage.

Trust is a key factor and the foundation of all negotiations. The more rapport and trust you can develop the better chances you have of a successful negotiation. Keep this in mind throughout the process. Always focus on building trust, even if you can't agree on all items on the agenda. And always be authentic.

For negotiations to work, both parties need to enter into discussions in good faith, even if you are trying to strike a deal from opposite ends of the business space. Make sure that more than one person from your team is involved in the talking process. A main person must be appointed, and another one who backs up the main negotiator and affirms his or her positions.

This means that your sales or buying strategy will not sound dictatorial to the other party. It will come across as more of a team effort.

There needs to be a head negotiator with two or more assistants who are well briefed on their respective roles and what the talking points will be.

Make sure that your negotiating session has been well rehearsed. All of the members of your team need to be 'singing from the same hymn sheet', so to speak. There is nothing worse than team members questioning each other in a negotiating meeting; this immediately weakens your position.

Make sure that the negotiating team comprises 'people persons'. The people you bring to the negotiating table need to be likable, professional individuals. In a business world that is increasingly diverse, it is also important to take gender and culture into account. For example, if you are negotiating with an Asian company, then make sure that you have an Asian person on your negotiating team.

If you are negotiating to buy the rights to a product in the women's market, then ensure that your team includes one or more women and is not male-dominated.

Cross-border considerations also come into play. For example, if the other party is coming from England and (based on your research) happens to enjoy football, then you will want to make sure that someone on your team has a good knowledge of the international football space.

This creates common talking points which can be used to develop a more relaxed atmosphere. Again, this ties in with building trust between both parties.

Let's look at several strategies you can employ when embarking on a successful negotiation.

How will you know if you are in a situation which will allow for negotiation? Only call for a negotiating meeting if you are able to gain an advantage on a project, product, campaign or company on the business front. If not, don't.

Double check your objectives. The only reason you are negotiating is to get what you want in the deal, so always double check and triple check your objectives. Never give up until you have obtained that which you set out to gain.

Negotiate with your team prior to meeting with the other party. This tactic aligns with the preparation phase mentioned earlier.

Use your colleagues as a sounding board to make sure that you and your negotiating colleagues are ahead of the game event before you step into the meeting.

Make sure you're in the right frame of mind going into the meeting. You need to be 'in the zone' when going into a negotiation. Professionalism and positivity are two of the biggest elements that are required in such instances, so stay relaxed and never show any sign of nerves, even though this is often easier said than done when discussing large contracts.

Be tough and business-like, after all that's why you are there.

Always make sure that you have a 'Plan B'. If the party you are negotiating with does not want to buy or sell, then make sure you have another option in the market to which you can turn your attention. This will also stop you from being desperate in buying or selling.

There is no difference between big or small negotiations. The principles of negotiating remain the same irrespective of the size of the deal, so you can never afford to relax even if you are negotiating a deal worth a small amount of money.

Once again, that modest deal could lead you into negotiations for a much bigger transaction with the same party in time to come.

Don't be shy. If you don't ask, you will not get, so you need to speak up for what you want from the deal.

You never know, perhaps the other party will think that your asking price is much cheaper than they thought and will agree without even thinking twice about it.

Life can be stressful, and some people abide by the principle of 'keep a low profile to retain sanity'. Unfortunately, keeping a low profile in business circles is not the way to go. One needs to be visible in order to attract attention to your business brand's services and product.

Listening will often give you a good advantage. Sometimes you will pick up on elements that you hadn't thought of going into the meeting. Don't move too much off course from what you and your team had planned during the preparation phase ahead of the meeting, but if you do pick up on something that could swing a deal in your favour, then use that to your advantage.

Always be willing to walk away if the deal is not going your way. Don't sell or buy just for the sake of it, simply because the other party is being difficult, and you want to conclude the process due to frustration. Always be open to walking away and using your 'Plan B' in the form of opening talks with other potential buyers or sellers.

Don't give anything away without getting something back. They say there is no such thing as a free lunch in the world of business. Yes, by its very nature negotiating does involve a bit of 'give and take', but make sure that you are in a position to receive more than you are giving away.

This is a business deal not a social club activity!

Remember that negotiating is a 'I will do this if you will do that' scenario.

So decide in your own mind what piece of cake you are negotiating for, be very precise about the outcome you want and then take time to understand the result the opposing party might want. This will help you to narrow the gap and edge discussions towards a mutually agreeable solution.

Never be afraid to call for short breaks during negotiations. These breaks can be used to caucus with your colleagues to discuss certain points that were discussed at the table.

Two or more heads are better than one and the greatest of negotiators often seek advice before making decisions. Emotions cannot be a part of the mix, so having more than one mind to think things through is a big bonus.

In conclusion, when it comes to negotiating remember that you are playing a hardball game that often involves big numbers that could impact your staff's livelihood. So don't be too hasty or too greedy. Negotiations take skill and a special type of person, which is why it is so important to choose your team with care.

Remember that there are two types of people in business. One is the strategic (salesman) type, and other is the operations (non-client-face) sort. Some people are the right ones to interact with clients while others are just focused on getting the job done as best they can.

Some people can be taught how to negotiate and could be groomed for greater things on this front, but generally speaking, the skills of negotiating come from within a person.

Negotiating is not necessarily an easy art, but it is a super skill to have in your arsenal. Having good negotiators on your staff is a major asset to your company and can help your company to grow and flourish in the long run.

Ultimately, successful negotiations involve staying one step ahead of your opponent at all times.

It requires hard work, market knowledge and learning to see things from another's perspective. Yes, there will also be times when you may need to motivate other parties to negotiate with you. And sometimes other businesses won't want to buy or sell, and you will need to talk them into coming to the meeting table.

This is part of the negotiating dance. And, like most things in business, successful negotiations centre on saying the right thing, at the right time, to the right person.

CHAPTER 31

Capital Raising

Capital Raising can be defined, in simple terms, as raising funds from investors to finance your projects or other business endeavours.

Remember that in trying to raise capital for your business, the product or service offering that you are tabling is only as good as the business plan that you are putting forward with it. Elsewhere in this book, we have mentioned Colonel Sanders of Kentucky Fried Chicken, who got turned down by 1008 investors before the 1009th one believed in his eleven herbs and spices formula, which allowed him to build the brand into what it is today.

We all know the popular taste of Kentucky Fried Chicken, but had he worked his business plan to perfection, I am sure that he would have only had to present to three or four potential investors before getting the financial backing.

The same applies to Walt Disney, who followed a similar path to the colonel in knocking on the doors of 301 potential investors before investor 302 believed in his dream of Disneyland, Disney World, and much, much more.

I must give these gentlemen full marks in terms of persistence, but the fact remains that in my view, they needed to box in a cleverer way. When one spreads the net as wide as they did, one tends to rely more on luck landing the 'yes' decision rather than the product and business plan.

It's a lottery, rather than aiming for a smaller group of investors and refusing to give in until a deal was clinched. So based on the above, you need to find the right investor for your product or service and not just throw the net as wide as possible. Think of it in terms of a heart transplant. If the heart is not suitable to the body, then why force the operation to happen?

You need to find the correct heart that will be a match for the body. The same applies to capital raising.

There needs to be a major link between the concept and the investor before the latter will buy into the idea and make the funds available.

If you are in the food industry, would you send your proposal to over one thousand potential investors when you know that three-quarters of them do not finance products or services in your sector?

If Colonel Sanders had gone to a park to sell samples of his product and gathered two to three hundred reviews and included this information in his business plan as proof of the success of the food, things could have been different much earlier in his quest to find an investor.

Imagine how impressed the potential investor would have been if the colonel was able to table a document containing future orders for his food.

The business sector can be an unpredictable space on any given day, so an investor will have to think things through quite carefully before opting to put money towards a product or service.

The 'how' question is probably the most important when it comes to approaching a potential investor. The investor will want to know exactly how their money will be allocated on the project. There needs to be a system of 'checks and balances' all the way. Accountability is key.

Now let's have a look at the importance of analysing the market and timing. Is the market ready for what you have to offer? Perhaps your concept is a superb one, but many have failed because they are simply too advanced for the current moment.

If you put your concept out there in five to ten years from now, you may make a fortune. You could well be one of those unlucky ones who is simply ahead of your time and rather than being a trend-setter, it comes back to bite you.

So before going after the investors, take the time to evaluate the market. Is the industry ready at this very moment for what you have to offer? The investors that you are about to approach probably have seen many, many proposals so it is not only about your super concept.

More important is the question of how your concept will make money in the short-term, before looking at the long-term picture. Always keep an eye on the opposition. Just like you, they probably won't sleep much either because they are also looking for that gem that will knock the socks off of the investors.

Think carefully about who will talk the presentation through when you are allocated the meeting time with the investors. Some people are better at convincing investors than others.

In life, there are people who excel in putting concept documents together, but they might not be the right ones to talk it through in a meeting room. Look for those exceptional people with passion and the gift of the gab.

Let's put things into perspective. Very, very rarely is there a case of a start-up company making a success of business without some form of capital being injected into the company at the start. It is not possible to say just how much money needs to be invested into a business at the start as circumstances differ according to the respective business industries.

However, without the financial input at the beginning, your chance of getting out of the proverbial starting blocks and making it big will be tougher without help up front.

I often get asked if approaching friends or family members to invest in a business is a no-go area or it can really work. The answer is a simple one. Your friends and family are closer to you than most so it's a good call as long as you treat them like investors.

They are not doing you a favour because they like you. They want to make money as much as you do, so treat them as business people and not as friends or family.

Approaching banks or micro-lenders for help can be a tedious process. The numbers that you will be requesting will be gauged against the type of collateral that you can put up and of course, judged against your credit record. If your credit record is clean, this is probably your best chance of getting financial backing at relative speed.

If you do pitch to the potential investors, which in my mind is probably the toughest route to follow, be prepared to answer a list of questions as long as your arm.

Keep in mind that if the investor is going to put funding into your concept, they have every right to ask as many questions as they like.

First, what type of business is being generated and what are the minimum and maximum sizes that it could be? Taking the short- and long-term pictures into account, what type of start-up costs are being talked about? How long after starting up will it take for the business to reach break-even point? What form of process will be in place should an investor wish to exit the business relationship a few months or years down the line?

It is always difficult to find finance for a start-up business because there is no form of track record for the investors to gauge. All they have to go by is a pie-in-the-sky idea that all parties hope will work big-time.

For example, it will be far easier to find finance for a new restaurant than trying to convince an investor to be the backer of a whole string of restaurants. Reality needs to be considered.

What if you have a niche market product like continental charter jet travel for business executives who make up only 5% of the industry? There is nothing wrong with that. As long as you are convinced that the 5% will buy in bulk and continue buying since at the end of the day 5% of sales is still business. Getting clients to return to purchase more of your offering is essential if your market sales percentage is aimed at the niche end.

Let's get back to the boardroom table. When talking to potential investors, keep the concept documentation and presentation as simple as possible. Remember that the investors won't understand the concept as well as you do, but if you lose their concentration along the way, how will the potential buyers in the market relate to your product or service?

So the business plan doesn't have to be a forty- to sixty-page one. Keep things simple. If the investor is really interested, he or she will send you correspondence afterwards requesting further information.

If the potential investor wishes to take things further, he or she will request all sorts of documentation from you so that they can have peace of mind that your business is in a safe and secure position for them to get involved.

Audited accounting documentation is usually the first paperwork to be requested. Then the financial backer-to-be will ask for financial projections. This flow graph should give them a good indication of just how soon the concept they are backing will reach break-even point and they will be able to gain sight of dividends.

An Asset and Liability statement will also be required which, according to law, will need to include outstanding business credit, debt and any loans which your business is currently in the business of repaying. Coupled to this will be the request for the past six to twelve months of company bank statements.

It is easy to get over-excited and to jump at the first investor deal that comes your way.

However, you will need to be cautious as the first investor to agree to finance your concept might not necessarily provide the best solution. Never forget that the investors are there for one reason only—to make money. So exercise patience and wait for two or three investors to respond with options. If the first investor is serious about being a part of your concept, they will hold on until you have made your decision final.

If you are not the right person to handle the business financing part for your company, you can always hire a Business Finance Specialist. Many companies specialise in these areas of the industry to are there to provide their knowledge and experience to make sure that your business will be on the receiving end of the best possible outcome.

So, in conclusion, how can you make your pitch to investors stand out more than others who are also striving to seek financial backing for their concepts?

Make sure that your offering is so unique that it is very hard to copy. You are selling a unique concept that will change the way of doing business forever.

You need to make the investor believe that if he or she misses out on this opportunity of financing your offering someone else will take it and strike it rich. Push the principle of higher profits and fewer overheads in terms of production. Show the investor that you have identified the perfect market for your concept.

Table a powerful CV profile of yourself and your senior colleagues. Having a classy concept is one thing, but the investor will want to know that the offering can be actioned without any hiccups that could jeopardise their investment. Always be open and honest.

If you try to hide a weak senior management member or a weakness in your offering, it will be exposed sooner or later and could cause a great amount of embarrassment.

The biggest sell that you can do in raising capital is convincing the investor of your professionalism and passion. These two principles are part of your genetic make-up since birth and cannot be bought or taught.

Remember that getting an investor to believe in your concept is not an overnight happening. The investor is taking a risk and will want to get to know you and your offering as best as possible.

Capital Raising can be as much fun as it is stressful. It's all about saying the right thing to the right person at the right time about your wonderful, unique, cutting-edge offering.

CHAPTER 32

Running a Business

Running a business is not something that one can learn from a textbook. It is really based on experiences that one has gone through, thus learning the dos and don'ts of the industry. This is why it is important to put experienced people into key positions in the business.

From the *Entrepreneurs* chapter in this book, you will know that I am not a fan of the entrepreneur style of business. Further, I am a firm believer that entrepreneurs don't make good CEOs as they are not very good at running matured businesses.

Running your own business is not as easy as it sounds. Everyone wants to be their own boss, but it is much more stressful than most people can imagine. One needs nerves of steel to survive and some have these, while others don't.

So based on this, if you have a brilliant idea, don't throw in the towel at your paid salary job tomorrow and follow your dream.

Rather let common sense prevail and set up your brilliant idea business model in your spare time before taking the plunge in resigning from your bread-and-butter post to run your own business.

Nobody, outside of the lottery, makes big bucks overnight. A business takes a good few years to stabilise so don't be fooled when people tell you that it took them a short space of time to set their own businesses on course to financial success. If running a business was that easy, everyone would be doing it.

Taking a business or brand forward requires leadership with clear vision and the ability to remain on course with the vision despite the challenges that may come with it.

Managing a business is more about dealing with people or products and market knowledge. If the business has staff, it is the role of the leader to motivate the workforce to get the best form of productivity out of them.

As mentioned elsewhere in this book, the leader also needs to ensure that the work environment is of such a nature that it allows for a positive vibe among the staff.

In sports terms, keep in mind that the best footballer in the world is not necessarily the best team captain in the world. Some people can lead while others can't but are excellent at what they do. A leader needs to be trusted and looked up to for inspiration, particularly when times are tough.

The biggest mistake that a team leader or CEO can make is to get too involved in the day-to-day operations of the business, which should actually be controlled by others beneath the top person. The leader's role is simply to lead and keep moving the business forward.

If the business is correctly structured, this should allow the leader to do exactly that and not get tied up in day-to-day operations matters. The old maxim, 'a fish starts to rot from its head' is very applicable when it comes to bad business leadership. The leader is the one to set the good example for the others to follow.

When starting a business, you will soon find out that there is a huge difference between having a great idea and getting it set up in the marketplace. As a leader, you will need to keep your focus on a variety of elements. Of course, the search for new clients will be at the top of your list, but making sure that your product or service is superbly packaged and a step ahead of the opposition will be right up there, too.

Running a business is no place for the fainthearted. In most cases, success will not happen overnight. So the leader needs to have a great sense of energy and stamina and the ability to remain focused.

Building a team to take the product or service to the highest level is also a challenging task for the leader. You've heard before that 'good help is hard to find'. Well, sometimes it is, and sometimes it isn't, but the point is; the right people with the right attitudes need to be found and placed in the right positions.

Think of it as building a skeleton. Find those key people and build the rest of the team around them.

Elsewhere in this book, I have also mentioned that the ability to do the job is more important than the tertiary diploma or degree that gets put in a frame on the office wall. Many people out in the business world reached levels of success the hard way, through the self-taught process, which could well hold more value than their years of studies.

When you are in the real business world, it's not about the degree but about getting the job done to the satisfaction of the client, and this is what a business leader expects from his or her staff.

While operating at a top level, it is nearly impossible for the leader not to keep looking at the bottom-line figures. It's like a lottery ticket before a big draw—it will always attract your attention. There is always that element of temptation as one considers using cheaper suppliers, materials and more.

Be careful on this one.

The last thing you want is for your brilliant idea to fall apart because cheap goods were used during the manufacturing process. Your business name could go down the drain if more goods return damaged due to malfunctioning in the first week than what you are actually selling. Many companies fall into this trap in the quest for making a quick buck.

Let's get back to the all-important target-market element. Remember that not everyone will want to buy your product or service, so the market, albeit it more limited, needs to be carefully identified. It doesn't matter if your potential buyers' pool is smaller than you thought.

If those people buy your offering and are happy with it, they will tell their friends and other associates who, in turn, could very well buy from your business. So how often do you need to revisit your business model? As often as possible. You will never have the perfect business model as the industry keeps changing and your mind will always think of new ways to do things. This is good.

Remember, we are in the era of modern technology. A leader should use the available resources in running a business. If a leader shies away from the prospect of change, he or she shouldn't be a leader in the first place.

Let's look at the element of outsourcing. Finding suppliers who won't drop the proverbial ball is the key here. Of course, you get suppliers with many strengths, but they have weaknesses too. Some are excellent in manufacturing products or providing services, but then are slack on the timeline element.

This doesn't help at all so quite often the appointment of suppliers to assist with the running of your business is done on a short-term contract before going into longer working relationships.

A leader also needs to take care of his or her health. Sometimes, this gets forgotten as the hours, days, weeks, and months tick by, but one cannot work long hours forever without the body giving in one way or another.

In many cases, customers will come to do business with your company because of you and not the company. If you leave, they may too.

Remember to always think like a customer, not like a business owner. What does the customer want? Most successful businesses have leaders at the helm who understand this principle. They look for the winning formula and when they have found it, they look for the next one.

Be streetwise when you, as a leader, walk around shopping malls or visit other businesses for meetings. Think in customer mode as to what works for you and what doesn't. Look at how other companies promote themselves and their offerings. Take note of their websites and how they stay innovative in their offerings through social media and other platforms.

Two of the most important keys in any leader's personality are those of confidence and persistence.

The confidence element will put you ahead of many of your peers in the industry, while the persistence part – a never-say-die-attitude – is always good to have.

Knowledge is power. So the leader should always be open to learning new things and ways to do business.

For example, it is never good to get stuck in the mindset of the winning formula of 1980. Much has changed since then, so don't copy the business styles of leaders from not-so-recent history.

Regardless of your age, don't be afraid to enrol in courses and to keep learning new things. Now let's look at teamwork within the business.

The leader should be setting a tone for the staff to work as a unit. Project teams cannot work independently of each other when working on the same project. Everyone should have the same information on a specific client and be working towards a common goal. There needs to be a common thread between all workers on the project. Likewise, there needs to be a high level of consistency in terms of deliverables among all involved.

In conclusion, running a business requires leadership of a firm mindset and someone who is able to make instant decisions, fully realising the impact – be it financial or other – that these may have on the business, clients or marketplace.

Change of leadership in large businesses often happens because a highly effective project leader is elevated to the executive level.

A project leader or department head the person may be, but an executive not. Many decision-makers don't understand this principle. Running a business includes something called having a 'Game Plan', a principle built around forming an imperishable relationship with the client, to such an extent that the client will eventually feel that they cannot run their own business without your product or service offering.

While staff members are handling the day-to-day operational elements, the leader should be mixing with the movers and shakers where new clients can be signed up. The leader is basically the face of the company in the eyes of the clients. And he or she is the one to educate the market on the importance of the products or services being offered.

The key note is why these products and services are unique and one or more steps better than any of the others on offer in the industry.

Running a business can be a very stressful form of employment as the leader often spends more time being the problem solver rather than focusing on moving the business forward. A fine balance between the two needs to be found in order to ensure success on all fronts.

Of course, there will be a lot of fun times, too, when running a business. These will be when the pros outweigh the cons—all of which will happen if the principles of good business are followed correctly.

CHAPTER 33

Delegation

With regard to a lack of delegation, the old expression is that if your bathtub is too full, the water will spill over!

The art of delegating work is not an optional exercise but is instead a necessity for any senior business person who wants to get the maximum results out of his time and efforts. If you are a successful business person, your services or products will be in demand and there will not be enough hours in a day to do all the business tasks yourself, so you will need to trust your fellow workers and hand over some of your workload to them.

Naturally, it is of great importance that the person to whom you delegate the work has the necessary skills and passion to complete the job effectively. Basically, the person is doing the job on your behalf and your good name is attached to the outcome.

Delegation doesn't always mean that work is being passed to a colleague. It may be a case of work being outsourced to freelancers or other outside parties, or simply loaded onto software programmes for the computer to carry out the tasks.

Learning how to delegate properly is an important principle as it could keep the business leader from having an emotional breakdown somewhere along the line when the workload becomes unbearable.

It is easy to fall into the trap of wanting to do everything by yourself because you will have the peace of mind that all will be done properly. However, there are only so many hours in a day. So, it is better to work in an organised, astute fashion, than pull eighteen-hour shifts Monday to Friday and have no family or other time.

Being able to delegate in a competent fashion is a sign of true leadership.

Those who are in management positions and cannot delegate efficiently will not remain in top business positions for long.

Keep in mind that delegation is not just for senior management people. Lower level project managers, as an example, need to be able to delegate work to their colleagues too.

Just as a senior management person will not remain at the top level for long if he or she cannot delegate properly, a lower level staff member is unlikely to climb the ladder of success in a business if he or she cannot master delegation.

The beauty of successful delegation is that it frees up organisational leaders and results in a better organised business. Without it, one is often forced to work under pressure, making unnecessary mistakes and doing last-minute tasks.

By delegating work to colleagues, you open your mind for growth. Remember what I have often stated in this book that the next big money-making idea might not come from the CEO but perhaps the tea lady, receptionist or cleaner who are also ambassadors for your business brand?

The same applies here. Through delegation, you have created the opportunity for someone else's mind to run through the work. Who knows? This person may just come up with an even better way of handling the tasks than the experienced CEO!

Delegation allows one to develop the minds, and indeed the skills, of colleagues in the office. It is important that the business leader has a plan in mind when delegating work to lower-level staff. One needs to understand the capabilities of the person that the work is being delegated to.

The person receiving the task should be sufficiently skilled to complete the task successfully.

The work cannot just be passed out because the senior person has too much on their plate for the day. The briefing of the delegated work needs to be clear. The receiver needs to understand the objectives of the tasks and the standard of work to be carried out.

The receiver also needs to know what resources are available to complete the task. Think of it from the point of view of a plumber or an electrician. The boss cannot send the plumber or electrician out on a job without providing them with the necessary training and most importantly, the toolbox with tools in it to be able to get the job done.

It is always better for the senior person to brief the receiver of the tasks in a written manner rather than verbally to avoid any misunderstandings. There is an old saying in business—if it's not on paper, then it didn't happen. Too often, a verbal brief is misunderstood or misinterpreted.

Despite preferring to receive a written brief, the senior person's office door should still be open in case of questions. We have said before in this book, 'no question is a stupid question'. It is preferable to ask than guess. A wrong guess could be fatal to the task. If the receiver of the brief is going to the senior person with a question or a problem, rather formulate a potential solution than wait on the senior member to provide one.

Pro-activeness is always the best approach.

The person receiving the brief needs to understand that the completed work will be evaluated in line with the objectives. Irrespective of whether conventional or unconventional methods are used, the final work delivered needs to meet the goal.

Keep in mind that the lowest level of staff, are probably closest to most client projects, so they would be the best people to delegate work to.

An important point to note is that while the delegation process is happening, the senior management member cannot delegate away accountability for the end result. At the end of the day, the senior person will still be responsible for the final outcome of the project.

While delegating work is a good thing, there are certain areas which a senior management person cannot 'outsource' to his or her team. These include the reviewing of performance appraisals, disciplinary situations involving other staff, and personal information files containing sensitive information about other employees.

Of course, there are those who don't understand the importance of delegation and abide by the negative slogan of 'delegation is abdication'. Some see it as a way for lazy managers to pass their work on to lower level staff. Some go as far as saying that by delegating work to junior staff, a senior manager is actually relinquishing their control of a department or project.

Others will feel that they can do the work faster and more efficiently themselves, rather than delegating it and fixing the lower level person's mistakes afterward.

Many believe in doing business the same way that they have done for the past thirty years, in other words, 'If it ain't broke, don't fix it'.

As mentioned, it is all about how one approaches the delegation process and how serious a senior management person is about not only getting the job done but also developing the talent at their disposal. Business leaders need to be humble and embrace the ideas of those that they entrust with work.

Constructive criticism is always welcome. The process needs to be thought of as a form of mentoring as the receiver is entrusted with the work that the senior person should be doing.

Senior management needs to be ready to reward great efforts. Keep in mind that, through delegation, the lower level person is often taking on responsibilities that he or she does not handle daily. When he or she achieves success at this level, the efforts should be rewarded.

When choosing the person to receive the project brief, it is important that the senior person considers the proactive working nature of the person.

The senior would do well to hand important business briefs to a lower level colleague who is hungry to succeed in the industry. This person is more than likely an outside-the-box thinker who is ambitious and looking to climb the ladder in the company.

It is also important to be sure that, by loading the additional work on the shoulders of this person, he or she will also be able to carry out normal duties while handling the new workload.

Remember that when the senior management person first delegates the work, the receiver could well take much longer to get the initial tasks done as this work will be new to that person. The senior management individual is an expert, the receiver of the delegated work is probably not; or not yet anyway.

A good sign of a lower level worker who is passionate about the delegated task is when questions get raised. It is a way of showing that the staff member has an interest in the work received from senior management.

Time frames can often be a challenge.

When delegating tasks to a lower level staff member, the senior management person needs to be realistic in terms of the time that the staff member has to complete the task. Quite often, clients want the work turned around at speed or perhaps provide the brief late to the supplier.

There is a fine balancing act when it comes to working at speed since quality should never be compromised.

This brings in the question: is there time to redo the job if the first attempt does not meet with success? Quite often, there isn't time for a redo.

Now that we have looked at delegation from a business leader's perspective, let's put ourselves in the shoes of the lower level staff member.

When a senior person asks a lower level worker to handle a work brief, it can be seen in two different ways. Either it is a hassle as more work is being put on the desk of the junior member, or it can be seen in a positive sense in that the senior person is entrusting important work to the junior. This form of delegation allows the lower level staff member to feel like they are part of the team and not just a junior member.

Delegation of work will, in fact, produce a higher level of productivity in the business. It has the ability to decrease staff turnover because senior management is showing faith in the lower level staff who feel that they are working for a business that cares about their growth in the industry.

What is important is that delegating work should be done in a 'no-perimeters' manner. That is, the person receiving the work has the means to run with their own ideas and ways to complete the task. By doing this, the business is allowing the lower level staff to think and make their own decisions in order to reach the final goal.

In conclusion, delegation may look like more of a hassle than anything else, but if done properly, it can have a major positive impact on a business both over the short and long term. It is important to keep the workloads relevant and as close to the receiver's skill set as possible albeit allowing opportunities for growth. The staff with the right attitude will relish working on meaningful tasks that are out of their scope of work.

Delegation is a recipe that leads to success and saves a business leader and indeed a business, significant amounts of time, money, and resources. Most of the most successful businessmen are champions of delegation. They understand the principle 'time is money' and that the business world evolves by the second.

So let's summarise the art of delegation. Choose the right tasks and transfer them to the person with the right attitude and skill set. Get this right and you, as a business leader, will succeed much more in business by the day!

CHAPTER 34

Management

Simply put, management is the ability to deal with people and situations. Rule No. 1 for a manager to remember is not to get involved in things that don't pertain to your daily tasks. The manager has delegated tasks to staff, so let the staff run with the deliverables without interfering.

The two main principles that a manager should bring to the office space are consistency and quality communicating skills. In terms of consistency, the briefing of staff should be of a high standard, with the objectives always clear. Now that the briefing has been done, it is time for the manager to return to his or her office and let the staff get on with the business. A manager is not a dictator but a facilitator who has an open-door policy, if help is requested.

Managing a team of workers means that the person in charge must set the direction for the project.

So the manager needs to have leadership skills. Apart from having the vision to see the project to its completion, the person at the head should be able to draw up organograms, flow charts and more to keep the staff on the right track. It is important that the direction laid down is visual and not just a verbal brief; and as we said before, it should also be put in writing.

This will allow the workers to visit the charts on the wall on a daily or weekly basis to ensure that they have all of the bases covered.

Nothing should fall between the cracks. Visual correspondence is vital. Every member of the team is, in actual fact, a manager in their own right. If they are overseeing work deliverables, they are managing something or other.

So in summary, the manager draws up the plan, briefs the workers and then analyses the deliverables afterwards.

Of course, being a manager comes with a complete sense of responsibility as the daily tasks may not only revolve around managing people.

The managing of client cash and budgets is a key part of many managers' daily deliverables too.

Whether it's a case of being a portfolio manager and investing clients' cash to make more money, or buying materials for the production of goods, it is all in a day's work for the manager. If the manager is in the business of buying materials or equipment, it becomes a bit of a balancing act.

The manager has to find the best quality products to purchase but at the best price. This often leads to purchasing low-quality goods. Remember what I have said before in this book: 'If it sounds too good to be true then it probably is'.

The manager always needs to be seen as valuing the staff members. Each worker cannot be seen as just a number in the company and on the salary-sheet.

There needs to be some form of positive vibe between the manager and the staff member and vice versa.

Again, the next big money-making idea might not come from the CEO or the manager, but from a junior level person, so everyone needs to be treated equally.

When appointed as a manager, many let the title and status go to their heads and forget their colleagues who are now a level below them. Positional power is a privilege, not a right.

Now that the manager is in a seat of power, he or she should not employ favouritism when it comes to briefing work. Sure, some people are more suited for certain briefs than others, but the leader should not pick favourites for the plum tasks.

Managing people and situations correctly means that the leader will have fewer volatile situations to deal with.

A person who does not enjoy conflict will struggle to be a good leader as there will be several times when the person will be thrown into a volatile situation to act as a mediator between aggrieved people.

Solutions need to be found at speed and in a way that all parties will agree to and respect, before damage to the project and company is done.

New staff members are often afraid to approach the manager. Perhaps they think that the manager has favourites in the department or maybe they feel that the manager has explained the brief before and will get uptight in doing so again for clarity, as the leader is also pressed for time.

The answer is simple. No question is a stupid question, and the manager is put into that position to assist the workers as much as possible, in order to achieve the maximum result.

Staff members need to keep asking questions because that is how they will grow in knowledge and experience.

There is no cut-and-dried formula for effective management and the leaders need to understand this. They are there to help and empower the staff below them and cannot get emotional.

They need to answer business-related questions whether they like it or not, irrespective of how much they are pressed for time. A good manager always needs to be rational and open-minded or else don't take the job. There will always be obstacles for a manager to overcome which is why a good manager always works out a Plan A, Plan B, and Plan C and not just a Plan A. Things don't always go according to Plan A, so backup approaches need to be readily attainable.

Managers need to find creative ways to keep their staff motivated. Creativity needs to flow in the office and people need to look forward to coming to work to take their projects a step forward.

A sense of patience is also required. Sometimes, when the going gets tough, tempers may flare and this will only make things worse in the office. The business life is never easy. There will be a lot of ups and downs, but the manager and staff members need to remember that they are all part of one team striving for a common goal in the interests of the business and the client.

A manager needs to work off the back of confidence. Sometimes, the manager or staff may find themselves short of this special ingredient of life. There is only one way to fix this problem. Expose yourselves to the challenge rather than trying to run away from it. Remember that every time you are faced with a challenge, you probably won't enjoy it, but by finding the solution you are being groomed for something even greater.

As a manager, having confidence is crucial. Keep in mind those gut feelings that we have spoken about in this book. A manager needs to follow his or her gut feel often because instant decisions need to be made sometimes.

A manager also needs to have a balanced life. This person cannot work sixteen-hour shifts every day even if they are paid a huge sum of money per month. The mind and the body will simply give in to stress and fatigue at some time or other. Whether you are a manager or a lower level staff member, never forget the principle—you must enjoy what you do.

Try not to be a 'do it the way I tell you' type of manager. Always remember how your knowledge as a manager, was acquired and that others need to learn, so don't be too harsh and judge them too early in their careers.

This brings us to the point of mentoring. While a lot can be learned through the self-taught method, one always needs good mentors or managers to learn from.

Good managers will teach their staff the importance of the principles of business such as deadlines, what a client expects, and possibly even some shortcuts of the business world that were not taught in the university or college classroom.

You can think of the manager as being the coach of a football or rugby team. The person in charge needs to plot the path to victory. The workday, week, month or year is like a marathon in athletics terms. As an average athlete, you can't just train and think you can run a marathon at the same speed from start to finish. The hills will be tougher than the flats and there will be times when you will run slower or faster.

So the manager needs to understand the minds of the staff. Break the days up into smaller portions. Will a worker be totally effective if they work on the same client project for an entire day, week or month? Hardly likely, I would think. That is why school days are broken up into different periods with different subjects.

You are unlikely to absorb everything if you have mathematics only for an entire day or week at school. Things will become too stereotyped.

Some managers do believe in setting a brisk pace in terms of work. If the staff is experienced enough to handle this, it may work in their favour, but never put speed ahead of work quality. As a manager, keep in mind that you may be more experienced and slightly older than your staff members. So mentor them well because they could be around to add value to the company long after you have left or retired.

The manager should never be afraid to discipline staff members. Life revolves around principles, and these pillars cannot be compromised.

The same applies to the workplace. The moment that discipline drops off, the business will start to crumble, and more people will start to take chances. This is usually linked to having weak management or leadership.

It is always good for a leader to bond with the staff over a cup of tea or a bite to eat. Quite often workplace challenges may be mentioned to the manager in a non-office area. The truth often comes out away from the office, so these little get-togethers between manager and staff are always good.

The manager should run the department as a democracy. It won't be good if the manager uses an 'it's my way or no way' mindset. Rather, find out what works best for the majority. Carry out a vote if need be. The manager should be seen as a seeker of information as this will boost credibility and trust.

If the manager is really too busy to mentor people, then pair the inexperienced staff members with the more experienced ones and allow a transfer of skills to happen in this fashion. The manager needs to keep thinking in order to be one step ahead at all times. Quality management will result in minimal turnover of staff.

It is never good for a client to visit a company five or six times a year and on each occasion the person on their business account has left and they have to engage with someone new. It gives the client a sense of instability.

In conclusion, like anything, the success of a country, business or other organisation stems from its leadership. In general terms, if the management is strong, so will the day-to-day running of the business and the output to clients be.

Some people are born to lead, and others are not. The most effective worker in your department is not necessarily the best manager. Different people have different skill sets in life. Some are born to make money while others are more operations-minded and born to be the vehicle that drives the making of money rather than the strategist behind it all.

So if you are a manager, think carefully about which style of management is the best for you to adopt in order to bring out the best from those in your department.

Management is an exceptional skill that can make or break a business. Company owners need to think carefully before making such appointments due to the consequences involved.

CHAPTER 35

Luck

South African golf legend Gary Player once said, "The more that I practice, the luckier I get".

The fact is, in business one needs to be open-minded in order to gain the luck that is needed to get the edge over the opposition. Don't misunderstand here. You cannot run your business based on luck alone. It is not one of the principles that will solely bring you success.

However, luck tends to hang around certain people more than others, so cross your fingers and hope that you are one of those. If you are open to receiving luck, you will get it and possibly much more of it too than you may have expected.

The odds of having the luck to win the lottery are not great as I am sure you know, so many people have to live life the hard way and work hard to get what they want prior to retirement. Luck does tend to follow the hard workers as a sort of reward for all the blood, sweat and tears put into one's career over the years.

Of course, luck works hand in hand with something that many can't manage. It is that scary word 'patience'. Just how long must one wait for a lucky break? The question is similar to 'how long is a piece of string?' Many can go six to twelve months and end up being on the verge of throwing in the towel on a particular business venture before the phone rings with a caller giving a life-changing message.

Never be afraid to try new things. Reinvent yourself or your offering as often as possible. The more markets that you try, the more chance you have of finding the winning area that will make money for you. Never become complacent.

The day this happens is the day you should close your product or service offering file and look for something else. Luck and complacency don't go together.

Having strategies and plans that are not flexible can actually damage your luck. Don't become overly focused on certain aspects of your strategies as this could block the flow of luck. In other words, never think that your big idea or new wonderful product has reached perfection level.

There will always be room for improvement or perhaps taking it to a market that you never dreamed of. A touch of luck could open that door for you.

Think about the cellular telephone which was invented to be used as an instrument for verbal communication. A few years later, it is used for emails, text messaging, social media, games, mobile banking, online shopping, etc.

Again we return to that word 'patience'. Don't rush your product or service offering. Remember the golden rule of being in the right place at the right time to meet that key person or take that phone call that will change your business forever. Remember, too, that it is not always the big-time businessman that could swing the luck your way.

Perhaps you will bump into a random person on the street and you will find out while chatting that the individual knows people who are the perfect 'door openers' for your product or service offering.

Don't grade people according to their status. The insurance salesman could swing that luck your way even more than the multi-millionaire can.

Many business people or entrepreneurs will see their success stories as self-made because of hard work, but somewhere in the mix, there will be that element of luck which gave them the edge at the right moment.

Luck hangs with successful people so you need to get networking and find those gems to latch onto so the luck can spread to you as well. The more you are connected, the more knowledge you have; the more hard-working you are, the more likely you are to attract luck.

Always remain curious. Something you learn today will almost certainly help you in the future and could attract that special element of luck.

Let's not get too excited though, as the 'patience' element is vital. A stroke of luck doesn't mean that your business is going to make millions of US dollars overnight. There could well be a waiting period while the buyers slowly react to your offering before you hit the business jackpot.

Then comes the day when you finally find out that your wonderful product or service offering isn't quite as super as you thought it was. Sales are slow. Nobody is buying. Rather be the optimist than the pessimist.

The story of the two little boys sitting with a bucket of manure illustrates this. The first boy was the pessimist. "What am I supposed to do with a bucket of manure?" he moaned. The second little boy, the optimist, saw the manure and smiled. He put his hands into the bucket and threw the manure into the air, shouting: "Wherever there is manure, there has to be a horse nearby."

The lesson learned from the above point is that one often has to go the long route in business to get to the money. Perhaps there is a reason why your first product or service offering didn't reach the great heights that you thought it would.

You are now placed to put it behind you and to ride the luck on your next project, which could possibly make even more money that the first project would have done.

The moral of the story here is simple—don't sit around looking for sympathy after your initial project didn't work out like you thought it would. Dust yourself off, stand up and start on something new.

Never lose that spark or passion that set you on the road of business in the first place. Every member of your team is unique hence they are able to attract luck differently. If these people are serious team players, they will recognise the importance of boosting each other's confidence in a bid to maximise productivity in order to end up with the best possible result.

You will always be more successful at something that you enjoy. If you enjoy what you do, you won't think of projects as work, but rather, a hobby.

Some people will refuse to believe in luck. Be this as it may, I believe that through your attitude, work rate and skills, you make your own luck.

If you want something badly enough in life, then work towards it and you will not be surprised at all when those lucky breaks come your way.

If you give up, you will never know what was possibly around the next corner waiting for you. Never take 'no' for an answer. Business is all about perseverance. Keep knocking on those doors and eventually you will find the right one will open, and your dream will be taken to the next level.

Remember that luck also rides off opportunism. If you grab the opportunity, then you also grab the luck that comes with it. You need to be in place to capitalise on the opportunity before someone else does. Use that gut feeling that is mentioned elsewhere in this book. If it feels right, then it probably is. Luck is not predictable. You don't know when it will come your way so be ready for it.

Don't miss out because the next person is just waiting for your mistake in order to take advantage of the situation.

So let's look at a few ways in which you will be able to spot luck.

Focus on situations where you are more likely to make your own luck than those where you keep on putting time and effort in without seeing results.

Network as much as possible because the more people you meet, the greater chance you have of getting your brand into the right place.

Do your homework and go to conferences and other events with a strategy in mind.

Get your business card into the hands of that key investor. Remember not to overlook the smaller business role players too. The lucky break will come your way if you play your game-plan right.

Divide your business life up into terms. For example, if you are a first-year law student who is planning to study for seven or so years, it can be quite overwhelming to think just how long the study road is. So rather break the period up into milestones in order to retain focus.

The same applies in business. Where do you want your business brand to be in five years from now? Then work out what needs to be done in the first two years, the middle, and then the final two years of the milestone. By breaking your life into small chunks, it will make it easier for you to focus and for luck to find you as you work towards your goals.

The best PR person for your life is you. Don't be afraid to tell people what your goals are. At the moment, it is not about achieving them. It is about setting them and having something to aim towards. If you don't promote your image, nobody else will.

Many people just amble through their lives in the hope that tomorrow will automatically be greater than today.

It may well be, but in order to attract luck, a firm focus is required. Think of it as a landing area at the airport for luck to touch down on.

Some people like to keep a low profile in business to stay out of trouble. This might be a noble approach, but it certainly won't get you ahead in life, and it seems unlikely to attract any form of luck.

Work out the odds. Are you more likely to meet the right business-minded people at the tennis-club dinner with your friends or the community choir practice, knowing that three members of the choir are investors? There you have the answer. It is not about going to the place that you enjoy, but rather being in the right place. Quite often, sacrifices need to be made.

Lastly, to attract luck, one has to be strong-minded. Don't let anyone talk you out of your great idea or strategy. Sure, listen to common sense, but also listen to that gut feel. It's better to be be the one who failed while trying than sitting back in regret for not having tried at all—while watching someone else action your plan and cash in on millions from it.

Fear has no place in the mind of a business person. If you allow fear to run your life, you are in the wrong industry. Be positive and connect with the right people as there are many good human beings out there who will be keen to connect with you and to help you reach your objectives.

Always be open to new ways of doing business or new ideas. The business world changes by the second and luck moves just as fast to the ones who are ready to receive for the right reasons.

In conclusion, luck is a part of the world, be it business or other. Sure, some people are luckier than others. The lottery has been won twice in a row by the same person before just as some business people are able to land two projects worth millions in the same day. These are not everyday occurrences, but they do happen from time to time.

Train yourself to be better at recognising lucky situations and before you know it, the majority of them will come your way.

Be prepared to take risks, make use of opportunities and manage uncertain situations. If you do these properly, you will soon realise that luck is shining on your career much more than on others'. Some say there is no such thing as a stupid idea. Often the so-called stupid idea just needs some refining to become a great idea.

CHAPTER 36

Dishonesty

Dishonesty has no place in society. It can cause major havoc in the business space in terms of finances as well as the breakdown of relationships, both in the office and with clients and other stakeholders.

If dishonesty is the worst thing that can happen within a company, the second worst is how to deal with it. Often, when there is a form of dishonesty carried out by a person in the office, a blind eye is turned towards the incident by the spotter, who will try to convince him or herself that the incident is a small one and will have no major impact on the business.

This is the incorrect route to follow as the problem could well grow into gigantic proportions in time if the incident is not dealt with. There is only one way to handle the situation and that is through instant disciplinary processes.

Failure to do this could see dishonesty becoming a part of the company culture.

Some who may spot a person being dishonest may fall into the trap of thinking if this person can get away with it, so can they, and dishonesty becomes a part of everyday life in the office.

Dishonesty is temporary and high-level ethics is permanent. It's a simple principle but one that people tend to forget when temptation strikes.

In business, there are typically three types of people. There are those who are born to win. They just have the ability to make money, turning US$10 million deals into US$100 million contracts with effortless ease. Be assured these people operate according to high levels of ethics.

Then there are the temporarily successful ones. They strike a huge deal today, but that is it for the immediate future.

Lastly, there are those people in business who, for whatever reason, end up being unsuccessful. The common denominator here is character. Should ethics be of a limited standard, the second and third groups here are almost more likely to be open to forms of temptation than the first-mentioned type.

Companies that promote honesty and transparency are doing the right thing in terms of business principles. Plenty of people will benefit from honesty in the long term while only a handful will reap the 'rewards' from dishonesty.

Remember that no news spreads as fast as bad news does. If situations are not handled adequately, your company and brand that you have worked so hard to build over many years may be the talk of the town for all the wrong reasons.

Stay away from the 'G-word'. Yes, 'greed' has been the downfall of many people in business since time immemorial and probably will continue to be in the years ahead as many succumb to temptation.

Believe it or not, there are still honest people out there in this world and the job of a leader or human resources manager is to find the right people that will add major ethical value, as well as skills and experience, to the business before other companies sign them up.

What you do daily in the workplace becomes routine in your life, be it good or bad things. So, it is important to carry out your daily tasks in an ethical manner.

Remember, too, that *your* name, not only your company name, is a brand in its own right and people will be talking about it, particularly when you apply for new employment posts.

So it is best to keep a clean slate and to be in demand rather than having people being cautious of you because of rumours or negative facts floating around the industry.

The word 'ethics' is closely linked to the term 'integrity'. Integrity stems from leadership. A leader is there to lead and set the example. If the leader is involved in dishonest doings, again, others will believe that they can also take chances and get away with forms of dishonesty.

The best way for a leader to gain the respect of their staff is to be transparent and honest in his or her daily interactions with the workforce. A leader in the business sector needs to be known for fairness and for showing no signs of favouritism.

Some people tend to go the dishonest route for a variety of reasons. Perhaps they have financial obstacles in their private life and the salary that they are earning just doesn't cover all the bills that they have to pay at the end of the month.

Others may feel that their leader doesn't believe in them as much as he or she believes in others in the office. In thinking that they don't have a long-term future in the company, the work attitude drops and so, their level of ethics.

As a leader or junior staff member, the principle to follow is a simple one—always tell the truth. This does require a great deal of focus as the truth is based on facts and nothing else. It is not about how you work with a person or what you may think of their work or personality. Stick to the truth and do not deviate from it.

One of the key factors in building a successful brand or business, as mentioned elsewhere in this book, is trust. There needs to be mutual trust between the leader and the staff in order for growth to follow on all fronts. If there are any forms of suspicion on these fronts, then obstacles are in place to hamper the growth or at least the speed at which it will take place.

Some company information will always be more important than others. So the leader needs to keep the door to dishonesty closed by ensuring that only certain people have access to the private documents of the business.

The right type of person with the highest level of ethics needs to handle the business income-tax documentation, bank statements, and other highly confidential papers.

Let's look at some ways of curbing dishonesty in the office.

First, the leader should keep a close eye on office infrastructure from telephones to stationery and more. The leader should know exactly how much budget is allocated per item per staff member per month, and should any person exceed the limit, he or she will be required to provide valid reasons for having done so.

If the excuses are not valid, then the amounts of over expenditure will need to be recouped from the staff member's salary. If it can be proved that the staff member purposefully abused the resources in order to put the company in a bad light, then further action would need to be taken.

The leader also needs to work out the time allocations per staff member per project. Abuse of time is another form of dishonesty as a staff member cannot dawdle through the month and use up fifty hours of time on a campaign, whereas another colleague completed a similar task in twenty hours.

Visibility is required on behalf of the leader. The person in charge needs to have some form of a presence so that the staff will know that they cannot take chances and do 'go-slow' style work. Time is money in the business world.

By getting to know the staff a little better, the leader will get that gut feel as to which members are focused workers looking to go further in the company, and which are just there to bank the salary at month end. The leader will need to keep an even closer eye on those that could be potential chance-takers from a negative perspective.

The use of prohibited supplements and steroids is another reason why people's personalities and levels of ethics may change for the worst. The moment that a leader trusts a person too much is the moment that cracks in the business system begin to develop.

Sometimes, even the most loyal of people are tempted to take advantage of opportunities, like coming late to work or not showing up at all. How many of your staff phone in sick per month? It's horrible to think this way but how many of them were really sick or are on sick leave just a little too frequently?

We are in an era of modern technology whereby software packages can track the use of time and office resources mentioned earlier. The leader should not be afraid to make use of things that will be able to monitor the use or misuse of office equipment. The misuse of time is as dishonest as the misuse of office resources.

Here comes the big one. Who can a leader trust to do the purchasing of supplies for the business? Commission and financial kickbacks are ever present in the industry with staff often approached by suppliers and offered 'a little something' at the end of the month, if the supplier's products become the preferred choice.

The leader needs to be ever-present in monitoring the purchasing of goods in order to catch any potential activity of a suspicious nature. Receiving kickbacks from a supplier is dishonest as this could lead to inferior supplier products being used ahead of regular products supplied to the business.

The company rules need to be clear on all fronts, as should be the punishment if someone is found guilty of an offence. Now the staff member has a choice between ethics or lack of them.

When you are driving on the roads, you know that if you speed down the street and get pulled over by a traffic officer, there will be a price to pay. The same principle applies on the business front. A staff member should think of things this way. Is the risk of financial gain at the expense of losing one's job really worth it?

There is an expression in the world of detectives and investigating officers, namely: 'There is no such thing as a clever crook'. Honesty is always the right route to follow. Keep in mind that as word spreads, it is very difficult to get another job when the people in the market know that a person has been fired from the previous place of employment for dishonesty.

We are in an era where company budgets are much higher than they were in the 1960s, 1970s, 1980s, 1990s, and early 2000s, so the temptation for a staff member or even a senior management member to make that extra bit of cash at month's end is ever present.

There is also the factor of being in an office the whole day alongside people with 'long fingers'; namely, thieves. The selling of a colleague's mobile device or tablet has become far too frequent in recent times to such an extent that many businesses have gone to the extreme of putting security cameras not only in their parking areas but in their offices too.

Apart from fraud within a company, this is possibly the most serious offense that could lead to police action. In spending a large part of one's day in an office area surrounded by colleagues, a family-like atmosphere should be present, rather than one of having to lock all possessions away, in case of theft.

In conclusion, dishonesty has no place in business and will definitely not allow a staff member of such low-level ethics to progress very far from a career perspective.

At the end of one's career, one will want to look back on the road of life that one travelled and prison would surely not be one of the places that one would have liked to have on one's CV, to show their children or grandchildren one day.

Apart from the temptation element, morals are something that one cannot teach a staff member. When you first arrive at the place of work, you either have these high ethical levels or you don't as they are a part of your growing up and personality.

Dishonesty should be rooted out at all costs and staff members are encouraged to report any form of dishonesty or criminal activity in the office to their superior as soon as possible before things get worse

CHAPTER 37

People

Appointing people in a business is all about getting the right skilled people, in the right places, and keeping them motivated.

Remember the golden rule is to have specifically skilled people doing the things they are trained for and like to do! Having ideal people with the best skills for the job and the correct mindset for the position is more important than having great people!

There are two types of business people:

Long-term-minded people are the kind that often overanalyse situations and take a while before, if ever, putting plans into action.

Short-term-minded people are just the opposite. These people rush to implement plans without sufficiently considering the positives and negatives.

Because of this impulsiveness, things can sometimes go wrong, or the plans may prove to be ineffective in the long run.

However, getting a mixture of these two types of business people on board is important when it comes to achieving success. You need a balanced approach. In addition to the type of people you need to employ, it is vital that your employees understand that your business participates in a cycle of earnings and expenses every day.

Everyone in the organisation should always be mindful of this state. In doing so, they can ensure that the earnings are increased, and the expenses are kept as low as possible. Anything less puts the business under pressure. To get to this state of employee-focused input, you need to consider the following factors.

Business leaders need to clearly define and communicate the targets and objectives of the company to all employees and give the staff enough space (in the form of time and freedom to achieve their goals).

People need to be open to their managers when it comes to reporting back on the status of projects. You will find that truthful employees are the accountable ones.

They will say if they are behind on projects and explain why. Others will say that things are going well, even if they are not, just to get their team leader off their backs. Either way, honesty and integrity go a long way.

People will fail to perform at their best if their minds are not at ease in the workplace. If the employees are unsure if their work will be respected or if their efforts will simply be taken for granted, then it will be difficult for them to focus on producing top-class work and even going the extra mile.

If the employees do not fully believe their managers or team leaders, then this could hamper delivery, which, in turn, could have a negative effect on accountability. So it is important to ensure that there is constant peace of mind and growth in the workplace.

If your employees are trying to perform a bit of a circus act by juggling too many responsibilities and trying to meet too many goals, then the wheels could well fall off the proverbial wagon at some point.

The team needs to be well structured with everyone fully aware of what they need to achieve. Critically, each person should not be given more to do than they can realistically handle.

Quality communication from the top level is key. If people are kept informed of developments within the company and with respect to specific projects, then they will feel more relaxed and comfortable in their work environment.

The more surprises that come their way, due to inadequate communication, the higher the risk of staff looking elsewhere for employment instead of focusing on the work at hand.

People need to be taught how to handle tasks. There is nothing worse than throwing someone into the deep end and then complaining at the individual when he or she fails to deliver. Regardless of how talented a person is, mentoring and briefing need to happen for maximum performance.

Leaders who are open to change themselves, through accepting either positive or negative feedback on projects, will find that they get the best out of their people. Employees will show much more respect to leaders they feel are approachable when it comes to tabling new ideas, sharing criticisms and finding solutions to take projects or other business matters forward.

Quite often people find themselves competing with others in the workspace, usually in a bid to impress their leader and secure that all-important promotion. However, studies have shown that people who work as team players in a company actually achieve more than those who work as individuals.

Teamwork brings about another degree of accountability and should be fostered within any organisation.

Here are good tips when it comes to hiring the right person:

Define the job carefully before putting it out to market. If your job description is vague, you will waste your time when it comes to the reading all the applications since, in these harsh economic times, every Tom, Dick, and Harry will be sending in their papers in search of employment, even if they are not properly skilled for the job.

Analyse your recruitment strategy to ensure that the right people are at the table when it comes to interviewing potential candidates.

Creating a checklist for hiring will keep your hiring process on course. Also, don't deviate from your checklist.

It's my view that with every appointment there must be a two-way process. The candidate must like the business and interview the business as much as the business selects and likes the candidate. This makes for a solid foundation.

You want a situation where the potential employee doesn't just look at the position as a job, but as a place where he or she can enjoy spending time each day.

Through business networking in the form of meeting people at events and other functions, the chances are that you may have someone in mind for a job long before the job description is posted. There is nothing wrong in inviting someone to apply for a post as long as the employment process is done in an open and fair manner.

For all you know, the person you have in mind may not agree on the salary package, and you may have to go for the next option on the list, so don't limit your choice.

Some people like to inflate their CV profiles to such an extent that they actually become false. Always check all references provided and keep an eye out for other people who may know the candidate from his or her previous experience in the marketplace.

The truth will always come out, but sometimes this only happens after the offer has been made and accepted.

The last thing you want is to employ someone who has left his or her previous place of employment under a cloud. So it's important to review all candidates carefully.

To save time, pre-screen all candidates before calling people for interviews. If the salary expectation on an excellent CV profile is way beyond your budget, then don't waste his or her time by calling that person for an interview when you know the chance of reaching an employment agreement are slim.

Your hiring team's experience will come in handy here. People will always give the answers the hirer wants to hear, but experience and gut feel will determine whether the person is the right fit for the job or not.

The people process is, of course, a two-way street. So let's look at what a potential employee should be thinking about when taking on a new job and what their habits should be.

Perhaps the starting point is asking oneself what one would like to achieve at the company. There are a number of questions which you'd hope an employee considers when he or she takes on a new role.

For example: How long do I plan on staying with the business? Is my stay just a port in the storm after a bad experience at my previous employer? Am I just working for a salary or am I intent on laying down roots and spending a good few years at my new place of employment? If an employee is thinking broader than just a salary-to-salary approach, then he or she needs to consider strategic goals as well. For instance: Where do I hope to be in two or three years' time within the company?

Reading is vital to the growth of any individual. In this modern era, reading doesn't necessarily relate to books; instead it features Googling and harnessing the power of the Internet to keep constantly informed about what is going on in the market and the chosen profession. Business is a race. The one who stays ahead wins. Knowledge is power.

Staying physically and mentally fit comes easier to some than others, but being in a healthy state brings about a degree of positivity in one's mind. Smoking and too much alcohol intake, coupled with bad eating habits cannot be a good thing, even if done behind closed doors at home.

To make the best use of time, it is important to plan your days and weeks carefully. Create that hour each day for reading and researching; it will make the world of difference. Imagine how good you will feel when you are able to come up with the latest information on projects as opposed to other people who are out of touch with events in the world and in your industry.

Now let's look at what a client expects from the person they deal with in business:

Clients want to always feel special and as if they are more than just 'another client' to the business.

The business can achieve this by learning as much about the client as possible as well as having their customs appreciated and opinions respected and embraced. Remember the old adage 'the client is always right'?

Now, let's look at how these principles align what how a person (an employee) wants to feel in the workplace:

Employees want to be treated as individuals and be respected and have their ideas and opinions respected and embraced.

Did you spot the similarities?

For a person to have the vision to grow within a company, there are four main areas in which they need to have some sort of skill or interest in. These include technical, management, technological and leadership expertise.

The business leader regularly needs to take a close look at how he or she appoints people. Remember the company is your brand and employees are your ambassadors.

So it's important to consider whether or not staff members are appointed too quickly or if your HR department takes sufficient time to scout the market to find the most suitable people for the job.

Furthermore, it's important to find out if the bottom line of the business top-of-mind and if managers are opting to buy cheap rather than buy resources of quality because they could easily sabotage your brand and business.

Additionally, it is essential to look at the company's performance reviews when it comes to accessing the delivery of people in your business. This is so because a boss is not at the coalface of operations, he or she often gets out of touch with the business hence it is always better to let the direct managers, to whom staff report, handle performance reviews.

Another thing that can be taken as a universal truth is that almost every staff member employed in this world believes he or she is underpaid.

This is a common gripe across the globe, with youngsters often having the loudest voices on this front. What younger people will learn is that even if the above is true, the experience that they gain early on will be worth its weight in gold later, as they climb the ladder of success.

In conclusion, good help is hard to find. If you live by this adage, then it goes without saying that you don't want to lose good people. But, as a business, you also don't want to be held to ransom. If a manager or team leader has tried his or her level best to make an employee feel satisfied and comfortable, but the list of requirements from the staff member is just too long, then one has to assume a 'take it or leave it' stance.

What is also fact is that many business leaders run their companies better than they run their personal lives. This is because, in business, they are so focused on routines, deadlines and putting systems in place. They often even do a better job in handling their business finances than they do with their own money. It's all about focus.

The more a business leader is visible and shows interest in his or her people in the company, the more respect the workforce will show. It is important to deal with employees as people and not merely as numbers that make up a business team.

Remember: It's not always about amazing products and services. In fact, it is often about the amazing people who make the product, or the service, come alive.

CHAPTER 38

Getting it All to Work

Planning your business for the next ten years is a worthwhile and strategic aspect of business ownership which will stand you and your business in good stead. While this may seem like an intimidating exercise, it is not as difficult as it might seem.

After all, once all the pieces of your business are in place, then the wheels will start to turn on their own, and possibly quicker than you might have expected. Looking after staff members will play an important role in ensuring that your business maintains its momentum.

Maintaining staff in key positions is of great importance as they will not look elsewhere for career growth if your business leaders assure them of their future in the company, of continued growth and remuneration in line with their output.

Sometimes people aren't changeable (they lack the ability to learn and work through to the next level), and these individuals need to be moved out of the company in order for your business to succeed.

However, managers and business leaders need to be realistic about what they are expecting from staff before taking drastic decisions that could either take the business to the next level or, if not handled properly, make things worse.

The winning formula ultimately revolves around everyone coming together to work towards the business's success. Here, there is no better slogan than world-famous Nike's 'Just Do It' because, ultimately, success comes down to action and implementation.

At this important stage, there is no time for strategy sessions. The brainstorming should have been done and the focus now should be on making things happen.

Because no business exists because of a single factor or item, success often comes down to a combination of various tangible and non-tangible things and how they mesh together. The holistic whole must work, and must consistently be improved. Therefore, never discard the small things or focus less on some aspects of the business than others.

When in doubt go back to these key pointers to enabling action:

Don't spend too much time worrying about the risk of a decision; if you don't take risks, you can't seize opportunities.

Getting started is often the most nerve-wracking part as it's the beginning of weeks or months of strategic planning. Once the few days are done, reality tends to set in. So commit to getting started.

Stick to the deadline dates which were drafted in the strategy sessions. After all that is what they are there for. Now is not the time to start to make changes to the plan.

Errors will happen along the way, so be agile enough to be ready to fix them as you go along. You are a team player, aren't you? Show this through your actions and embrace errors.

Large projects will never be completed to perfection if staff members think large scale. Break projects up into days rather than weeks or months and get each portion assigned to the person with the best abilities for the job. Rather work in 'baby steps' than giant leaps.

After a few days of activation, the team at the coalface will soon work out what works and what doesn't. Remember that, sometimes, strategies work well on the big screen in the boardroom but not necessarily as well from a practical perspective. So learn from trial and error.

The 'business rule of thumb' suggests that in order to know whether the strategy surrounding a business or product/service has been actioned successfully or not, a thousand-day test period is a good yardstick to use. By then, one should have a good idea about the successes or challenges that are on the horizon.

I have tested this principle multiple times—with success. Stick it out, no matter what.

Remember that not everything will work from day one: it takes time to get all the pieces of the puzzle into the correct places, so don't get frustrated if everything doesn't work as you expected it to from day one. Often, patience is required. If you are not open to adjustments, then failure will be on the cards.

Because the market can be a tough place, trying out underdeveloped concepts is a huge risk. It's brilliant if they come off, but the chance of failure is ever-present. With lots of cash having almost certainly been used to take your business, products or services to the implementation stage, it would be foolhardy to push underdeveloped concepts to market too early.

Remember that knowledge is power. As a result, you can never do too much homework. Research is the key when it comes to success. Understanding markets better than your opposition leads to rewards. By the time you have gone to market, you should have a powerful message to share with the world, one which includes a tagline or few words that will be top-of-mind in the client's headspace. Give your message oomph.

Many clients will go the 'spin doctor' route and will sub-contract to a reputable public relations (PR) agency to manage the media affairs at the time of the launch of the business, product or service. This can work in two ways: Either you can appoint the PR agency to come up with a campaign to attract as much attention as possible to the business, product or service over the first few months, or you can enlist their help in assisting with any damage control should the business make headlines for the wrong reasons.

It is unfortunate in life that 'bad news sells newspapers' and these days, tragic, fraudulent or other controversial events make the headlines. Knowing how to react in times of bad press is an art and often requires the services of an expert.

I refer to risk management on many occasions in this book, because I believe in it so strongly.

This element can make or break a company in the long run, so it is a small amount to spend for what could be a big saving. Learn to manage risk.

Now, let's look at some ways to get your product or service offering into pole position in the minds of buyers.

All businesses, whether we like to hear it or not, have strengths and weaknesses, so as you take your brand to market you need to ensure that you are pushing toward your strengths. Any weaknesses can always be picked up as time goes by, preferably when business deals are in the bag and nerves have settled. So always work on your strengths.

It's important to fully understand the needs of your buyer. This can be achieved by focusing on the market.

Realise that there is nothing wrong with starting small as it means that there is room for growth.

The starting point will always be determined by how much budget has been allocated to launching the business, product or service.

As you go to market, you will still be learning things that could come in handy when taking your business, product or service to the next level. Never shut out advice or input, even if you think that your offering is perfect. Market trends change as time progresses and you will never know when that piece of advice will come in useful for putting your offering ahead of the rest. Be a seeker of advice.

Always stay flexible and be open to change, stay nimble and keep focused in order to seize opportunities. It's important to pay attention to the small steps, instead of only focusing on the end-goal. Your objective or dream will guide you, lest you find yourself lost in the vision.

Focus on what is at hand and work methodically towards success. Success hinges on everyone in your team pulling in the same direction. So keep in alignment.

Nothing fuels excellence more than inspiration. If you can create an exciting and dynamic work environment, then the natural energy will drive your company forward. We all want to work for a hero; make your company and its people that hero by staying inspired and inspiring.

You could be the most brilliant businessman in the world, but it is true that 'you are only as good as your last game'. You can be a world-class sportsperson, a leading politician or a top-rated business leader and you will be forever remembered for failure, rather than all your successes.

Fortunately, many people have short memories and bringing an extremely good service or product to the market a few months after a brand disaster will go some way to mitigating that negativity. But never rush to market. As competition around the world heats up and markets get tougher with each day, buyers are faced with more choices and an often-shrinking budget.

So it is vital that all the elements leading up to implementation and the action process are handled mindfully and with a focus on quality and perfect execution.

Once you've done your bit, then the proof is in the sampling. It either works for a buyer or it doesn't. There is no halfway on this. It is equally important to keep emotions far away from the business space. If the business, product or service fails to make the money that it was expected to generate, the business leader cannot necessarily put the blame on the project team that worked on the campaign.

There will, undoubtedly, be many factors relating to why a new release failed to live up to expectations, and these could include:

Timing. Did the timing of the big announcement clash with the launch of other business brands? Did this take some of the shine off your big moment?

Similar products or services sent to market by opposing brands. Did these put your new release on to the back burner? If so, why?

It may be that some information on your offering may have been leaked to the opposition prior to your launch, which may have consequently given your opposition a competitive advantage. In cases where information has been leaked, confidentiality clauses in staff contracts will need to be re-evaluated and tightened.

Perhaps your offering was simply not as good as you thought it would be. Be honest.

Should 'getting it all to work' ultimately not gel for whatever reason, it is important not to take things personally or make hasty decisions. Rather think through what changes can be made to the service or the product offered by the business before opting to make drastic staff acquisitions or cuts.

Try again with a renewed sense of confidence because the lessons learned the first time around will only have made you wiser and more prepared to take a second bite at the cherry.

Bear in mind that, if you find yourself in such a situation, now is the time to bring in risk management and the other safety nets you put in place as you look to get your product or service offering back on track.

When you are on the ropes, getting up to try again is the sign of a true champion. Remember a winner never quits, and a quitter never wins!

CHAPTER 39

Talent and Talent Management

Talent distinguishes business and plays an important role in empire building. Talented people need to be carefully managed and retained in the interest of the company.

Here is an example that many business leaders regularly experience.

A medical practice had five doctors and five specialists. One of the five specialists is very talented and brings in 65% of the revenue. However, this person is a law unto himself (he doesn't want to do meetings and doesn't fit in with the rest of the staff).

So what choice does the CEO have with regard to this person? Does the company boss dispense of the services of this individual? Or does the company leader find a way to manage this person so that his skills are not lost to the business, keeping in mind the large revenue percentage that this specialist generates?

The answer is a simple one.

Give this person a lot of rope and build your business around this talented person rather than forcing the individual into an environment that he or she is not comfortable in, as this could affect their output. This person needs to feel valued and should be given as much space as possible to perform at his or her best.

The problem often boils down to the fact that the most talented people in business (who generate the big bucks) are the ones that could quite easily be too talented for the company and hence get lost.

So what can we learn from this?

The more you give responsibility to talented people, the more they will grow. It is important to keep talented people motivated by giving them new work that other companies would only allow them to do when they have more experience. This distinguishes your company from others in the minds of these talented individuals

There is a fine balance in managing talent people as they may sometimes become too powerful and this could negatively impact on the rest of the staff, meaning that productivity could be affected.

Like most things in life, the final outcome depends on the individual. Some young workers can manage responsibility more than others, so there is no fixed way to manage a person.

Each individual needs to be managed according to his or her own talent and work ethics. Just like unique marketing strategies need to be put in place for each client, the same applies when it comes to managing talent people. This is linked to getting the right people into the right places in your business.

The effort that needs to be put into the recruitment of talent from the marketplace cannot be ignored, if you want your company to become the best in the industry!

So how does one spot high achievers in the workplace in order to identify them as the assets for departments or project teams to be built on? The answer is a pretty simple one.

These people usually stick out quite easily in a crowded workplace. They have high levels of self-discipline and are extremely focused. They always seem to be one step ahead of the rest in terms of knowledge and are always proactive rather than reactive in terms of approach.

They also require less supervision or management than others do, so they can run with a project without having to be managed 24/7.

What is key here is to make sure that these high-level achievers or assets receive adequate business resources in order for them not to become frustrated and go in search of another company that will help them reach their full potential.

Remember that these types of people see challenges as a happy space, in other words as a space for them to find solutions which further boosts their confidence. These types of people are great to have around and can only be of value to your business if managed and driven correctly.

Of course, they will never be the most popular in the office. Think back to your school days and how you hated those boys and girls who got 98% to 100% on exams while you did your absolute best and got stuck on 60% to 70%.

Business leaders who are fortunate enough to have such people on their workforce should keep an eye out for those special assignments which can be given to them. Even if the special assignment ends up being one step too far for them, they will accept failure at first but be assured they will dust themselves off and try again. They will not rest until they find the solution to the challenge. This is one of the attributes of a perfectionist.

It is great to have these people around, as while the business leader tends to be more focused on the balance sheet bottom line matters, it is a good feeling to know that there is someone else out there who is taking their task so seriously.

It is this sort of talent that makes a huge difference to a business at the end of the day.

So let's summarise the characteristics of these special 'assets'.

He or she will be an extremely responsible type of person who is not a clock-watcher.

The person will tend to go home when the job is done rather than when everybody else leaves for home.

He or she will also not be threatened by anyone else in the office. Why should the person feel threatened when his or her attitude and skill set is superior to anyone else on the team?

He or she will also tend to be very focused on detail. There is little room for error in most businesses with time being classified as money. So getting things right the first time is key in a fast moving, thriving business industry.

He or she will also have long-term goals. These people do not live day to day. They know where they are at the current moment and where they need to be in six months to a year or even three to five years from now. They think of their job as a marathon in an athletics event. They know where the start and finish lines are. They are in it for the long haul and are definitely not sprinters.

Everything about the person or persons will be done in a positive mindset, whether it is work-orientated or even making a cup of coffee.

They usually enjoy being the 'core person' in the team that others can come to for advice or assistance. They usually don't mind helping others, as again, they do not feel threatened.

He or she will also enjoy receiving regular feedback from the boss. They are usually open to criticism as they know that this is how they learn, rather than taking criticism personally like some people in the workplace do.

It is up to the business leader to make the workplace as fun as possible for all parties. Everyone loves incentives, so it is important to find ways and means to keep the spirit as high as possible among the workforce.

Month-end family meal vouchers or spa treatment vouchers (for the women) always attract much attention and will bring about that extra effort from the staff in a bid to win the prize. Of course, the high achievers will probably get to the prize first based on their attitude and ability, but the business leader will need to be wary that the same staff member (even if it is deserved on merit) does not win the prize each month.

Due to their high levels of confidence, many of the high-level talented people will also turn out to be the best marketers of your business brand as well as ambassadors for the products and services that your business is offering.

Not all of these talented people may turn out to be the best stand-up speakers, but it is the knowledge that they carry that will convince a potential client to go with your business.

In conclusion, talent management is an art. As much as a business wants to retain as many of the top assets in the industry as possible, it is not always possible due to many external factors.

Perhaps the husband of the talent person has just been transferred to another country by his work, and the wife has been left with no other option but to resign from your firm and accompany her spouse.

Maternity leave often comes into the mix as well, but here business leaders need to be smart and allow compromises to fly if it is felt that having the person behind the laptop, even if it is from home while on leave, is of importance.

These highly talented individuals are sorely sought-after in the business industry so don't let them slip through your fingers when the opportunity arises for your company to hire and retain them.

Remember, the next brilliant service or product idea might not necessarily come from the CEO's office but quite possibly from a staff member and more than likely from one of these assets who understand the business so well and is blessed with vision.

Look after your assets in the form of high-level talent and you will find that others in the workplace will also tend to obtain a renewed energy level by being around these people.

Even the most experienced of business leaders could be quite surprised at just how this type of person can lift the morale in the office.

As mentioned earlier, if you want to be like the best, then you must learn from the best, and when you become the best, keep learning, because the business industry changes on a constant basis.

CHAPTER 40

What is Success?

The most obvious way to determine whether a business is successful or not, is through examining the balance sheet and income-statement documentation. This should be done with the age-old philosophy of 'income shall always be greater than expenses' being front of mind.

If you ask a hundred leading business people for a definition of what success is, you will probably end up with a hundred different answers. There is no hard-and-fast rule. To some, it will be about making piles of money and turning a business into a success. To others, success could well be determined by how much a leader is able to grow the success of their workforce and others around them rather than the balance sheet or income statement.

By this, you can see that success is not always measured in monetary terms, as much as many of us would like it to be.

When a leader's business career is over, the balance sheet figures may not seem as important to them as in years gone by. They will be left with a list of questions and it could be a bit of a culture shock to many who will suddenly realise that they can't tick all the boxes as they thought they could.

Success in this instance is built around job satisfaction and knowing that one has made an immense difference to the industry in which they worked over many years.

It is like playing a role in uplifting the community in which you live, rather than going home after a hard day's work and locking the front door hoping that nobody will come and knock on it.

We all have goals that we want to achieve in life and business. I know many business people who have set goals of relocating to London or New York in the next five years.

That means that they have five years to finish the previous goals that they set for themselves in the place in which they currently are.

It is so important to finish off a stage of one's life on a positive note. I am sure you would like people to remember you for leaving a business department better off than it was when you first arrived? That is a form of success.

Of course, there are many other ways to measure if your business is successful. For instance, how does your business, service or product compare to others in your industry? You often learn more from your competitors than you will from your own product-development team.

Examine the debtors and creditors on your books. Take a careful look at your accounts and check out the state of affairs. Remember that some debtors may have been invoiced but could take ninety days or more to pay, while others may not pay at all, resulting in bad debt write-offs.

What are your capital requirements or loans? The best way to access this is if your business will be able to generate sufficient earnings and not have to borrow money. The year-on-year growth should be about 20% per annum, which is broken down into roughly 5% inflations and 15% net profit.

Social responsibility: Another way of measuring if your business or project has been a success or not is in working out how much difference your firm makes in the community. You will probably find when it comes to filling out large tender documents, that your company will have scored points for any form of value that it has added to the community in which it operates (e.g. cleaning up areas near rivers, or parks; providing employment opportunities to the less fortunate and so forth).

Generally speaking, if the gross profit is more than 30% per annum and the net profit is more than 15% per annum, these are regarded as minimum requirements.

It is important to define and to communicate what is success in your specific business, and it does not need to be a single item. As a minimum, it will always be a financial objective or ratio.

Let's get back to basics! Everyone, be it a CEO or lowest-level staff member, should have the aim of being number one in the market, irrespective of the industry. But how do you get there? And, once you do, how do you celebrate this success?

Remember that success inspires. Always take the time to determine what you can learn from a successful project, once it has been completed.

You learn new things every day of your life and these elements will add to your business experience, which will put you in a position to go to the next level when the right time comes.

Always have a positive mindset. Your mind is an important tool because it is the repository of vital information gained through experience, research, and mentorship. It is your daily business tool, so you have to care for this vital machine.

To do so, you need to maintain a confident mindset. One of the best ways to do this is to keep positive by focusing on your accomplishments to date, rather than thinking about what you still have to do. The pieces of the puzzle will fall into place if you think logically and without stress, and if you believe that you can succeed. These elements are the road to success.

Keep yourself motivated.

Small things that you learn along the way will amount to big wins when it comes to achieving success, so stay motivated and move forward one victory at a time.

CHAPTER 41

Sticky Situations

A 'sticky situation' is just what it sounds like: a tough situation to get out of. Finding yourself in such a negative bind certainly creates a sense of fear and trepidation, so getting yourself out of these situations is a skill in itself.

Some situations are created by us, while others come down to honest mistakes. Others are foisted upon us. There are numerous 'sticky situation' scenarios out there, many of which we've encountered in our business careers. For example: Say you paid a supplier's money into the wrong bank account. That's a sticky situation. Say you lied to a client and find your untruth unravelling, leading you to being exposed in front of senior management. That's a sticky situation.

When you find yourself in a sticky situation, two principles apply when trying to get out of the embarrassing circumstances: Always be honest with staff and clients. Honesty is not a rope to hang yourself with but a principle which will gain you much respect in the long run. And when there is a 'sticky situation' problem, stand together as a team of staff members and fix the situation rather than pointing fingers at each other in a bid to shift the blame.

Let's look at some potentially sticky situations that could have a major impact on your business career:

You have been approached by another company

Conundrum: While you are happy with your current place of work, you are always on the lookout for other, more lucrative opportunities in the marketplace. One happens to come your way and now you are tip-toeing around how to tell your boss – who values and trusts you – that you are leaving. Things become worse when you tell your best friend at the office. He or she tells the next person and soon everyone in the office knows about your pending departure, except your boss.

Solution: Be honest from the start. A small problem will only grow in size if you don't honestly communicate the situation. Inform your boss that you have enjoyed working for the company, but you have been approached by another firm. Perhaps your boss will try to increase your salary in a bid to retain your services if he or she feels that you add that much value.

Presumption

Conundrum: It is often said that presumption leads to the worst of all mistakes. You are working on a project as part of a small team of consultants. You think the person next to you is picking up on certain responsibilities and he or she thinks that you are. The ball gets dropped rather badly.

Because deadlines have been missed, pressure builds up and, angered, you don't speak to your colleague for the next week as you presume he or she is trying to make you look bad. The only problem is he or she is thinking the same about you.

Solution: Every group should have a leader who sets out the roles and responsibilities from the start. Follow these roles and responsibilities carefully to avoid any form of embarrassing situation.

Disorganisation

Conundrum: You are falling into bad habits, including showing up late for meetings and not putting as much effort into your work as you should. When it comes to work, you look for every available short-cut—and it shows in quality of your work.

Solution: Pay attention to details at all times. If you are a business person, then act like one.

Don't take on too much

Conundrum: When committing to work, always make sure that you have enough time to deliver to the very best of your ability. Don't take on too much and end up close to having a nervous breakdown because you are worried that if you delegate work to colleagues, it may not be done according to your high level of expectation.

Another concern that you may have is that some of your work is of such a high level in terms of confidentiality, that information may leak out if you delegate the work to another colleague to handle.

Solution: Try to avoid putting highly confidential information into emails which could be maliciously forwarded by others. You need to stress the importance of confidentiality to your colleagues because your client has trusted you with their sensitive documents. Also, no gossiping about work in the corridors or during a smoke break is allowed. Gossip travels in 'broken telephone' style. Before you know it a concocted version of events has hit the streets or, even worse, has reached your client's ears.

Bosses who take credit for your hard work

Conundrum: This is a frequent occurrence in the marketplace with some bosses specifically asking junior employees, public relations firms, design companies and advertising suppliers not to put their name or logo watermark on certain documents. This usually means that the boss is planning on passing the documents off to the bigger bosses as his own work.

Solution: Make subtle mentions of your work during meetings so that those around the table who are bright enough will understand who did the work. Copy (cc) key members on certain documents via email.

If your boss freaks out about this, apologise but at least you have achieved your objective as the email is out there and people now know who is doing the work.

Expecting a child

Conundrum: You are a key cog in the business wheel but are now pregnant and in the middle of a multimillion-dollar project. Given the timing, it is understandable that your boss won't be too thrilled, but there are ways and means to work around this.

Solution: In this era of modern technology, including laptops, mobile phones, the Cloud, and flexible working arrangements, many people can and do work from home and are able to provide as high quality a service as they would if they were seated in the office.

You were promised a promotion and suddenly things with your boss have gone quiet

Conundrum: This happens frequently in business. Perhaps your boss understood that a major client was about to sign with the company and jumped ahead in mentioning your new role to you.

Solution: You will need to handle this in a sensitive manner. What if this amazing new client has done a U-turn on your company in terms of signing? It is not your problem but has now become just that.

It's annual bonus time

Conundrum: You receive your much-anticipated bonus and guess what? It is much smaller than you expected or than your boss had led you to believe it would be!

Solution: You will need to be cautious in handling this. Weigh up your options. Is it worth 'starting a fire'? Perhaps your boss could only get this size bonus agreed to by the company's board because they are about to promote you to a new, better-paying position in a few weeks' time? Check out the terrain before rocking the proverbial boat, as things could turn out in your favour if you play your cards right.

Your boss is sharing personal issues with you

Conundrum: Either your boss really trusts you, or he or she is keen on mentoring you, or your boss is developing feelings for you.

Solution: Tread with care as this could either grow your career or possibly jeopardise it. You need to draw a barrier between business and personal matters when it comes to discussions with your boss. It may even be a good idea to identify another person on the staff for your boss to take his personal problems to. Gossip spreads quickly so be careful that it is not too obvious that you are the boss's 'favourite', as this could ignite jealousy in others.

Yes, there are sticky situations around every corner – be they personal or business-focused in nature – but if you play your cards right and stick to your principles then you will be respected at the end of the day. And that 'sticky' incident will become a growth experience.

In conclusion, being honest and truthful is the best way to handle any sticky situation. But there are things that a company can do to foster this sort of attitude. If a business can create an environment where employees can be honest without fear of repercussions, then this will put difficult situations out in the open.

If you have an open work environment, then problems can be fixed, and if they can be effectively addressed, then you can take the 'sticky' out of anything.

CHAPTER 42

Indicators

Indicators measure value and performance in a business, and measure whether or not a business is able to achieve its objectives. As a result, business indicators can often be used to determine a company's success levels in reaching important targets.

Since these indicators can also be 'triggers' within a business, relating, as they do, to both positive and negative aspects of health, they should be properly defined and applicable to your company's line of business. Critically, these indicators should be well communicated and understood by all staff.

Let's look at some performance-level targets that can be used to analyse a company's position in the market.

Debtors of over ninety days are the most common indicator of poor corporate health because cash flow is impacted directly. A ratio needs to be set that if debtors reach a certain mark in outstanding payments, then the matter must be escalated. Keep in mind that 50% of debtors pay around 90 days with some, possibly, not paying at all.

If debt levels reach a certain amount, it is a clear indication that some specific actions are required to remedy the situation.

Depending on the type of business, certain 'triggers' should be built in to give the business leader a good idea (at monthly or quarterly meetings) of whether the business is showing growth or if there are negative elements which need attention. For example, for a retail concern having outlays of stock (for example, foodstuffs) that have not been sold within a certain amount of time will create a negative impact on the business. In such an instance, a decision needs to be taken as to whether carrying levels of the stock in question is viable or not.

If the competition issues a new product, for instance, this could also be a trigger which sparks a review of your current product line. Similarly, if competitors achieve market share above a specific level, then this could also be an indicator.

Now let's take a closer look at the most famous word in business and one of the most important business indicators: Budget.

Budgets are the lifeblood of a company's planning and performance because they are living documents which – much like a pulse or a heartbeat – give you an indication of the health of your company.

As such, it's vital that every good business person understand how to read and apply budgets, to understand them and consult them. One of the first starting points is to appreciate the difference between Gross Profit (the cost of making the product or providing the service) and Net Profit (gross profit less operating and other expenses), as well as the margins involved in both instances.

It is difficult to judge just how much of a cash buffer is needed in your business, since this depends on the type of product and service being offered, as well as the state of the market at the time.

Other budgetary considerations include considering:

Average annual expenses per customer: This is quantified by the average amount of cash needed to serve one customer.

Earnings before interest, tax, and depreciation: Income is measured, and interest, tax, and depreciation are deducted from the amount.

Research and Development indicator: I can't stress sufficiently the importance of this element, despite the fact that many businesses seem to ignore this investment completely, to their detriment. An R&D amount needs to be a serious line item in every company's budget and can usually be worked out in a percentage format for the whole project.

Keep an eye on inventory.

When it comes to business indicators, keeping data on your inventory is extremely important. This can help you with estimating which of your offerings to market are popular and which are not.

Neglecting oversight of your inventory can lead to theft or damage to stock and a shortfall in popular items (you may be carrying too much stock that is not selling at a reasonable speed and too little stock of products that are in demand).

One of the best ways to access the popularity of sales items is through the use of the Point of Sale (POS) unit. This programme will allow stock to be automatically removed from your inventory list the moment it is sold.

All hands on deck.

Your staff contingent must be involved and educated when it comes to understanding business indicators. You can handle this in various ways.

Staff members need to understand POS and other systems that have been put in place, as otherwise the stock vs. cash scenario will not balance.

Modern-era computer technology is great, but nothing beats the good, old-fashioned hand count. This will give you the best form of indicator. Understand the possibility of stock damages, swaps or returns because these will impact on the figures, so do take them into account.

It's important to establish a loss prevention department. Some companies, particularly retail stores, establish a loss prevention department or unit.

Elements that fall under this department include extra security, video surveillance, and any other safety means that could help to reduce the risk of goods leaving the store without being paid for.

Be equipped to track sales.

Sales statistics represent one of the most valuable indicators in any business, and are deserving of special attention. They show you the bottom line (real world) figures of what is actually going on in the company. Having a handle on these statistics will help your business stay on track.

While budgets, sales statistics, and inventories are vital business indicators, there are myriad other potential indicators which require your attention.

These include:

Keeping an eye on the amount of quality active proposals that have been sent to market over the past three to six months and how many positive responses have been received. Maybe you need to up your game?

Monitoring the number of discussions that take place with existing clients with regard to potential new projects is important. This could show a great sense of interest as far as new business is concerned.

Exploring how many new relationships have the potential to become long-term clients. Some clients will naturally have bigger budgets to spend on your products or services than others, but monitor this situation as it will be a good indication in terms of growing your business. Some clients may opt to get involved with your business on a six- to twelve-week starter project before committing to a longer relationship with your company.

The best way to gauge satisfaction is to ask customers or clients to fill out a short survey form. Their answers will also give you a good indication of how people perceive your product or service offering.

Be open to criticism. Even though you may have put in a great deal of hard work into your offering, it is important to see how customers rate your product or service. Criticism will only help you to grow your offering to the next level and have your business make a greater impact on the market.

Web traffic is important because it gives an indication of the market's reaction to your offering. Your webmaster will be able to advise how much traffic your website is generating. If this is not translating into business, then consider what information you are sharing and how to entice potential customers to linger longer on your site.

Your business's PR person or company needs to keep an eye on this key area as it could bring about major positive or negative publicity for your brand. People are quick to move to post comments on Twitter and Facebook or photographs on Instagram if they find something new and innovative in the market that can change their businesses or their lives.

Unfortunately, they are just as quick to post information or images if they find a service or product that they feel is not living up to expectations.

Productivity is vital. So ask yourself: Do the hours that my business puts in on a product or service align to the hours put in by my competitors?

This is not always easy to work out since your opposition won't be open to sharing their information, but you can find out one way or another. Once you do, be honest about how you stack up against the competition.

In conclusion, indicators are crucial elements when it comes to monitoring your business growth and your company's position in the marketplace.

Many companies overlook or misunderstand the importance of monitoring indicators as they are too focused on strategic elements or just swamped by getting the job done.

Intelligent businesses pay attention to details, and they have the ability to learn and are capable of reading the market for signs of new opportunities or chances to take current products and services to the next level. Understanding what the indicators are trying to tell you boils down to having the right staff in the correct positions in order to provide the necessary input to senior management.

The wise take indicators seriously, while the foolish will ignore them.

If a product or service is not working out, act swiftly by paying attention to the indicators. Be careful not to let a faltering offering stay on the market for too long while you look for solutions since the damage to your brand could be so great that it may even become irreparable. If you pay attention to the indicators, you can catch potential problems swiftly and act quickly to steer your ship in the right direction.

CHAPTER 43

Risk

Nobody goes into business with a mindset of losing money, so when this happens, it can mean only one thing: that the risks were not identified up front and were, therefore, not avoided.

It is impossible to do business without any risks. The trick is to identify potential hazards and, if you detect these early, determine how to mitigate and deal with these problems.

Your downside should always be protected, but never overprotected. Some businesses believe that the appointment of a risk officer will safeguard the company against potential risk, but that is only the beginning of the damage control process.

Business leaders need to remain involved in the risk management process, irrespective if they have appointed a risk manager or not.

Remember that the risk element might not always be external, as many business leaders are inclined to believe. It could well be internal in the form of fraud or theft, or possibly a cash-flow-cycle problem.

One of the biggest downfalls in a business occurs when company departments don't communicate well with each other. This is a risk that should not be present as it is a basic, controllable element of everyday business.

While it is necessary to look both internally and externally, it is on the latter consideration where the business needs to continually assess the risks. Ask yourself, for example, what will happen to your business if your top ten clients decide not to make use of your services of products anymore?

Similarly, what would happen if your country's currency devalues drastically due to political or other reasons?

When assessing risk, a good place to start is by dividing up risk elements according to the basics. Note the risks that are distant (e.g. highly unlikely risks). Then make a list of the more likely risks.

Next, list your most important risks. These are almost like business bombs (unpleasant surprises) waiting to explode and damage your business. Be sharp and identify your specific risks accurately.

When it comes to managing risk, it is always better to be proactive rather than reactive. At a minimum, it is important to do scenario planning to help you deal with potential situations. If, for example, we discover massive fraud of 30% of the company's value then this approach can help to determine how you deal with this practically.

No one really prepares for such instances, which is why these matters are often not dealt with properly. Doing so is good business practice.

Let's be honest. Running a business can be dangerous, with many unexpected risks appearing out of the woodwork. This is why spending time assessing risk is so important. The best way to evaluate risk is to get an external person to analyse the situation because the person is not emotionally connected to your business or the project.

If you do not go through these steps, you run the risk that your business will spend double the amount of cash on risk management out of concern for what the future may hold.

Your business's reputation should be of paramount importance to you. Remember, it counts on two fronts: your personal reputation as a worker or leader and your business reputation. So risk statistics need to be taken seriously.

This relates to precious data that can make or break your business. While most people are focused on strategy and implementation processes, the risk element probably ranks second equal to the 'Research and Development' aspect in terms of perceived importance.

Insuring against risk is an expensive exercise, but also a highly necessary one. If your warehouse that is filled with stock goes up in flames tomorrow, then so do your dreams, ambitions, and bottom line if your stock is uninsured.

Theft and fraud are other risk elements to insure against. Fortunately, there are many insurance brokers in the market who are able to provide packages loaded with benefits to give the business owner peace of mind.

As a potential risk area, never underestimate the data that you have on your computers. Accounting information and other data relating to existing clients, potential clients, debtors and creditors will be of major value to unscrupulous individuals who are looking to make off with this information, be it to start their own business in opposition to you or mischievously sell it to opponents.

Of course, there is also the risk of your office computers simply being stolen in a normal robbery situation. Irrespective of the reason for the breach, guarding against a data breach makes good business sense.

There are some serious factory risks that also need to be managed. Acids, fuel, gas and toxic fumes are all realistic risks that could wipe the smile off of the face of a business leader at any given time. Staff members who work on these fronts need to be properly trained and provided with the correct equipment since accidents do happen.

The location of your business could also be risky if it is not well thought through.

Be careful not to start a business in an area that is known to flood or is situated on an unstable geological fault. Similarly, if you are working with fire or heat in your manufacturing process then make sure that you are not too close to your thatched roof or chemicals business. The proximity could be explosive.

From a staffing perspective, always remember that people will be people. Some will take their jobs more seriously than others, so be aware of personality trends and even the potential for alcohol and drug abuse, which are a very real part of modern-day society. Some insurers even provide policy cover to assist businesses with staffing problems of this nature.

Because people are unpredictable, always keep a shortlist of subcontractors whom you can call in if some of your staff are booked out on sick leave, or if a national strike protest action takes place and causes a potential delay to your service delivery.

Businesses put a lot of time and energy into new innovations, be it new cleaning chemicals, a pharmaceutical range or more. Should any of these fail, it could bring major financial loss. Again there are insurance packages available to safeguard against major investments laid out on these fronts.

Much capital is often ploughed into the purchasing of seemingly endless amounts of equipment for work purposes. These will inevitably need to be insured against fire, theft or other forms of accident. From drought to endless days of rain, these could have major impacts on your business. Consider if you are a farmer and don't get rain for three months, so the local dams are on the brink of running dry. Your crops are about to be ruined or your stock is about to perish.

Likewise, flood could have just the opposite impact, with the crop not being able to withstand the long periods of rainfall while some of the animals could well have perished in flash-flooding conditions.

Once again, risk insurance packages are available to cover you in the event of these natural disasters.

Let's look at ways and means to try to avoid risks:

Employ staff who are good at their jobs and understand the marketplace. Don't always employ workers on the cheap, this will ultimately come back to bite you.

Rules and regulations: Before you try anything in life ensure that you know the rules or perimeters governing your business and influencing your road to success. Know the lay of the land in which you operate.

Don't go overboard in overcapitalising or taking out too many loans that could result in a repayment issue down the line. It's important to keep loans and capital in hand.

To avoid unnecessary internal complications between staff and suppliers, the business leader should be on top of his or her game in understanding the deliverables of all concerned. Never push the boundaries too far by asking for favours at no additional value, since someone else may do the same to you, one day.

The word 'confidential' is there for a reason. Some information on your business, services or products should definitely *not* leave the CEO's office. It is up to the business leader to make sure that all documentation is water-tight and that business formula secrets are sacrosanct.

In conclusion, managing business risk is something of an art.

Just like the rest of the world, the business sector changes on an hourly and sometimes a by-the-minute basis and it often turns into a bit of a hustle to get to the top. Wide-awake business leaders manage to achieve this mainly through a twofold approach: First, keep a close eye on trends and changes in the marketplace. And second, by being well-connected through business networks which allow them to be one step ahead of risks that could potentially damage their business or their reputation.

All in all, risk management remains one of the most important aspects of any business. Those who get it right tend to stand head and shoulders above the rest, and it is not impossible for a small- to medium-size company to succeed on this front ahead of a large corporation whose management may have overlooked certain key risk element areas.

The old saying that 'time is money' is always applicable. The bottom line is not to hold back when budgeting on the risk management front. Think of it as a cornerstone or a fundamental rather than an additional expense or a peripheral.

Risk should be understood for what it is. Unfortunately, some companies are excessively risk evasive, which is as problematic as taking on too much risk.

A long-term vision is required when gauging risk management on businesses and projects. Many of the current staff may well not be working for the company five years from now, so it is important to put a long-term strategy in place that includes insurance packages that will give all involved peace of mind if things go wrong.

CHAPTER 44

Hopeful and Staying Humble

This may sound quite strange to you as you may not have thought of the terms 'humility' and 'business persons' in the same sentence, yet this chapter will show you the importance of staying hopeful, humble and on top of your game in tough times.

The reason why the link between humility and business may sound quite out of place is that many people associate the term 'humility' with a sense of weakness. However, there is nothing wrong with a business person being humble and there is definitely no need for business people to be arrogant.

You will be surprised to know how many people think that arrogance will carve down their business opponents and will pave their way to the top. This is definitely not the recipe for success. Rather stick to having a positive never-say-die attitude than being known across the industry for an arrogant approach.

Humble leaders are more respected by their workers while arrogant decision-makers are feared. The arrogant ones are perceived to be one-person-shows while humble leaders are seen as team players that promote unity among staff.

Being humble does not mean that you lack confidence. Humility is actually an essential part of the business person that encourages those around them to grow and flourish. Here is a thought on humility for the arrogant ones—it does not take away power from a person in charge but actually increases the leader's authority in the eyes of all.

In business, you may often find that the only constant is change. There are always ups and downs, but it's important to stay positive and to remember the idea that 'tomorrow will always be greater than today' in order to make sure that you remain sane in stressful times.

It is very important to be honest and truthful in everything that you do. If a client criticises your offering, would you say the criticism valid? Don't go into a shell and believe that you are always right and everyone else is wrong.

Yes, you put so much time and effort into your offering and you are more emotionally attached to your work than anyone else, but answer the question—was the client's criticism valid or not?

Just like summer, autumn, winter, and spring, the world of business has its own seasons and quite often you will get bad news or blessings when you least expect it.

Regardless of the season, it's always important to approach business with a positive mindset. Be the hopeful one, while bearing in mind that being and staying hopeful doesn't exempt you from making tough decisions.

If you are the decision-maker and after consulting with your gut-feel, common sense, and your most trusted consultants, you decided not to proceed with a certain supplier or business deal, then just remember that 'when one door closes, another will open'.

Cash flow is king, so when business is good, then build up that cash-flow cushion to survive those 'rainy days'. No matter what the situation, always stay humble.

In most cases, it was a sense of humility that got you to the point of success so don't throw that element of your personality and business culture away just because you are now going through tough times.

Remember that your personality and attitude attract luck through various elements, including saying the right thing at the right time and being at the right place at the right time. These have one common denominator—a positive approach to business. If you don't believe in yourself and your offering, then don't expect others to.

When the going gets tough, it is time for the leader in you to stand firm because showing that you can handle major responsibility in stressful situations can be one of the biggest growth phases in life.

When a business is facing immense challenges, it is important to take a step back from the problems and view the situation with a clear mind. Has there been too much focus placed on smaller details rather than on the bigger picture?

Or is it the other way around, in that too much focus has been placed on the larger picture and a lack of focus on some of the smaller details have caused the business to travel on stormy seas?

In tough times, it is often easy to close the cash tap completely instead of bringing in some specialist consultant to help put solutions in place. Remember that there is no business person out there who has 100% knowledge of how the market works.

Every day brings something new in terms of knowledge and experience even for the most successful of business people. So, don't feel like you are falling a million steps behind the best.

When the heat is on, small problems will start to become big obstacles in your mind. The way forward is not to let this happen. Sure, it is easier said than done, but keep in mind that in a business day you probably have much to worry about, and while the small issues need your attention, you can't afford to let them consume all of your energy and then be found wanting on the bigger problems.

Due to the nature of this book, my next sentence may sound rather strange to you. Believe it or not, there is more to life than just business and working. If you are the leader, then your business needs you to be strong. So don't work yourself into the ground and end up in the hospital with a nervous breakdown, because you are the cornerstone of the business. Without you, it will crumble to the floor.

You need to live a healthy lifestyle. Eat regular meals and exercise as often as possible. Your home life is just as important. Make sufficient time for your family and friends. Who knows? Time spent with them may stimulate the next big business idea in your mind. Try to leave your work at the office as much as you can so that home time will be private time.

It is not always easy to do this, especially if you are the business owner. Many clients don't believe in business hours and will want access to you when they feel like it.

Be open to new ideas.

Your way of doing things may have been the right way in the 1980s but times are changing. We are living in a fast-paced world where today's business innovations are old news this time tomorrow. Failing to plan is planning to fail and failing to change falls into the same negative category.

Let's take a look at some positive tips that will help you to surf over those tough waves and head back up to the top.

The best way to keep the mind busy is by finding some form of business rhythm. When the wheels of the business are turning with confidence, things will start to pick up again.

This means the business must have the right staff in the right places and hope that there won't be any delays on the side of the client in terms of sign-offs on projects.

Delays in the starting date of projects cause a huge amount of stress and strain on budgets. Imagine if you brought in extra staff to help handle the workload and now the client has advised that they will continue with the next phase of the project in six months' time?

So there you go—carrying additional staff wages for another six months!

This will almost certainly lead to a break in the business momentum and it won't be your fault. If you are new to leadership in a business, you will soon work out that many obstacles in the workplace are actually not your fault. This is why you need to stay focused, be positive, and have that never-say-die attitude.

Due to budget constraints, you may be forced to cut back on staff and other resources. Think this through very carefully as you don't want to retrench people today and then an opportunity comes your way tomorrow and you don't have the personnel with the right skill sets to handle a large contract.

Keep an eye on your competitors. Stay positive and be first to get to the opportunity while the others enjoy a siesta. The business picture may be even bigger than you think. Perhaps through your company, you are the one to lead the nation, if not the world, out of the economic crisis that it finds itself in. Your positive attitude and humility, in alliance with your offering could be just the tonic to change the way that people around the world do business.

Always keep thinking about ways that you can do business better and faster than anyone else—even when the market is asleep. The market sleeping doesn't mean that your mind should also sleep.

The best way forward to turn things around in tough times is to be on the look-out for new opportunities.

Remember, the business owner's job is not to implement but to lead and keep the workforce motivated.

Even during tough times, keep working and be ready for your season. Work on the next big idea rather than becoming immersed in self-pity. Remember that the end of an economic recession sparks a renewed spiral in the industry.

It is, therefore, important to make sure that you have the perfect offering and strategy so that when the window of opportunity opens, it finds you ready and eager.

While the window of opportunity is closed, you may find yourself in a do-or-die situation. Stay focused and keep your mind working.

Challenges are put into a people's lives to make them stronger and to teach them the steps that are required to take them to the next level be it in business or life, in general.

Irrespective of whether a business is going through good or bad times, the leader will always be accountable for the goings-on in the business. So, having a cool head is required.

Believe in yourself and show that sense of humility and positive attitude that you are known for.

If you have been following these good leadership habits and the future of your business looks bleak, remember that you are going this is just a season, which, I promise, won't last forever. Remember that the down seasons are much shorter and relatively scarce. In fact, you will have more good news than bad news. It is all about your outlook on life and business.

CHAPTER 45

Communication

The ability to communicate clearly and decisively is an important part of any business. Analysing information and passing the results on to another party is a form of communication. How this is managed could have a huge positive or negative effect on the bottom line of a company.

A leader will struggle to achieve his objectives if he or she is unable to communicate clearly to the employees in the office. Communication entails conveying the deliverables for a project to other staff members. Clear communication is required right up front when it comes to appointing staff or putting contractors or suppliers in place.

Communicating is a skill that needs to be constantly worked on. Like most things in life, some people are better at it than others, while the latter need to keep working at their written or non-verbal skills so as to master the art.

Remember that communicating is not only about a boss talking to the workforce or an employee consulting with a client. The picture is much bigger than that. Any form of social media usage (Facebook, Twitter, Instagram, LinkedIn or your website) plus content conveyed via platforms such as email, text messaging or WhatsApp, also fall into the communications category. One-on-one verbal sessions with colleagues, is another form of key communicating.

Let's break it down for easier understanding.

A business leader should be looking for the easiest route in terms of communicating briefs to staff members. A business leader needs to be streetwise when finding the best form of communication. This doesn't happen overnight. It is often done on a trial and error basis before one comes up with the winning formula that brings about the most success. In being one of the basic elements of business, CEOs should realise the importance of it as far as production and profitability are concerned.

When it comes to the global market, things can become quite tricky as your New York, US office may be speaking to your Beijing, China office, and there could be a language problem. If you are communicating about huge sums of money, it is always best to put it down on paper and not just go the verbal route. At least there will be a paper trail to follow in case things go wrong.

Keep in mind that the staff in your office could well be of different age groups. The young people will usually be much more in touch with social media that those in the fifty-plus category. Even the tone of messaging needs to be taken into consideration. In this era, people use shortened words for social media and may accidentally drop them into client communication. A sense of focus is required on all fronts because the workplace is, after all, still a professional setting!

Just as it is important to use quality communication to take a project forward, the same applies on the problem-solving front.

In most of these situations, employees work under huge amounts of stress and will be looking for simple flowing communication to work from, and not pages and pages of documentation.

Let's take a look at what a human resources manager will look for when hiring a project manager to head up a department.

Not all world class footballers make great team captains and vice versa. The same applies in the sense that not all great world class footballers make great coaches.

It has to do with one's ability to impart knowledge to the others, and not everyone is born with the drive to do this.

Some people are naturally better at planning their lives than others, and this will filter through when appointed to manage a project individually or as a project team. The ability to motivate through communication is vital and again, some are born with the ability to do this, while others may struggle or be unable to achieve this at all.

Studies have shown that a quality manager spends between 70% to 80% of his or her day communicating with his or her team members, so one can see just how important this element really is. If you are still a junior employee and have dreams of climbing the ladder in the company where you work, my advice to you is to focus on the communications element and use it as a form of foundation.

Think of it as a kind of image which is seen by your bosses, colleagues, clients and more. Even if you are still that junior staff member, take charge of situations. Show those around you that you are excited to learn and explore new opportunities. This is a form of communication that shows that you are up for the challenge!

The best bosses in the world are the ones who realise that communication is a two-way street. It's not about the CEO handing out the briefs and locking him- or herself inside the office until the workers have done the job. There needs to be open communication, in case the staff have questions about their tasks.

If the CEO or project leader has provided well-planned goals for the tasks and has provided detailed job descriptions, the communicating factor could well be on the right path.

Here's a tip for people who receive written briefs from their bosses. If you receive the brief in the form of an email, always respond to the sender with the word, 'noted'. Nothing annoys a boss more than receiving the silent treatment. By this, the boss is left in an uncertain mindset as to whether the staff received the brief via email, or even more importantly, whether they understood it.

Never be afraid to ask questions about a document that you have read, even if you are sitting in a meeting and everyone else seems to understand.

The chances are, they probably don't understand the document either but don't want to be the ones to put up their hand. Rather look silly and understand than keep quiet and go down the road of failure.

A good communicator is always filled with confidence. Although you may not see yourself as a strong communicator, your confidence may just be what is winning you support among your colleagues.

Here's a thought that many people often forget. Listening is a sub-form of communication. Yes, your lips might not be moving, but by taking in vast amounts of information, you are setting yourself up for your reply. Again, not all people are great listeners. It is something that needs to be worked on.

The chances of growing in this area are really good as most people prefer talking to listening so you will have many candidates to listen to as you look to perfect your listening art. Thank goodness for modern technology since as the business leader's list of deliverables keeps on growing, the need for quick forms of briefing staff has become inevitable. The ability to communicate is no longer a special gift or a major talent. It is a 'must'.

Quite simply put, if you don't have good communication skills, the chances that you are going to succeed as a manager are pretty slim. There is no room for error either. All communication coming from the CEO or project leader's desk must be 100% accurate.

The team on the ground should have full trust in their superiors and the communication that they receive from them. The CEO needs to make sure that the computer servers used by your business are up-to-date. There is no time in the business day for the loss of communicated material, information or data.

You will also find that each business leader will have his or her own style of communicating. Some leaders are very quick on communicating by text message while a few are good at using the good old phone call to convey messages.

Some bosses prefer sending out their messages at 6am. Many employees appreciate this and find it better this way than getting messages at 10pm.

There are basically two types of leadership and both are related to communication. The one is business-aligned, and the other is person-aligned. The main thrust in any business is to get the work done. Some managers tend to get too focused on their own deliverables as well as the ultimate goal and simply run out of time to communicate sufficiently during the business day.

Those who are more individual-aligned tend to be more popular among the staff as they are more focused on ensuring that the workers have the correct instructions, resources, and realistic deadlines to get the job done.

As I am sure that you have worked out here, being a leader is not the easiest task in the world. While doing his or her job, the leader still has to communicate, monitor, and be accountable for the tasks handled by others.

Another important point is criticism. Some staff can handle this better than others. Some workers will take a leader's criticism personally and friction in the workplace will follow as a result.

Criticism is a form of communication, but it needs to be carefully controlled. Leaders cannot let their frustrations boil over when communicating in a critical fashion as staff personalities and outlooks on life differ.

A strong barrier that may negatively affect good communication is the inability to adapt to change. Some workers are too set in their ways. They lack flexibility and cannot implement the communication notes, as desired by the boss.

A leader cannot be indecisive when communicating. The goal that has been set must be the firm target at all times. And so, vital information cannot keep changing during a project as this will create uncertainty and a lack of confidence in the minds of the staff.

It's important for communication to be clear, concise, structured, and relevant. As mentioned elsewhere in this book, the leader needs to be open-minded. He or she cannot adopt an 'it's my way or the highway' approach. The door to the office of the boss needs to be open for staff to bring new ideas or thoughts.

Communication is vital when creating and upholding respect between all workers. It's important to ensure that interactions among workers remain transparent and in the interests of advancing the business or client's project to the next level. A good leader will have the ability to communicate without thinking that the project could backfire.

Yes, mistakes do happen and risk-taking is a part of the business world, but sometimes key decisions need to be made and communicated.

The leader is a leader for a reason. Besides being 'captain material', he or she should also be the authority in the area of expertise that is at the core of a project. Hence, communication relating to the business or project should always be clear.

Spending less time in meetings means that there is more time to carry out the day's work. Hence it's important for the business to stay updated with modern technology to ensure that communication in the office is instant, clear, and concise.

All businesses should have an internal and external communication strategy. If time is a problem, a public relations communications company can be paid a monthly retainer to manage the communication elements of your brand. An example of this would be writing press statements when new or current staff take up top positions in the business.

If your business is serious about being involved in social responsibility in your community, then press statements in this regard would also come in handy because the business could take advantage of the press and social media to be in good light in its buyers' eyes. Also, as a result you will generate good publicity for the business and attract more buyers.

In summary, communication is an essential tool for a business.

CHAPTER 46

Work Environment

The work environment is where we spend a large part of our lives, so it needs to be a positive area. Think of it as a place for extramural activity. You go to the golf course or the tennis courts because you enjoy the game. It's not that you must be there, but you have chosen to partake because you like the sport, the people and most importantly, the environment.

My advice to business owners, who sometimes get irritated when staff want to brighten up their work area with pictures, flowers or other items, is to relax. Use a degree of leniency with the employees and let them make the most of their workspace if it means that it is going to make them as productive as possible.

Open-plan office space generally allows for greater growth and teamwork than floor space divided up with employees placed in cubicles.

If, as a business owner, you notice that one department is outshining the rest in terms of productivity, take a look at their work set-up. Do the other departments need to follow in this regard?

Gone are the days of grey-walled, government-style offices where staff members sit with long faces, showing their boredom to anyone who cares to notice.

A good starting point is to find out from the employees what type of work environment they would like to be a part of. Some employees prefer working in larger teams while others are more effective in small- to medium-sized groups. Naturally, the work office space would need to cater to the choices made.

Another good point is for regular feedback sessions to take place so that the senior management can get a good understanding of the feelings and needs of the staff towards their managers. It needs to be a 360-review approach, so all can speak freely about their managers or vice versa. This all contributes towards finding ways to have the best form of work environment for all.

While a large salary is a huge incentive to join a company, it is important to check out the work environment. Will you be able to fit into the culture of the company? So you are a Monday to Friday person and your new job will require you to work on weekends. Do you still take the job opportunity knowing that you don't quite fit in?

What about the scenario where you have just recently got married and don't want to travel? You guessed it, your new job not only includes regular travel but international trips too. It all sounded quite good until you found out that you would be sleeping more in hotel rooms than at home.

So you have worked out, I am sure, that the work environment element is broader than just the desk area where you sit in the office. In order for you to perform at your peak, you need quality briefs from the client and top-notch direction from your project leader. Is that all in place?

What is the team spirit like in the office? Is everyone upbeat about their tasks or are they just doing the old 'offering time in return for a salary at the end of the month' thing? In other chapters in this book, I have written about the importance of incentivising staff be it financially or through vouchers, to keep them focused on not only doing their jobs to the best of their ability but also to bring in new clients or increase business with clients currently on the company database. There is more chance of top-level productivity if the workplace offers diversity.

The creative spirit needs to flow amongst all and employees need to encourage each other. Remember that happy staff members tend to be loyal ones.

If the business owner can get the right sort of work/environment mix and manage people correctly, then the staff turnover is unlikely to be that high. Happy workers tend to take pride in their work and will look to go the extra mile.

A good working environment will also play a major role in keeping stress to a manageable level. Conducting business can be pretty nerve-wracking at the best of times, so a good positive working environment will help the cause.

Now let's look at the leadership that is offered to your employees. Are the briefs just dished out to such an extent that some staffers just can't cope with the quantity or does the business offer sufficient support to help the staff to achieve the success?

Sometimes senior management get so bewildered by the bottom line of the balance sheet that they forget to offer sufficient resources to the people who need it most, namely the workforce.

As a business leader, you need to keep your team motivated. The new ideas need to keep flowing in.

As stated elsewhere in this book, the next brilliant idea might not come from the CEO but from a junior staffer or even the tea lady as they all carry the company brand. So keep everyone in the office environment as happy as can be.

In an ever-changing business world where many people are going towards the 'online build your own business work-from-home' route, it is becoming more and more important for bosses of corporations to see the bigger picture as far as the work environment is concerned.

Some of the larger corporates even go as far as to have on-site catering and laundry outlets to make life easier for their employees. After all, people do have families and other commitments outside of their jobs, but by providing these forms of support, it means that the workforce will feel more comfortable in spending the maximum time at the office knowing that certain services are just down the hall.

The business owner should be careful in selecting these additional offerings. If your business is in the line of selling health supplements, it's hardly a good idea to have a pizza or hamburger caterer nearby, even if that is what your staff wants when working long shifts.

Don't hold back on computer equipment either. Make sure that your workers have the latest in software packages (and indeed, hardware itself) to bring about the best form of outcome in their work. Your work environment will go a long way towards gaining that all-important edge over your opposition through the superb work output of your employees.

So let's break it down to the five senses. The work environment revolves around what the employee touches, sees, and hears. Of course, the taste element might not come into the picture just yet, but the smell in the form of aroma can give the worker a nice feel-good aspect.

Now that you have modernised the pictures on the wall and changed the furniture from old steel filing cabinets to more current wooden furniture, what more can be done to make the employee feel that this is the right place for him or her?

Here's the worst-kept secret in the workspace. Most employees sit at their desks for less time than one thinks. So it is not just about making the workstations pretty but placing focus on other areas of the office too. What about those auditoriums that have super top-of-the-line modern technology projectors, computers, and other equipment, but are as dull as can be in terms of décor?

Once you have come up with a way to liven up the auditoriums or meeting rooms—which are, after all the place that major decisions are taken, it's time to brighten up the hallways. Out with the artwork which wowed clients in the 1960s and in its place must come pictures to which the modern-era business person can relate.

For example, if you are a sports marketing consultancy, it's time to put up some football, rugby, cricket, track, and field or American gridiron memorabilia depending, of course, on the country in which your office is based. If you are a lawyer, it's time to bring out those framed photographs of your CEO shaking hands with top politicians or business people.

The employee needs to know that he or she is working for a firm that is serious about finding solutions for its clients.

Don't forget those much-frequented coffee areas too. Position some key images about business success next to the coffee machine and they won't go unnoticed.

Many businesses like to use words of wisdom to inspire their staff. There are some great utterances from US and British presidents plus sports and other stars that have stuck in society for years.

Martin Luther King's "I have a dream" is just one of the motivating phrases that have stuck around for decades. As any good business person will tell you, the day that you stop dreaming is the day that you should be closing your laptop for the very last time in the industry.

In whatever one does to brighten up the workplace, the key goal is to make the employee want to come to work the next morning and do their best. There is no hard and fast route as far as formatting the 'Ultimate Staff Member Experience' is concerned as this may differ depending on the line of work that the business does.

Improving the work environment does not mean that staff members will stay with your business forever, but it will play a role in improving positivity, focus, and productivity.

Keep in mind that these are changing times in the business sector. Looking after staff to this extent was not on the table in the 1960s, 1970s or 1980s—nor was beautifying offices.

The businesses who don't take this aspect of the industry seriously are the ones who will end up with huge staff turnovers. The employees are not robots or just numbers on the payroll. They are human beings who want to do their best in a friendly, positive environment.

Caring for working environments is what differentiates great companies from the ordinary ones. Staff will think twice before taking an offer elsewhere, as they may earn more at another company, but will the environment be the same? Many believe the old notion that 'the grass is greener on the other side' but soon find out to their detriment that this is not always the case and soon request their old jobs back.

Many bosses go out of their way to make the company perks that accompany the salary to be so juicy that staff do not want to leave, or cannot afford to move on. If the employee had to pay for the perks such as medical aid and pension fund out of his or her own pocket, it could well add up to way more than what the company is offering as the business is probably getting a discounted group deal.

This links in with the work environment element and how a business looks after the workforce. The work environment needs to be thought of in the same way so as to ensure that the employee care part is not neglected.

It might be a good learning point for the boss to spend an hour or so in the office space once all the staff has left for the day to get a feeling for just how it feels to work there. Of course, the boss will only be there for a short time compared to the staff, but it will give the leader a good idea of how the employees may feel too.

Attention to the work environment is something that often gets overlooked and then impacts negatively on the business over time. Don't fall into the trap. Instead, make that small spend which could net you big money on the profit line.

CHAPTER 47

Gems

'Gems' is a key business term that is used when it comes to finding that special ingredient that will take a company to another level. While many do also refer to exceptional people as 'gems', the meaning of the word goes far beyond this as it also applies to the spotting of opportunities, bonuses and other benefits—in other words, all the good things in business.

Spotting potential business opportunities that other people may think will just be a loss of money, is a major talent.

Some people have this gem of a gift in them and can turn that US$10 million piece of business into a US$100 million one with effortless ease. It is these types of people that are marketing managers of firms today and multi-millionaires a few months later because of their ability to sell an idea.

Many such people naturally prefer to go off and make money for themselves rather than work for a boss, but it is always great to have such individuals in one's business even if it is only for a short time.

Naturally, it is always a good thing to network and stay close with such individuals in a sense of building long-lasting relationships with winners in the world of business.

These people don't focus too much on the risk element when working towards unearthing the gems that nobody else seems to notice, but rather go full force towards the end result knowing that it is a win situation all the way.

They have the ability to change their own destiny and circumstances seem to always work in their favour because of their positive attitude and outlook on life.

An example of this type of gem is the one who is sitting in a lengthy meeting about the invention of the mobile phone. Most around the meeting room table understand the phone to be just that—a tool for communication.

However, the gem sees things differently. Surely if the device can be used for verbal communication, it can also be used for text messaging and the sending and receiving of emails?

A gem-type of person also finds it easier to identify with the market needs and hence can also spot the shortcomings of the opposition. This creates the gap for the new product to enter and no second invitation will be required.

Like precious stones, gems are hard to find, hence within a company, these special ones often get overlooked. One would think that people would latch on to the gems and learn from them, but the 'blinkered' approach is often present.

You will be surprised at how many people think that they are a million times better at their job than the person sitting next to them, rather than adopting an approach of learning and taking advice to improve their own level of performance.

Let's look a bit more at the opportunities called gems rather than the individual. Just like finding high-quality gem-like staff, the opportunities of making money or doing business are out there but can only be spotted by companies with vision.

Again we go back to the 1009th investor who had the vision to understand the value of Colonel Sanders's Kentucky Fried Chicken recipe.

Did the Colonel say something different to what he mentioned to the previous 1008 investors who turned him down, or did the 1009th investor simply understand the bigger picture?

The second part is the correct answer with the investor clearly seeing an opportunity bigger than selling chicken. If the business strategy was to be planned correctly, then Kentucky Fried Chicken would not only make huge cash out of going the franchising route, but it would also expand its sales offering by way of chicken burgers, salads, soft drinks and more.

The opportunity was a gem which was spotted by a gem of an investor. The benefits of the investment far outweighed the cash outlay in the mind of the investor. The old saying of 'if you don't take a ticket, you can't win the lottery' is ever true in this case.

At this early stage, did the gem of an investor think that the gem of an opportunity would grow into a multibillion-dollar food empire in the US? Yes, probably, but in those early days, it was highly unlikely that the vision saw the brand taking over the fast food industry across the globe.

That 'lotto ticket' in taking the chance to invest in Colonel Sanders's recipe changed the mindset of food and business forever.

So is the gem the person, the opportunity or the marketing strategy? Generally speaking, a mix of all three is what it takes to get a brand to global levels, as Colonel Sanders found out. Who would have thought that restaurants, which used to rely on customers to pay their meal bills by cash or cheque, would one day have credit card swiping machines?

Let's take that a step further, now not only restaurants but entrepreneurs and other business people are walking around with wireless credit card swiping machines in their jacket pockets. This allows them to be paid by customers on the spot with the machine working in tandem with the business person's mobile phone to allow the transaction to take place.

Clearly, a gem of an investor bought into a gem of an opportunity, which was backed by a gem of a marketing plan which has made millions or billions for the production companies.

A business owner worth his or her salt will tell you of the importance to always invest back into the business after the big deal has been done. Don't go out and buy the mansion, holiday penthouse, and Porsche to show the world that you and your company have arrived in big-time business!

Always look at your business needs in terms of infrastructure and staffing before you book that holiday trip to Hawaii. Your goal should preferably be one of, "where am I going to be ten years from now?" instead of resting on your laurels.

The competition out there in the business world is fierce and your opposition will not only be trying to better your super-duper product offering, but they will be looking at ways to steal your gem staff away from your business.

Now that your business has gained a greater source of profitability from the big deal that you did, it is time to look after people before you lose them. Do some individuals need to be raised to business-unit heads with their salaries to carry additional benefits that will make them stay at your company?

The last thing that you want is for people to think that you, the business owner, are living a life of luxury while everyone else in the business is still a slave to the system.

You need to box clever on this one.

If the senior gems that contributed greatly to the huge deal are getting twitchy, and you are willing to do anything to retain their services and entrench the longevity of the company, it may be time to work out some form of shareholding with them, albeit in a division or subsidiary company rather than the actual company, which is the 'baby' of the business owner.

A business owner should always go the extra mile to make the gifted staff members feel like they are stakeholders in the business and not just a number on the month-end salary list.

Sometimes, bold decisions need to be made. Yes, it's great to keep as many gems on your staff as possible, but it comes at a price. The business cannot hoard top talent forever unless the income allows this to happen.

While this comes at a huge cost, keeping top talent happy at your business does mean that there will be many fewer resignations in your business.

If the staff are well looked after, they will soon realise that the 'grass is not always greener on the other side' and will hang around at their current place of work for longer than they initially intended to.

What a business owner now needs to be cautious about is to not overload their gems with too much work.

While the gems could potentially handle this, the briefing in of top-level work to a handful of select individuals could result in the boss being seen as having favourites on the workforce.

Be careful when it comes to setting boundaries for your gems on your workforce. You don't want to restrict them too much as that will mean you could potentially be restricting them from finding the gems in the marketplace too.

Think of it as a gold rush. Everyone wants to find the gems, be it staff or business opportunities so the competition is fierce. As happened in the days of the gold rush, the jewels aren't found every day, so the staff needs to be strategic as to how they go about things, but gems in the workplace will understand this better than most as they will know what they are looking for.

The gems on the staff might not necessarily be your leaders. They may well be more operations-minded; as in get-the-job-done type of people.

They may be much more valuable to a company on the strategic and operations side than as administrative heads of a department.

This doesn't mean that gems on the staff are not team players. There will be many occasions when the gems cannot do a whole mind-blowing strategy on their own. This opens the door for others to work with them and learn from them.

Although developing gem staff members is not an easy task as it comes from within a person, teamwork relationships between other staff and the current gems are probably the best way to uncover the next range of exceptionally gifted people.

In closing, finding gem opportunities and capitalising on them is what brings in the big bucks. This is more about identifying an area in which to 'fish'. It's a niche way of doing things rather than throwing fifty baited hooks into the water and hoping that a fish (in the form of a business deal) will bite.

For the business owner, the strategy is a simple one. Always stay one step ahead in the business rat race. A proactive approach gets noticed by clients, potential business stakeholders, staff members and yes, you guessed it, staff gems. If a business leader adopts this approach and looks after the workforce, everybody will want to work there.

***

www.ingramcontent.com/pod-product-compliance
Lightning Source LLC
Chambersburg PA
CBHW021810170526
45157CB00007B/2530